Full Gas

PETER COSSINS

Full Gas

How The Race was Won – Tactics from Inside the Peloton

YELLOW JERSEY PRESS
LONDON

1 3 5 7 9 10 8 6 4 2

Yellow Jersey Press
20 Vauxhall Bridge Road,
London SW1V 2SA

Yellow Jersey Press is part of the Penguin Random House
group of companies whose addresses can be found at global.
penguinrandomhouse.com

Penguin
Random House
UK

First published in paperback by Yellow Jersey Press in 2019
First published in hardback by Yellow Jersey Press in 2018

penguin.co.uk/vintage

A CIP catalogue record for this book is available from the British Library

ISBN 9781787290204

Printed and bound in Great Britain by Clays Ltd, Elcograf S.p.A.

Penguin Random House is committed to a sustainable future for
our business, our readers and our planet. This book is made from
Forest Stewardship Council® certified paper

To Anabel Hernández, an inspiration as a
journalist and writer

CONTENTS

'Cycling is a living, breathing art. Those cyclists who forget that are halfway to becoming sloths'

Laurent Fignon, *We Were Young and Carefree*

It's late on a baking mid-August afternoon in the French city of Nîmes, which is hosting the start of the 2017 edition of the Vuelta a España. Team buses and trucks are lined out beneath the trees flanking the city's main boulevard on the western side of the old town, famed for its Roman amphitheatre. Next to some, mechanics are carrying out final checks on equipment, while others provide shelter for riders warming up on stationary turbo trainers for the team time trial that will provide the first test at what is one of cycling's three Grand Tours, alongside the Giro d'Italia and the Tour de France.

With the final reconnaissance of the route already done and an hour until the start, there's not much for team directors to do except soak up the Midi sun. Wandering through the crowds, I spot Patrick Lefevere sitting in a deck chair doing exactly this outside the bus of the Quick-Step Floors team he has managed under different sponsors for almost thirty years. The silver-haired Belgian is famed for his tactical acuity.

— Excuse me, Patrick. Do you mind if I ask you a few questions?

— What about?

— I'm writing a book about tactics in cycling—

– Hah! Good luck!

Lefevere's booming voice, as deep but not as sonorous as that of Johnny Cash, almost knocks me back and draws the attention of the Quick-Step mechanics and soigneurs, *who turn and stare. What have I done to provoke their boss? they're wondering. And I'm thinking the same.*

Lefevere pulls off his mirror shades and looks at me for a few moments, his stare as glaring as the sun. He then points to his right, towards the bike stands and pressure washers where his mechanics have been working.

– See that chair over there. Bring it over here next to me. Let's talk …

Bike racing has been described by American writer Owen Mulholland as 'chess at 150 heartbeats a minute', the depiction neatly combining the strategic complexity of trying to outwit 200 other riders when the messages your brain is receiving from every part of your body are telling it 'slow down!' Yet, talk to the riders who battle each other within the peloton, that wonderfully seething mass of mayhem that is so mesmerising when seen from the TV helicopters, and to the team directors who are lined out in convoy behind them, and the comparison is more often made to poker. Bike racing is all about bluffing, about hiding what you've got in your legs and what card your team is planning to play, about alliances that come together in an instant and are dissolved just as quickly, about keeping your rivals guessing. In the Netherlands, long one of cycling's heartlands, they have a saying that encapsulates it perfectly: 'First eat what's on your neighbour's plate, then start on your own plate.'

Fundamentally, road racing is a very simple sport. Once the riders are waved away, there are essentially just three different scenarios that can be acted out: a small group of riders escapes and end up deciding the day's spoils between them; that small group is reeled in before the finish and the best sprinters in the bunch decide matters between them; or the break goes clear but is chased by the teams of the strongest riders, who then dispute the finish between them on a climb.

Its complexity derives from each of as many as twenty-two teams beginning the race with a specific strategic objective, which might be as straightforward as ensuring one of their riders is in that break, or more far-reaching with the stage victory or the leader's jersey as their ultimate goal. Once the race referee has signalled the start of racing, the twenty-two tactical plans, which will have been agreed on just a few minutes earlier at the briefings held behind the tinted windows of luxury team buses, start to impact on each other like water molecules bouncing around a saucepan over a flame. That there will be a result is inevitable. But what happens in between that flag being dropped and the finish-line banner cannot be predicted and can be totally incomprehensible, especially to the occasional fan but even to someone like me who has spent a quarter of a century watching and writing about bike racing.

In an attempt to better understand and explain the constantly evolving and frequently quite exquisite tactical puzzles that every bike race sets and every rider within it contributes to, I've spent a season watching races with a different perspective, focusing more on the various processes that lead to a rider winning a race, and less on the finale and the words and personality of the winner. It has been enlightening and captivating. In doing so, I've fallen back in love with the sport that drew me in during the early 1980s, and much more passionately than before. Indeed, I confess that I've discovered the full scope of its beauty for the first time.

The result is *Full Gas*, an explanation of the how and why of bike tactics. It delves into the sport's history to understand where tactical thinking began and to highlight its development over a century and more. More than anything, though, *Full Gas* is an experts' guide into the intricacies of top-level bike racing in the modern era and the tactics that are both its essence and provide so much of its colour. The expertise is not mine, but comes entirely from those who know bike racing from the inside – as racers and team directors. I am extremely grateful to each and every one of them.

And why *Full Gas*? It is the in vogue term for riding flat out, giving absolutely everything left in the tank. It is the most fundamental tactic of all.

CHAPTER 1

WHAT ARE TACTICS?

Ally MacLeod thinks that tactics are a new kind of mint.
— *Billy Connolly*

Before getting too deeply into the subject of cycling tactics and how they have developed, a more fundamental question needs to be tackled: do they actually exist? To be precise, are tactics any more than a rider's instinctive reaction to what is happening around them, a response that is impulsive rather than pre-planned?

In order to answer these questions, it is useful to understand the difference between strategy and tactics, terms that are frequently used interchangeably, but are significantly different in what they describe. Strategy defines a long-term objective and the plan set out to achieve it, a mission statement, if you like. For example, a team might begin the Tour de France with the aim of winning the yellow jersey in Paris. Each morning, almost as soon as the team's bus arrives at a stage start, the staff who direct the team on the road hold a briefing to provide the riders with the strategy for that day, framing it within the longer-term view for the race as a whole. So, for a flat stage that is likely to end in a bunch sprint, their sporting director would probably define the strategy as ensuring that the team leader finishes up towards the front of the peloton so that he does not lose any time to his rivals in the battle for the general classification.

Tactics are the more concrete methods that are employed to guarantee that this strategy is carried out successfully. On this hypothetical sprint day, these tactics might include certain riders being designated to set the pace on the front of the peloton, or others riding close to Froome with their bikes set up in a similar way so that they can be quickly exchanged if the Sky leader suffers a mechanical problem. Smaller in scale than strategy, tactics happen within a shorter time frame, they are the initiatives intended to achieve the next step towards the overall objective.

In sport, a team or an athlete's strategy is usually very easy to define. Most obviously, it is victory, although for some it might be a top-three finish or a place halfway up the table or division. Tactics, too, are generally quite easy to decipher. A football team might, for instance, line up with five defenders against a better or more in-form team, or the coach might ask two of their players to double up on an opponent who is particularly vital to the success of the rival team.

In cycling, however, although a team's strategy is often clear-cut, tactics are much less so simply due to the number of teams trying to implement tactics designed to achieve their strategies. Almost from the very start of a race, the strategic plans drawn up by many of those twenty-odd teams will be in tatters, perhaps because they haven't got a rider in the breakaway and a rival outfit has, or they've been affected by one of the many unpredictable factors that can always affect a bike race, even on a day when there is not a great deal of action – the punctures, the crashes, the weather changing, a rider not eating or drinking enough.

Does this therefore mean that much of what then happens within a race is instinctive rather than tactical? For instance, when Mark Cavendish is asked about his tactics when sprinting, he insists that he has none, that everything he does in the final 200 metres of a race is completely instinctive. Is a rider attacking on a climb or a descent responding to reflex rather than reflection? Are riders who react to a change in wind direction by moving up through the peloton to ensure they are at the front in case it splits also acting in the same intuitive way as the likes of Cavendish and Marcel Kittel do when a gap opens up amid the mayhem of a bunch sprint that provides them with a clear run to the line?

While readily accepting Cavendish's perspective, I would suggest that almost everything else that takes place within a bike race before it reaches that point 200 metres from the line is the result of the strategies that the riders are given before a race being applied by means of tactics that are skilfully and often subconsciously employed. Indeed, Cavendish's ability to employ his unparalleled intuition as the best sprinter road cycling has ever seen depends on that strategy and those tactics working almost perfectly time after time. In short, they provide the opportunity.

There is no better way to illustrate both the existence and necessity for tactics than by looking at a masterclass in their planning and implementation.

It is the afternoon of the nineteenth stage of the 2017 Vuelta a España. The 149.7-kilometre route that meanders from the tiny village of Caso in the remote Parque Natural de Redes through a series of steep-sided Asturian valleys to the port and resort of Gijón on Spain's Atlantic coast offers a final opportunity for glory to the 150-odd riders within the peloton who aren't specialist climbers or lightning-fast sprinters.

It will be, says Tejay van Garderen, one of the climbers saving his reserves for the following day's stage to the summit of the Alto de l'Angliru, a day for 'some of the savviest guys around. The breakaway artists who know how to win from a group on a stage like that are the riders who are blessed with real tactical skill. They have to know how to expend as little energy as possible when trying to get into the move in the first place and how to save all the resources they can when they're in the breakaway. Crucially, they also have to know how to win out of that breakaway move, be it in a sprint or by escaping with an attack at just the right moment.'

A little more than three-and-a-half hours after the peloton has rolled away from Caso, after crossing four categorised climbs, the last of them a mere fifteen kilometres from the finish, victory in Gijón will go to Thomas De Gendt, one of the canniest of breakaway specialists. 'It's very simple for me,' De Gendt says of his approach. 'If I stay in the bunch then I can't win the stage. It doesn't matter how good my form is, I'm never going to win a mountain stage because there are so many other good climbers. The same goes for a sprint. I can't contend with those guys on a sprint stage. As a result, the calculation is effectively made for me: if I want to win, I've got to be in the breakaway.'

As the Vuelta peloton gathers at the start line in Caso in the early afternoon, De Gendt's task is complicated by the fact that he is the one rider every other breakaway hopeful has in his sights. Winning on days such as this has become his signature as a racer, the reason for his renown and popularity among cycling fans. Having already claimed stage wins at the Tour de France and the Giro d'Italia, the rider in the red, white and black colours of the Lotto Soudal team is looking to add his name to the elite group of racers who have won stages in all three Grand Tours. But how do you win when everyone has you down as the man to beat?

For a start, it certainly helps if your team has won three stages of the race already. Thanks to the bouquets claimed in earlier breakaways by teammates Tomasz Marczyński (twice) and Sander Armée, the latter coming just the day before, De Gendt is under less pressure to succeed, from his team at least. Three wins for a line-up that lost its nominated leader, Rafael Valls, in a crash just before the Vuelta and started without a recognised sprinter is an exceptional haul.

'When Valls couldn't start we were all asked to focus on winning stages,' De Gendt explains. 'When Sander Armée won our third, the morale within the team was very good, as you can imagine. Not having a leader makes it easier to get into moves like that – you can do whatever you want – and the stage into Gijón gave us our final opportunity to take advantage of it. It was mentioned in the team briefing that a lot of guys from other teams would also be keen to get into the break, and that this would give us a real chance of winning the stage.'

During the briefing, Lotto Soudal's sporting directors gave their riders vital information about the stage route, including the difficulty of the climbs and descents, as well as likely tactical scenarios. But De Gendt's personal plan of attack was already extremely well formed, the seeds having been planted as early as the day of the announcement of the Vuelta route just prior to the start of the season.

'You look at the stages a bit when they first announce the route and think about possible days that might suit you, but you can only start to make a firm plan once you get the road book and have a good look through that,' De Gendt says of the race 'bible' that all riders receive from race organisers. 'At the same time, though, you don't want to look too many days ahead of where you are because you don't want to lose your focus on the days that are coming. It was only two days before that stage to Gijón that I thought it would be a good one for a breakaway. I think I even said after stage sixteen that stages eighteen and nineteen would be very good for a breakaway, and both times they went to the finish. So I just look two days ahead. Then you need to have the legs in the morning and it's only then that I make the decision whether I'll go or not.

'That day was a good stage to choose because it was a bit too hard for the sprinters, but not hard enough for the climbers. It was typical of the kind of day when breakaways often go all the way to the finish. Usually there's a big group on days like that. There tend to be three, four, five days on a Grand Tour like that, and on those days it's just a case of being in the right place when the break starts to form.'

From the start in Caso, the route initially takes the Vuelta riders on a steadily descending and very fast road past a series of hydroelectric reservoirs to what is now the rather inappropriately named town of Rioseco. Within moments of race director Javier Guillén brandishing the flag to signal the official start of racing, Juan José Lobato (LottoNL-Jumbo), Edward Theuns (Trek-Segafredo) and Laurens De Vreese (Astana) accelerate away from the peloton. Within a minute or so, three have become nineteen as De Gendt and fifteen others bridge across to the breakaway group.

'Being in the break is half the task,' De Gendt continues. 'If you're one of ten guys in the break, then you've only got to beat nine other riders rather than the whole bunch. But the key thing about getting into the break is that you've got to have the legs to go. If you're feeling a little bit tired from the day before then you're better off holding back. But if you've got the legs, then any stage is a good one to go.'

As Orica-Scott don't have a representative among the nine-teen-strong group, Chris Juul-Jensen is given the thankless task of achieving the same junction on his own. The Dane makes little headway until the cavalry arrives in the form of a clutch of riders whose teams either ended up with not enough or, like Orica, not a single rider at the front.

The opening climb, the Alto de la Colladona, is the toughest of the stage's four categorised ascents, rated first-category and, therefore, significantly more difficult than the three third-cat-egory tests that come later. Davide Villella (Cannondale), wearing the blue polka dot jersey as leader of the King of the Mountains competition, is first over the summit, with De Gendt second over the top.

'I came into the Vuelta a little short of my best form, but I knew it would come. When it started to come good, I could see that other riders were realising I was in good shape because they started to watch me much more,' De Gendt explains. 'That was the case when I got into the breakaway on stage seven to Cuenca. That day I was with

Alessandro De Marchi, Alexis Gougeard, Arnaud Courteille and Davide Villella, and we made a little plan. We decided to go steady until we got to the final fifty kilometres, then we'd go full gas.

'We all knew what we had to do and by collaborating it gave us the chance to surprise the bunch, but when it's a flat finish like that then in ninety-nine times out of a hundred there is no chance you will be able to stay away. However, there is that little possibility that the sprinters' teams may not have enough power to close the gap or they allow just a little bit too much of an advantage to the breakaway. That's what you're always hoping for. Unfortunately, it didn't work out and I didn't end up winning. But missing out that day may have helped me at Gijón as some of the riders perhaps thought I wasn't up to it any more and were looking at other guys in the break, which suited me perfectly.'

While he missed out on that stage to Cuenca and the energy expended meant that he had to sit in the pack for the next few to recover his physical resources, De Gendt believes that all time spent in breakaways is useful. Some breaks may be dismissed by commentators and fans as kamikaze, as offering those involved no more than the chance to position their jersey and its myriad brands and logos in front of the television cameras, but he laughs that off.

'Every time you get into a break you're giving yourself a chance of going for a good result. I also think you need to be in as many breaks as possible to get the experience you need to win. If you only get into a break three or four times a year, I don't think you're going to get enough insight into what it takes to win from a break. That's why I'm always looking for opportunities to join a break and why I went in the break so many times in the Tour de France,' says the Belgian, who featured in half a dozen in the 2017 race.

'By experience, I mean not only the simple fact that you're fighting for a possible victory, but also that you're getting a look at the other riders. At the Vuelta, for example, I was in the break with De Marchi two or three times, and that enabled me to see not only how strong he was in that race, but also how he reacts in certain situations. That's vital when it comes to knowing how they might react if, say, another rider in the break attacks, whether they're good in a sprint, or if they climb well, and whether they do their share of the work. I know that some guys who get in breaks won't do that many pulls [on the front] until the last thirty kilometres. But you need to be in the break to see all of those things. If you stay in the bunch you've got no idea at all.'

Although there are riders who track De Gendt's intentions when they are sizing up whether or not to get involved in what can often be a drawn-out and extremely draining battle to get into the breakaway, he dismisses any notion that he's distracted by such calculations. 'I don't look at certain riders trying to get into the break and think, "He's usually a good guy to work with so I should follow." It's more a case of getting into the break and then seeing who's there with you.

'That said, usually when I go, other good riders go as well. At the Tour, for example, you tend to see the same selection of riders in the break, the same six or seven names – not in every break, of course, but I guarantee you'll see very familiar names in the big breaks that have a good chance of making it. Once they do come together, I know who'll ride full [gas], and which are the riders like Rui Costa who won't fully commit,' De Gendt says of Portugal's 2013 world road race champion.

'He's one of those riders who's always more towards the back of the breakaway group, looking at other riders to do the work and saving as much energy as possible.

'When someone like Rui Costa is in the break with me, I try to save some strength for when they attack or I push a bit harder on the climbs so that they also have to suffer. On flat sections, you can save some energy when you're on a wheel, but if you go really hard on a climb they have to go hard if they want to follow, even if they are on a wheel. It's not so nice for someone who has been saving energy to suddenly have to go full on a climb. It's hard on their legs, so I'll do that a few times and see how they react.'

De Gendt's presence close behind mountains leader Villella at the summit of the Colladona highlights that he's already putting this tactic to use. With nineteen riders at the front and French star Romain Bardet part of a chase group that is only a minute and twenty seconds behind, De Gendt is already pushing on strongly. Every time a rider drops out of the break-away group, the Belgian's chances of prevailing improve.

'Once you are in a group with just six or seven riders you have to do some pulls. But when you are in a group of, say, twenty riders it's a bit easier to hang around at the back without anybody noticing that you're not working. If there are lots of guys in the group, I always try to lose as many of them as possible on the hills or over the last fifty kilometres so that I can ride with a smaller group in the final part of the race and it's easier to see who is working and who is not.'

Despite De Gendt's efforts, the breakaway group re-forms on the descent of the Colladona and the valley roads beyond it. Bardet's hastily formed gang is closing in too. With sixty kilometres covered, the leaders reach the base of the second climb, the third-category Alto de Santo Emiliano. Here, Trek's Edward Theuns decides to keep the chasers at bay and splinter the lead group again by pushing hard as the road ramps up. When De Gendt's compatriot is two kilometres from the top, Villella joins him. But he's not arrived with the intention of collaborating. Instead, the Italian swishes away from Theuns to amass maximum mountains points, his advantage at the summit a minute on the now twenty-six-strong group just behind that's been boosted by the arrival of Bardet's little band.

As well as the Vuelta's King of the Mountains, the break also features Matteo Trentin, leader of the points competition. Winner of three stages thanks to his finishing speed and, it has to be said, the lack of distinguished rivals in that area, the Italian wants to strike a double blow in his attempt to secure the green points jersey in Madrid. Firstly, he wants to secure maximum points at the day's intermediate sprint at Pola de Siero, which lies in between the final two climbs. Having achieved that objective, he will then turn his focus to the stage win in Gijón. Consequently, while Trentin sits in the big breakaway group, his Quick-Step teammate Bob Jungels ups the pace on the front of it in order to bring Villella back into line. Soon after the group passes the MUMI, the Museum of Mining and Industry, housed in one of the many derelict collieries and factories located rather incongruously at the bottom of what are otherwise beautifully wooded valleys, Villella is reeled in by the group with Jungels still in the vanguard.

German climber Emanuel Buchmann is the first to upset Jungels' shepherding work with an attack as the road heads up the third climb, the Alto de la Falla de los Lobos. Bardet breezes across to him and pushes on harder, with De Gendt also quick to help with sustaining this injection of pace. Lobato, De Vreese, the now tiring Villella and, crucially, Trentin are the first to yield at the back of the group. When De Gendt leads over the pass, he has just seven riders for company.

'I was looking at the battle for the green jersey and I knew that Trentin would want to be in the break because if he could win in Gijón, then pick up some points at the intermediate sprint on the Angliru stage, he would only have to be in the top seven in Madrid to edge out Chris Froome for the points title. So, I was watching him closely right from the start,' De Gendt reveals, highlighting the calculations that are often required when assessing who is going to do what. 'When the group swelled to almost thirty riders, I pushed up the pace on the climbs a little in order to try to get rid of some of the sprinters and also even the odds up in my favour because there were some teams who had four guys in the break and several that had two, and I didn't have anyone from my team there with me. I deliberately tried to drop the guys who were there to help their teammates win the stage. Unfortunately, they all came back after the climb so my plan wasn't a total success.'

Although De Gendt is eager to press on, when other riders at the front won't commit fully the group swells again to number more than twenty riders. By Pola del Siero, Trentin is back with them and is first over the line at the intermediate sprint.

Once again, there are too many hangers-on, too many riders sitting in the wheels and waiting for the final climb before showing their hands. Cannondale's Simon Clarke and Villella attempt to take advantage of the lull by attacking, but each is chased down. Young Spaniard Iván García is luckier, though.

Racing towards his home city in his first Vuelta, which still awaits its first Spanish winner, the UAE rider manages to make his attack stick. His lead has reached almost forty-five seconds when the Quick-Step duo swap roles, Trentin setting the pace for Jungels, who will be the stronger of the pair on the final climb.

Ascending the Alto de San Martín de Huerces, García pushes his advantage out to almost a minute. 'By that point I was keeping a close eye on Bardet. I knew that he was going to attempt to get across to the lone leader on the final climb,' De Gendt continues. 'However, when he did make his move he went so fast that there was no way that I could follow him, and I couldn't go with Rui Costa and Nicolas Roche either when they started to chase after him. So I started tracking Bob Jungels and that proved to be a wise move.'

Bardet, Chris Froome's most dogged rival at the Tour de France just a few weeks before, trims back all but a dozen seconds of García's lead by the summit of the final ascent. A brilliant descender, he soon bridges across to the youngster with Roche and Rui Costa fifteen seconds behind. For the next few kilometres, the race becomes a two-up time trial, the Frenchman and Spaniard sharing the pacemaking in order to keep the Irishman and the Portuguese at a distance. The chasing pair win that little battle, though, and two becomes four at the front.

With half a dozen kilometres to the line in Gijón, Roche attacks. Thanks to his show of force on the final climb, Bardet has revealed he's the strongest, and Rui Costa and García look to him to respond. The Frenchman does, and Roche is reeled in with four kilometres left. The quartet barely have a chance to size each other up again, though, before Jungels bridges across to them with Navarro, De Gendt and two others glued to his wheel.

Roche, once quick in a sprint before a greater focus on climbing drew much of the speed from his legs, signals his lack of confidence in this critical skill by attacking with a little less than two kilometres remaining. Navarro and De Gendt jump across to his wheel. The trio have a small gap racing into the final kilometre, although neither the Spaniard nor the Belgian comes through to help the Irishman with the pacemaking.

Tactics may not play a significant role in a bunch gallop, but De Gendt now demonstrates the advantage they can offer when contesting a sprint within a much smaller group. Like Navarro, he keeps glancing backwards as Jungels closes the gap, with four riders on his wheel. The fact that they've not assisted Roche suggests they are both confident that they've got the resources and fast-twitch fibres in their sculpted legs to give them an edge. Both men are breakaway specialists, but Navarro's a typical Spanish climber, light in weight and dangerous in an uphill finish. He's not used to sprinting for victory on the flat, and his window of opportunity closes when Jungels brings the chasing quintet back on terms just before Roche leads around the sweeping left-hand turn with 700 metres to the finish.

With eight riders trailing him, Roche is now in the worst place, with everyone in his slipstream waiting for the right moment to attack off his wheel. He ups the pace, making a long effort that plays even more into the hands of the riders lined out behind him. With 250 metres to go, García accelerates from eighth place with all he has left. He gets two bike lengths clear before De Gendt darts leftwards from third in line and begins to open up his sprint. For a brief moment, we appear to be on the verge of a fairy-tale result in Gijón. However, as García's speed drops, De Gendt's increases and at the line he's two bike lengths clear, clenching his fist to celebrate the victory that completes his Grand Tour set.

He barely has time to enjoy the moment before he's guided into the TV interview area. 'That last climb was really steep and I had to go full just to keep on the wheel of Bob Jungels,' he explains. 'There were four guys away so I thought we were going to ride for fifth position but the gap was never more than fifteen seconds and we were going full to catch them. Nobody was skipping a turn. Once we caught them, it was like poker. I had good cards so I had to go all in when Nicolas Roche went in the final. I have a fast finish but I didn't know all of the guys. I just went full and did the sprint of my life.'

Reflecting on the victory a few weeks later, De Gendt insists that he was lucky that his group managed to catch the four leaders in the final couple of kilometres, but agrees with the adage that sometimes you make your own luck.

'I went in the breaks at the Tour almost every day and that was too much. But at the Vuelta I was a lot more selective and that's probably why it worked out,' he says. 'That's the key to cycling, that you can always learn and, if you pay attention to those lessons, you will benefit in the end. Experience counts so much when it comes to winning.'

CHAPTER 2

THE DEVELOPMENT OF TACTICS

Strategy without tactics is the slowest route to victory. Tactics without strategy is the noise before defeat.
> — *Sun Tzu*, The Art of War

Across a century and a half, bike racing has developed from a primitive state, where racers generally rode with pacemakers and time gaps were measured in minutes and hours, to become what many perceive as a rather bewildering sport, where the leader is rarely seen at the front and a three-week event can be decided by a few dozen seconds. Over that period, the fundamental development has been the primacy of the team over the individual, a change that the UCI is attempting to counter with a series of initiatives intended to shift the sport backwards towards an age when the major events weren't so controlled, when technology had less of an impact and when racing, we're often led to believe, constantly thrilled.

Racing began with Paris–Rouen, the first recognised event to cover a significant distance – 123km – and provide a coherent structure. Held in November 1869, its organisers laid down that 'All velocipedes, all mechanical machines moved by human force, either by use of weight, by action of the feet or hands, monocycles, bicycles, tricycles, quadricycles or polycycles are eligible for the race. They will only be able to carry a single person, who will drive and steer them, and changing the instrument employed during the event is prohibited.' The rules added, rather confusingly: 'Riders are allowed to ride in company or in caravan, but without giving each other any assistance. Two or more riders can't ride at the same speed or provide each other with mutual assistance via the use of ropes or chains.'

Did this prohibit or permit drafting behind another rider, taking a position in their slipstream in order to avoid cleaving the wind, the first and most fundamental tenet of road racing? Rule-making over the next half-century would suggest the former, but at this point the regulation was ahead of its time. The winner, Paris-based Englishman James Moore, covered the course at an average of just 11kph, well below the speed at which any following rider would gain significant advantage by 'sitting in' on a rival's wheel. Indeed, when it came to tactics, the 118 men and two women who lined up had very few options. The race essentially boiled down to one simple strategy, and Moore undoubtedly spoke for most of the competitors when he described: 'As soon as the signal was given I pressed on the pedals with all my might.'

On rough roads that became very cloying in the wet weather, Paris–Rouen proved little beyond the fact that velocipedes were liable to frequent breakdowns and that bicycles rather than tricycles were the most efficient racing machine.

Crucially, though, it triggered enthusiasm for the sport in France and beyond.

It is difficult to establish who provided the first demonstration of physical strength allied to tactical insight in the nascent sport. Among the most celebrated illustrations of what could be achieved by marrying brain and brawn during that era occurred in the inaugural edition of Bordeaux–Paris in May 1891. Established by Bordeaux-based newspaper *Véloce Sport* with the aim of increasing its circulation, the 600-kilometre race was also pitched as a duel between the best French and British riders. However, Britain's top racers, who were all amateurs, were prohibited from competing against France's top men, who were professionals. In order to guarantee the international flavour of the race, the organisers yielded to the British officials, which left George Pilkington Mills, Montague Holbein and Selwyn Francis Edge as the favourites in the thirty-eight-rider field.

Twenty-six hours after the 5am start in Bordeaux, Mills was the first to reach the Boulevard du Porte Maillot in Paris, with Holbein next to finish an hour and a quarter later. Yet, Mills' success was no solo grind to victory in the way that James Moore's had been in Paris–Rouen, and for two reasons. Firstly, although the British riders were not allowed to race against professionals, they were, however, quite happy to employ them as pacemakers and draft behind them. Secondly, thanks to his collaboration with one of these pacemakers, Mills, a colonel in the British army, pulled off road racing's first significant strategic coup a few kilometres beyond the control point at Angoulême. Mills got back under way following this enforced stop after only a few minutes, to the huge surprise of spectators and officials who were expecting the racers, having covered 127 kilometres, to take a nap. However, while his rivals dallied, Mills rode off to rendezvous with champion racer Lewis Stroud, who was both speedy and very durable. By sitting in Stroud's slipstream, Mills built up an unassailable lead.

Later that year, France's leading rider, Charles Terront, produced a performance that eclipsed that ground-breaking success and led to him becoming his country's first veritable sporting star. Competing in the first running of Paris–Brest–Paris, a 1,200km race that would keep Terront on the road for just thirty-eight minutes short of three days, the Frenchman adapted Mills' tactic in a manner that would be extremely familiar to riders and fans in the modern era. Rather than using one or more pacemakers to 'break the air' ahead of him, Terront sat in behind one pacer while a second man rode on whichever side of him the wind was gusting from, providing him with additional shelter. Incidentally, the same man also carried an alarm clock, letting it ring when Terront appeared on the verge of dropping off and only relenting when the Frenchman was roused from his drowsiness to shout 'Enough! Enough!'

Three years later, the growing importance of tactical insight in racing was highlighted in two very different ways. The first occurred in the French national kilometre championship at the Vélodrome de la Seine in Paris. Six riders lined up, including Maurice Farman and the favourite Lucien Louvet. All six started off at walking pace and got progressively slower before rolling to a halt and doing a track stand, poised almost stock still and perfectly balanced on the pedals.

Farman was the first to yield, but only made a couple of pedal strokes to take him up to the top of the track's banking, inviting his rivals to take his place at the front. As he waited for them to move, Farman realised that, with his rivals almost stationary and with the track's gradient in his favour, he had an opportunity to ambush them. He accelerated hard, gaining twenty metres before his rivals even realised what he was doing. When they did, none of them were keen on taking up the pursuit, and Farman extended his advantage to fifty metres before Louvet finally reacted. At the bell, Farman led by forty metres, but Louvet was gaining, towing the other four riders on his wheel. Going into the final bend his lead was twenty metres. Coming off it, Farman's rivals were almost on him when Louvet, exhausted by his 600-metre effort, threw in the towel. Farman held on to win by ten metres.

Writing in *La Bicyclette*, A.M. Peragallo commented: 'The end of this race seemed to have conclusively proved the result of the championship was false, because Louvet had shown clear superiority, not only over the five [sic] that he had led for more than a lap, but also over M. Farman, on whom he regained more than half of the distance initially lost. However, like the hare in the fable, he had set off too late! Louvet demonstrated the power of his thighs and M. Farman showed the power in his head.'

Fittingly given Peragallo's conclusion, the publication of Henri Desgrange's seminal training manual, *La Tête et Les Jambes* (*The Head and the Legs*), took place that same year. Although it was six years before Desgrange took up the position of editor at *L'Auto-Vélo*, which would later become *L'Équipe*, and nine before he announced the first edition of the Tour de France in the pages of that yellow-papered publication, Desgrange was already well known in French cycling thanks to his racing exploits, which included setting the first Hour Record in 1893, when he covered 35.325km on the Buffalo track in Paris.

Based on his competitive experiences, Desgrange structured the book as if offering guidance to his teenage self on how to train and race in order to reach the top level of the sport. Featuring a good deal of the misogynistic hokum that would later be common in *L'Auto-Vélo*'s pages, Desgrange also included a good deal of advice that is still fundamental when training and racing now. In his preface, fellow journalist Ernest Mousset stated: 'The head and legs! It is impossible to express in fewer words and in a more effective manner what cycle sport demands of those who want to devote themselves to it, two qualities that are quite different to each other in nature, but which complement one another. One must have both in equal measure if one is to become a complete racer.'

Desgrange expanded on this, affirming, 'An intelligent man always beats a brute. The great racers are all intelligent: what I mean is that they all have their special kind of intelligence, clear and lucid understanding of the precise means that they must employ to attain their goal.' To back this up, he advised: 'The way in which a rider finishes a climb is, for me, an infallible indicator of their intelligence. And I will even add that it's at the end of climbs that road races are always decided. The rider who knows how to stay within his limits on a climb, who saves himself for the final metres, who can finish without being overly breathless and is quickly onto the descent or the flat section that follows has victory within his grasp. He will perhaps not drop his rivals the first time, but he will do the third, the fourth or the fifth time.' More than a century later, this remains an essential piece of advice for road racers.

Desgrange's instructions on how best to select pacemakers and employ them during competition now reads like a basic guide to building a strong team around a general classification rider. Middling riders are well suited to this role, he suggests, as they tend to take better care of the man they're pacing. He adds that one of a team of pacemakers should be riding a bike that matches the rider's own, so that they can swap in the event of a mechanical incident.

He suggests that adversaries be sized up at any sign of fallibility. 'You must quickly learn to recognise his weak points, test them out from time to time, push the speed up on a climb, in the corners,' Desgrange advises. These words could equally well have been uttered by modern-day *baroudeurs extraordinaires*, such as Thomas De Gendt, Jens Voigt or Thomas Voeckler, breakaway specialists renowned for their ability to go clear of the pack and then pick off their rivals in that escape one by one.

While *La Tête et Les Jambes* does drift into the ridiculous on frequent occasions, Desgrange counselling his charge, for instance, to practise holding his bladder for as long as possible to avoid the need to stop to relieve himself and to get used to parching heat by rinsing his mouth with water and a touch of vinegar after training without swallowing a drop – 'Only when you can withstand thirst for eight consecutive hours will you no longer need to worry about this,' he instructs – there is much that evokes comparison with contemporary training and racing, and some sections that offer food for thought about current racing practice.

For example, he rebukes his rider for waiting for a rival who has punctured to fit a new tyre. 'In racing, as I told you recently, there is never any room for sentiment ... The fans will perhaps whistle at you, but what does that matter? You know all too well that the fans know nothing and only focus on the trivialities of racing … It's necessary for your rivals to think that you are a single-minded man, as someone who can't be swayed, has no weakness and from whom nothing can be expected. Once that's been established, they will never ask you for any concession again.' What, you wonder, would Desgrange make of today's unwritten rule of racing that results in riders waiting if the race leader is set back by a mechanical problem or a crash?

Desgrange then presses home his belief that riders always need to be cunning and ready to mislead their rivals. 'If you feel a little under the weather, that's the moment to proclaim that you've never felt so good. When you're in good form, I can see good reason for loudly stating that you are ill or that you can't be bothered … don't let anyone know your true feelings,' he advises.

Given that long-distance races on the road were still relatively rare, Desgrange's perceptiveness when explaining how to best prepare for an 'endurance race' is startlingly correct. 'The pace at the start is always terribly quick and we've often seen the best being dropped in the opening laps because they've been in a bad position,' he says. 'Mistakes that often pass unnoticed in a sprint event cannot go unseen in an endurance race … Most of the time it's the excessive pace being set by a rival that stands out, even though they're completely unaware of it. You will spot this mistake easily … you will see your man tire bit by bit, struggle to follow the pace; his movements will be erratic, and quickly incoherent. That will be the moment to give a nod to your pacemakers and say goodbye to him in the most gracious way.'

Towards the end of the book, Desgrange exhorts his rider, who is now in his mid-twenties and racing at the highest level, never to allow himself to be dropped. 'Fight with all you have for as long as you can. Who knows, the rival who drops you may perhaps have made an effort that is beyond his means,' he asserts with power meter-like prescience.

Desgrange's insight appears to have influenced racing for a considerable time, or at the very least corresponded closely to tactical thinking in that period, especially in regard to getting the most benefit from pacemakers, who were then very much part of the sport. 'It's not just a case of being strong and skilful if you want to win Paris–Roubaix, you also have to select your pacemakers very carefully,' said Frenchman Maurice Garin after finishing third in the inaugural 1896 edition of what quickly became one of the landmark events on the racing calendar. Seven years on, Hippolyte Aucouturier employed no fewer than thirty-five when he triumphed in Bordeaux–Paris.

During the years either side of the start of the twentieth century, racers and their sponsors focused on boosting speed, generally with little regard to safety. Tandems, triplets and even quadruplets were introduced as the search for speed dominated. Horse power then superseded leg power, as manufacturers provided their star riders with motorbikes and cars to pace them. Run on terrible roads, races such as Bordeaux–Paris and Paris–Roubaix became a dangerous lottery, where being the strongest often didn't count for much, assuming the riders could see where they were going in the choking, blinding dust.

Given the frequent chaos that beset races at that time, it is impossible to overstate the extent by which the Tour de France changed road racing. The first multi-stage event, the first race to completely do away with pacemakers, the 1903

Tour may not have looked much like the modern-day race, but it provided the foundations for that and every other road-racing event. The participants lauded it as the event that 'levelled the playing field' by allowing the humblest roadman to take on the best road riders of the era as an equal – in theory, at least, since the manufacturers still provided their top performers with the best equipment and backup, and that still counted for a lot.

The sixty intrepid racers who lined up in Villeneuve-Saint-Georges, on the southern edge of Paris for the opening stage to Lyon all adopted the same every-man-for-himself approach, riding right to their physical limits. This one-dimensional tactic was effectively a crude forerunner of *la course en tête*, the uncompromising strategy of making the race from the front that would be so devastatingly employed by Eddy Merckx sixty-odd years later. When race official Georges Abran fired his start pistol, every one of the five dozen starters went full gas, unconcerned that 467 kilometres and a full night of racing lay in front of them on roads that were sometimes cobbled but mostly no more than packed earth, and were either dusty or muddy, depending on the weather, pitted with potholes and open to slow-moving horse-drawn traffic as well as motor vehicles kicking up even more dust or spraying mud. For the pick of these racing pioneers, the rush continued for most of the next twenty-four hours, becoming less madcap as it went on and their resources dwindled, but interrupted only by brief stops at control points to sign their names and stock up with food. They tackled the remaining five stages with the same blinkered approach.

As road racing's popularity soared on the back of the Tour's success, it was very much a sport of breakaways. Being in the vanguard allowed the leading professionals the clearest view of the road ahead and made it more likely that, when delayed by a puncture or mechanical setback, which were frequent, they would have other strong riders around them when they got back under way after a minute or two of fettling their machine. Starting slow and pacing your effort wasn't a practical tactic for a good rider because it relegated them to racing with weaker rivals. Race reports prior to the Great War suggest that the peloton only existed as an entity at the start of an event. Once racing began, the peloton split immediately. As a consequence, bunch sprints were extremely rare. Some events bucked this trend on occasions, notably the Tour of Lombardy and the Tour of Flanders, which weren't then blessed with the hills that make them so distinctive now. However, even at those two events and other similar ones such as Paris–Tours, lone winners were common and sprints between groups of ten or more were very much the exception.

As for the racers, the best were all-rounders who could climb a bit, sprint when needed, but, more than anything, depended on brute strength to power them for hour after hour over treacherous surfaces on weighty bikes. The introduction of the high mountains to the Tour in 1910 offered climbers such as French winners Octave Lapize and Gustave Garrigou an advantage, but often not enough to compensate for losses sustained on the flat. It wasn't until the late 1920s, when manufacturers had finally recovered from the impact of the Great War and the sport took its first great leap forwards technologically, that the specialisation of riders, to them being labelled as sprinters, climbers or *rouleurs*, became more pronounced.

The establishment of more and better organised teams increased the depth of competition, which was further heightened by the increasing use of the derailleur. As a technological innovation, the ability to change comparatively easily from one gear to another is probably the most important the sport has ever seen, and certainly had more impact on bike racing than the introduction of race radios or power meters. Coincidentally, given the fierce debate in contemporary times about the use of those devices, Henri Desgrange dismissed derailleurs as an aberration that falsified competition by giving weaker riders the ability to compete with the strongest. He consistently refused to countenance their use by the leading riders in that event, insisting the Tour would become a race between bikes rather than riders if he relented.

French cycling writer Pierre Chany offered four reasons for the derailleur having an impact on racing, particularly in races on flat terrain: firstly, they allowed the regularisation of pedalling cadence, thereby reducing the influence of resistance; secondly, they enabled the use of big gears, resulting in higher speeds on the flat, descents and in sections with favourable wind; thirdly, higher racing speeds meant greater wind resistance, making it harder for solo riders or small groups to maintain their advantage over a peloton where the pacemaking is shared between many fresher riders; and fourthly, the ability to change gear enabled riders to produce a short, intense effort to regain sanctuary in the bunch. By the time that Jacques Goddet took over from the ailing Desgrange as the Tour boss in 1937 and finally allowed use of the derailleur, bunch finishes were already commonplace in most of the other major stage races and breakaway victories were increasingly measured in seconds rather than minutes on flatter stages.

This immediate pre-war period also witnessed the start of the rivalry between Gino Bartali and Fausto Coppi. Not only did it dominate Italian cycling on either side of the conflict, but it also marked road cycling's transition into a sport much more familiar to contemporary fans. Bartali, the older of the pair, who won the Tour in 1938 and 1948, three Giro crowns and just about every other title of note, was the traditionalist. 'He came from an era when cyclists simply got on their bikes and rode,' Paul Foot writes in *Pedalare! Pedalare!* Coppi, on the other hand, was, according to his teammate Raphaël Geminiani, the man who invented cycling. 'Coppi was the avant-garde of cycling. First he got to know himself, how far he could go physically, then everything else followed that. Every cyclist since has been inspired by him. Nothing fundamental has been invented since Coppi,' Geminiani says in William Fotheringham's biography, *Fallen Angel*.

Italian teams had long been organised around a single *campione* surrounded by faithful *gregari*, or *domestiques*, and Bartali's teams certainly followed this pattern. Yet Coppi adapted the model, making it more sophisticated and demanding far more loyalty from the riders who were brought in to do everything from push him up climbs early on in races so that he could preserve his energy to running errands for him around his Piedmont home town of Novi Ligure where they were all based. Tactics changed, too. According to Italy's 'third man' of the post-war era, Fiorenzo Magni, 'Coppi started from the principle that having riders behind is useless so he needed riders in front. That way, when he attacked, he had support ahead of him: one or two riders who could pull a bit, help for fifty kilometres perhaps, then he would leave them.' As Fotheringham points out, 'They would also give moral support or offer up a wheel if he punctured or had mechanical trouble. These are the fundamental tenets of cycle racing as a team.'

The two men's influence wasn't limited to their own teams either. Rival riders would ask Coppi, Bartali and other leading *campione* for permission before joining a breakaway or going for a stage win. Threats to this hierarchy were stamped down, emerging riders suddenly finding they had a good part of the Italian *gruppo* riding against them. During the 1946 Giro, for instance, in the midst of one of their most hotly contested battles Coppi and Bartali agreed a deal to suppress the emergence of Vito Ortelli, after the youngster led the race for several days. These strictures also applied to the *gregari*, who were obliged to ride for their leader in every circumstance. Dubbed *cyclisme à l'italienne* by the French, this approach to racing was brutally disciplined but supremely effective. The top teams and their *campionissimi* ruled the roost, relegating the rest of the riders to a supporting role as *gregari*, racing in what was effectively a state of serfdom rather than as plucky *domestiques*, never granted even the occasional opportunity to ride for themselves. By colluding with each other, the established stars ensured a closed shop.

Coppi amassed dozens of titles, including two Tours and five Giri. Perhaps most astonishing, though, is his number of solo wins: he claimed fifty-eight, clocking up, according to one calculation, no fewer than 3,000 kilometres on his own in the process. His team's equipment, efficiency, loyalty and tactical know-how offered a foundation from which this majestic stylist could impose almost at will, especially on his home roads. It didn't work so well in France, where, says Geminiani, it was harder to control rival riders and the approach to racing was quite different. 'In the Giro there would be a kind of arrangement between the riders that you wouldn't really race until the feeding station, whereas in France we would attack as soon as the start flag was dropped ... because everyone went from the gun, everyone was a danger, breaks could get a huge amount of time; it was more chaotic.'

Coppi's innovations, which covered diet, technology, training and staff, also extended to adopting a set strategy for Grand Tours rather than just taking each day as it came and responding to opportunities when they arose. 'He would plan to *"fare il vuoto"* – open a huge gap – on two or three major stages, and then control the remaining stages.'

Having worked so effectively for Coppi, the Bianchi model was adopted throughout the sport by Louison Bobet and Jacques Anquetil, the latter under the management of Geminiani, whose Saint Raphaël team gained the nickname 'the Real Madrid of cycling' as it scooped title after title. Their strategy at stage races was simple: neutralise every break that offered a potential threat and never offer any assistance in any break they did join, with the aim of ensuring that Anquetil could clean up the title in the time trials. Geminiani acknowledged it wasn't pretty, but it was effective.

Rik Van Looy tailored it to suit his particular strengths as a Classics specialist and sprinter, amassing almost 400 victories from the late 1950s during a lengthy career when the ambitions of his teammates were completely subordinated to his own. Many of them were gifted riders who could have won decent races, but opted to join Van Looy's 'Red Guard' because they could boost their earnings by helping him win more often and, just as significantly, count on his influence to gain lucrative contracts for criterium appearances.

'I believe in having a top man in the team. I'm a born leader. It's my nature,' Van Looy said of his team's structure, which was replicated at almost every other for the next two decades. 'In the Classics, everyone had to race for me. In the other races, they were to ride for whoever was in the best position on the road. It was that richness [of talent] that produced so many successes, many for my teammates.' His *domestiques* had a quite different perspective, though. They ended up fighting among themselves for the scraps their leader allowed them. After he spent a fraught professional season sharing leadership at the Solo team with Van Looy, Eddy Merckx said his compatriot preferred a rider on a rival team to win rather than one of his teammates.

In *Cycling is My Life*, Tom Simpson offers a succinct insight into Van Looy and the Red Guard's tactics when racing at the Circuit du Provençal in 1965, when he found himself in a breakaway with Belgians Joseph Timmerman and Roger Baguet. 'Timmerman did his share of the work but Baguet, who was in Van Looy's team, would not do a stroke. They always claim to be protecting their leader or they have a man off the back. Anything to save them from working. Anything, in fact, to block the race,' says Simpson, highlighting how Van Looy's teammates would sit in and not collaborate, keeping them fresh if the escape stayed away, but simultaneously stifling the break's progress to Van Looy's eventual profit.

Having started his professional career in uneasy alliances with Van Looy and then Simpson, Merckx opted for a hybrid of the Coppi and Van Looy systems when he became a leader in his own right at Faema in 1968, mixing humble *domestiques* with more talented riders, all devoted to him. As with Van Looy, when the opportunity arose and Merckx viewed it as appropriate to take it, these riders could savour success of their own, but the money that came from the prize money 'The Cannibal' reaped and the contracts that he was able to assure them meant their loyalty was guaranteed. By the early 1970s, when Faema had morphed into Molteni, Merckx's team had the biggest wage bill in the sport and, as Geoffrey Nicholson notes in *The Great Bike Race*, had become so strong that it was accused of stifling competition in some races, four decades before Sky were depicted in the same way.

'Not only does every member of his team put Merckx's interests first, but collectively they dictate the rules to everyone else in the race,' says Nicholson. 'Even a great individualist like Coppi, celebrated for his long, lone attacks, depended on the support of his team until the moment came for him to break loose. What Merckx has done is to build around him a team of even more gifted riders and persuaded them that it's in their interest to work for a common cause – himself.'

Other teams tried to emulate Faema and Molteni, but all came up short simply because Merckx was incomparable as a leader, racing and winning from one end of the season to the other, an almost inexhaustible phenomenon, a rider so strong and single-minded that he could do what he wanted almost whenever he wanted. According to his sporting director Bob Lelangue, 'There were no tactics with Merckx. He was so strong that he would improvise during a race and his teammates had to be prepared to back him up in every decision. He was like an artist, a filmmaker or a painter. You could guess which way the work of art was heading but you didn't quite know how he was going to get there. He just followed what inspired him on the day.'

That inspiration became known as *la course en tête,* 'racing from the front' as Fotheringham puts it in *Half Man, Half Bike.* What it portrayed was an approach that hadn't been seen since the very early days of the sport, when racers would try to create openings at every opportunity rather than being defensive for the most part and waiting for favoured terrain to seek out an advantage.

'As a way of racing it is pro-active,' Fotheringham explains. 'It is centred on the premise that as much physical and mental energy is used in chasing down moves as is spent in making them. Attack becomes the best form of defence: you need to crack a climber such as [José Manuel] Fuente, so you harass him on the flat then frustrate him in the mountains; you have to beat a sprinter so you burn him out beforehand. A star's team is there not merely to control the race but to destroy rivals' minds and bodies before the leader puts in the *coup de grâce,* or to be sent up the road to act as decoys: the leader bridges to them when he makes his move or forces the opposition to tire themselves out chasing. *La course en tête* calls for resourcefulness, inventiveness, complete determination, total concentration.'

Merckx's rivals quickly learned they had to be ready at all times to respond. There was no predicting when he would go on the offensive, only that he almost certainly would. An offensive might come when the wind changed, after a crash, in a feed zone, on a hill or a descent. 'Merckx would attack anywhere,' his Italian rival Francesco Moser recalled. 'In my first Giro in 1973, when the bunch had stopped to get water – that still happened back then – he attacked at full speed. Imagine the chaos! We were a long way from the finish and there were riders everywhere – that was Merckx. He was terrific ...'

Explaining his approach, Merckx said, 'There are a lot of things in a race that you can't control although you have to be aware of them. The main thing you can count on is yourself. And that's what I always put emphasis on.' He reasoned that by controlling the rhythm of a race, he inevitably forced his rivals to follow. Consequently, at the day's end he was no more fatigued than they were. This approach was particularly effective in the mountains, the one area where Merckx felt he was lacking compared to the specialists. By harrying the likes of Fuente and José Jiménez on the plains, obliging them to push big gears to stay with the pace, he sucked most of that advantage away from the climbers by the time a race reached the mountains. 'They may not be defeated in the mountains in the strictest sense but they are no longer able to create huge gaps,' said Merckx, aware that physical strength now mattered as much as endurance, and that this would inevitably suit all-rounders in his mould.

Merckx's rivals responded not by ganging up on him but by sitting on his wheel, effectively handing the initiative to his team. If Merckx couldn't attack, one of his *domestiques* would, and they were classy performers. Far too dangerous to be given much leeway, they would have to be chased down, with Merckx tracking the pursuers and already plotting his next move. 'It was classic cycling team tactics: a decoy out front, teammates behind monitoring the chase, ready to take advantage of the chasers when they tired or when the junction was made,' says Fotheringham, who goes on to describe *la course en tête* as 'the benchmark for the entire sport. The way he raced is the gold standard to which all professional cyclists and all their victories are compared.'

CHAPTER 3

THE MAKING OF MODERN TACTICS

Tactics mean doing what you can with what you have.

– Saul Alinsky

From the mid-1970s, the strategic approach to racing began to take on what would be, to contemporary fans, a far more familiar shape. Previously fiefdoms built around one out-right leader, the so-called 'giants of the road' such as Merckx, Coppi, Van Looy and Anquetil, teams switched to a focus on the collective. While they still depended on a star name to carry their attack in the biggest events and to draw in sponsors, the primacy of 'the group' became fundamental.

The impetus for this model came from a new generation of sporting directors, all former riders with strong personalities, each of them more influential than any one rider on their roster and most of them superlative tacticians. In the forefront were Peter Post, Giancarlo Ferretti, Jan Raas,

Patrick Lefevere and Cyrille Guimard, who described the transformation as one that took the sport away from the 'artisanal, old school, empirical', methods where everything was learned on the job to a new approach where the focus was more on technical aspects, on training, technology, and specific racing targets, resulting in increasing specialisation among riders. New giants did emerge, none bigger than Bernard Hinault, but as would be seen when Guimard unceremoniously sidelined the Breton, his first protégé, to bring through his second, Laurent Fignon, all were expendable when it came to ensuring a continuity of success within a team.

In this era where the sporting director was king, 1976 was a particularly significant season, marking the appointment of recently retired French sprinter Guimard as *directeur sportif* at Gitane and the first major road race successes of ex-track star and 1964 Paris–Roubaix winner Peter Post's TI-Raleigh team. In essence, the Anglo-Dutch TI-Raleigh squad, backed principally by British money and featuring mainly Dutch riders, implemented what was broadly the *la course en tête* strategy embodied by Merckx, but honed it to suit the all-round talent of their squad. It was, says sports writer Richard Moore, 'democratic, meritocratic and fluid. Post's riders were encouraged to be aggressive, to attack, to bend the race to their will; and then to support whichever rider happened to be in the best position or shape to win.' According to Marc Sergeant, who rode for Post for five seasons when TI-Raleigh had become Panasonic, his attitude was, 'I don't care who wins, but it has to be one of us.'

The strategy was brilliantly effective. Typically, Post's team would line up at any major event with two or three protected riders, who would carry responsibility for leadership at that race. Another half a dozen riders were all primed to join the breakaway. Once into the front group, any TI-Raleigh rider would sit in, telling the other escapees they were defending the interests of whichever combination of Jan Raas, Hennie Kuiper, Dietrich Thurau, Gerben Karstens, Gerrie Knetemann, Peter Winnen and Joop Zoetemelk were in the peloton behind. Between 1976 and Raleigh's decision to pull out of the sport at the end of 1983, when Panasonic stepped in, Post's team, which rarely featured a specialist sprinter, won fifty-six Tour stages, the yellow jersey with Zoetemelk in 1980 and a host of Classics victories. 'One year at the Tour they won eleven stages. Incredible,' Kuiper recalls. 'That was a real team, with real team spirit. Everybody worked for everybody else. If somebody got away, the others protected him.'

José De Cauwer, a TI-Raleigh rider who went on to have an illustrious career of his own as a sporting director, notably guiding Greg LeMond to success in the 1989 Tour and Tom Boonen to the world championship in 2005, confirms the simple tactic employed of putting a rider in the break at almost every opportunity. 'That guy would say he couldn't work because his leader was behind, and the result was that if they stayed away he would be fresh and would win the race. We always used that same excuse,' says De Cauwer.

'Everyone thinks that it was Peter Post's idea to have a team with lots of winners and give them all a chance, but I recall that the idea came from the riders, from Jan Raas, Gerrie Knetemann and a few others. Rather than being Peter Post's idea, it was the tactic of Peter Post's team. We had incredible success. Of course, that was down to the fact that we had good riders, but the team spirit was so high as well. There was such confidence.'

The obvious question given the blatancy and regularity of the tactic was why did teams allow them to get away with it? 'It wasn't too long before the other teams started saying they wouldn't work with the guys from TI-Raleigh because things always went the same way,' De Cauwer explains. 'They'd say, "We set up the break, we do the work, and then it's one of them who wins the stage." But the more races we won, the harder it was for the other teams to change tactic. Once they got into the break with one of our riders, they knew they would have a chance to win and they worked again because they had that opportunity.' It's worth noting that teams had often worked with Merckx's for exactly this same reason.

De Cauwer stresses, though, that there was more to the strategy than simply ensuring TI-Raleigh was represented in the break. 'The other key to that team's success was that they always got the right rider in the breakaway. If you put a *domestique* in a break who can't sprint and finds he's up against three or four quick guys, he's going to really struggle to win, even if he hasn't done much work. The big advantage that TI-Raleigh had in a race such as the Tour was that most of the riders selected for a race like that had the potential to win,' he says. With that expectation came pressure. It was not for nothing that the riders at TI-Raleigh altered the company's 'TI-R Group' abbreviation to *Tirgruppe* – firing squad.

Post's constant demands for excellence continued when TI-Raleigh became Panasonic. Sergeant admits that when he joined them in 1990, he struggled to cope with Post's incessant hectoring for success. 'He expected you to be one of the best. We were always expected to carry the weight of the race.

There was always a moment when we had to start pulling, when they would depend on your qualities and the time had come to deliver. Sometimes it was quite hard to live up to that,' he recalls.

'I think I got very strong on the tactical side when I was a rider. A lot of the other teams just used to watch us and wonder what we were going to do, and we took advantage of that. We'd think about how the other teams would react if we employed a certain tactic, and how we could then benefit from that in a way that they perhaps hadn't foreseen. It was an interesting way of looking at racing.

'He was quite special,' Sergeant adds with a rueful smile, offering an illustration of how Post would keep his riders on their toes. 'I used to do quite a lot of work, bringing the bunch back up to the breakaway and helping our sprinter Olaf Ludwig in the final, and I remember him saying to me on the morning of a time trial, "You don't have to go full today. You've done a lot of work already and tomorrow's another important day." I ended up in eightieth or ninetieth position, and that evening he came to the riders' table with the results sheet and ran his finger down it. "Sergeant, hmm, you were ninetieth today …" Then he named a few riders who had finished ahead of me, and declared, "Those guys are quite cheap …"

'There was always pressure there, Post playing with your mind, so that you were never at ease. I enjoyed riding for him, but he had an image and he completely lived up to it. I remember him wearing white shoes one day, which was quite something in cycling back in those days. That was all part of it.' Sergeant, now a team manager himself at Lotto, adds, though, that Post did have a more considerate side. 'You could say to him, "Peter, I've got some trouble with my knee or with my stomach, and I'm not sure I'm going to be able to start tomorrow," and he'd say, "Don't worry, that's fine. I need you for later." You couldn't do that three or four times in a season, but if you really had a problem, he would listen to you. That's another good quality which I learned.'

However, Dietrich Thurau insists that the Dutch team boss's munificence only stretched so far. 'I remember saying to Peter Post that I wanted to focus on the Tour. "You're mad," he said. "I pay you every month, so you'll ride every month." So I raced in Holland, in Belgium and in France – I raced everywhere. But it was exhausting,' recalled the German stage-race specialist, who was clearly ahead of his time with that kind of thinking.

Thurau might have found Cyrille Guimard offered a more sympathetic ear, as the Frenchman became cycling's most assiduous innovator since Coppi. Forced to retire at twenty-eight due to knee problems, Guimard fitted the pattern that produces the best sporting directors. Although talented and determined enough as a rider to wear the Tour's yellow jersey in 1972 and engage in a hard-fought battle with Merckx that ended prematurely only because his knees became so bad he had to be lifted onto and off his bike, Guimard quickly realised after turning pro that tactics was the one part of racing in which he excelled. As early as his debut season, he often found himself acting as road captain and even deciding strategy at his Mercier team. 'I was making some decisions on everyone's behalf. I've got to admit that I liked that role, as would be proved in the future,' he revealed in his autobiography, *Dans Les Secrets du Tour de France*. Lucien Van Impe, his first team leader at Gitane, admitted the Frenchman's insight was uncanny. 'Everything

Guimard said at the briefing came true by the end of the race.'

The Gitane team Guimard took over in 1976 was built around Van Impe, an anomaly as a Flandrian, as he was small and thrived in the high mountains, where he could turn big gears with such unparalleled ease that he had already captured three King of the Mountains titles at the Tour. The rest of the sixteen-strong roster principally comprised young French riders, of whom the most promising was the youngest, twenty-one-year-old Bernard Hinault. Guimard's first task was to persuade Hinault to stay as the precocious Breton felt the team was so poorly run.

Gitane had bagged just five wins, plus Van Impe's third mountains crown the year before, only three the season earlier. Yet, the bullish and extremely self-confident Guimard immediately set his sights not on the Tour's polka-dot prize, but on Van Impe winning the yellow jersey. For a rider turned director, whose most renowned successes occurred when he refused to yield to Merckx's supremacy and desire to dominate, there seemed no reason to aim any lower, particularly when the Belgian phenomenon finished the Giro with a painfully debilitating saddle sore that obliged him to miss the Tour. Van Impe, though, was a follower rather than a leader, a rider who was never keen to take the initiative. He'd turned pro in 1969 and had a single day of racing before making his Tour debut, witnessing first hand how Merckx delivered a textbook demonstration of *la course en tête*, winning by eighteen minutes, taking six stages and all of the classification jerseys, with Faema also the best team. Although hugely impressive in finishing twelfth, Van Impe was one of those most affected by a Merckx complex, so intimidated by 'The Cannibal' that he seldom attacked if there was a chance of upsetting his compatriot, happy to pick over whatever crumbs Merckx left.

'How do you go about winning the Tour de France with a rider who doesn't want to?' Guimard asks in *Dans Les Secrets du Tour de France*, before going on to detail how he managed to achieve this, showing not only tactical insight and brilliance on frequent occasions, but also pulling off what was arguably the greatest bluff in cycling history.

Guimard began by bending Van Impe to his will, making the sylphlike, bubble-permed climber more afraid of his boss than his rivals. Stubborn and easily swayed by his wife Rita, with whom he would spend hours talking on the phone each evening, Van Impe defied and contradicted the Frenchman, the younger man by three months, it's interesting to note. In what would become trademark fashion, rather than yield to his star rider, Guimard issued an ultimatum: fall into line or miss the Tour. Reluctantly, Van Impe acquiesced.

It wasn't only the flakiness of his leader that made Guimard's ambition appear excessively optimistic. Gitane's roster didn't inspire confidence either, the Frenchman admitting that it, 'wasn't the crack squad I'd be working with in future seasons with Bernard Hinault. It wasn't capable of imposing itself on a three-week race. So I had to stake everything on the high mountains and protect our leader up to that point.' Merckx's absence helped, though, as did weaknesses in each of Van Impe's likely rivals for the Tour title.

Guimard's plan to try to keep Van Impe out of harm's way during the Tour's opening week wasn't radical. It is now the standard formula. Gitane's leader reached the first rest day without a notable setback, then unveiled his almost inimitable talent for racing in the high mountains as he captured the yellow jersey by finishing a close second to Joop Zoetemelk at Alpe d'Huez. What surprised even the clairvoyant-like Guimard were the losses sustained by the rest of the yellow jersey favourites. As Van Impe and his teammates celebrated, their French boss contemplated how his brittle team could possibly defend the jersey through another half dozen mountain stages. He came to the conclusion that they couldn't.

There are plenty of instances in Tour history of riders relinquishing the yellow jersey with the aim of regaining it later in the race. But this tactic is generally employed during the first week. At that point, the yellow jersey favourite can select from any number of stalking horses for a few stages – waiting for a suitable candidate to infiltrate a breakaway, which is allowed its head and finishes several minutes ahead of the main pack. Over the following days, the new leader will assuredly make the most of their moment in the spotlight, doggedly defending the yellow jersey and taking a good deal of the media and popular attention. All the while, the race favourite and his teammates can hide in the peloton, save their resources and wait for the right moment to assert their authority.

However, as Van Impe led the race out of the Alps, already halfway through, the leader board featured only well-established names. On the face of it, ceding the Tour de France's yellow jersey to one of these riders would be madness, even heretical for the French manager of a French team. It could well have been career-ending. Yet, thanks to his Kasparov-like facility to see several moves ahead of his rivals, Guimard could see a way to make this lunacy work by instigating a breathtaking bluff.

Guimard weighed up the strengths and weaknesses of the riders just behind Van Impe on the leader board. 'One name stood out for me – Raymond Delisle, who was about four or five minutes down on GC. I knew the Peugeot riders very well and felt that he was one of the few riders who could get into a long-distance breakaway in the mountains and stay the pace to the finish,' he explains. 'So I called him on the phone – yes, I actually called him! – and had a bit of chat with him about this and that and then slipped in the fact that if he was considering attacking on the stage to Font Romeu then we certainly wouldn't chase him down.' Guimard was also well aware that if Delisle followed up on the hint, his bid for success would neuter the rest of Peugeot's team, including defending Tour champion Bernard Thévenet.

Persuading his own riders, and particularly the jubilant Van Impe, of the necessity for this strategy was harder, though. Guimard, who had sarcastically dubbed Van Impe 'Monsieur Bien Sûr' because he always gave the impression he agreed with what was being asked of him even when he didn't, knew his leader was unlikely to follow instructions. His bluff had a fundamental flaw.

Guimard's ploy began well. Delisle joined the break and opened a decent lead. It then became apparent that Belgian riders from other teams had started the chase behind them. Van Impe was implementing his own strategy. Livid, Guimard let his leader know there would be serious repercussions if this continued. Soon after the chase stopped. 'Guimard est Guimard,' Van Impe explained with a shrug, having confirmed that the Frenchman threatened to pull him out of the race.

As Van Impe sulked, Guimard was exultant as stage-winner Delisle's winning margin reached seven minutes at Font Romeu. He recalls it being one of his happiest days in cycling, especially when he heard the reaction of race followers. 'They couldn't understand what was going on. Some of the Belgian press looked like they were going to attack me. They were shouting: "How could you lose the jersey in these circumstances?" Their stories said that I "lacked experience", that "it was the mistake of a young *directeur sportif*". Of course, I played up to that. "Yes, I've made a stupid mistake because I didn't want to over-exert my team," I told them. I could barely keep a straight face. It was beautiful.'

Guimard now had one move left to make, and everything was staked on it. It depended on Van Impe not only gaining time on the Pyrenean stage through the heavily wooded peaks of the Couserans to Pla d'Adet, above the town of Saint-Lary Soulan, but attacking from a long way out to maximise his gains. He gambled on Van Impe's rivals seeing him as 'almost a sprinter in the mountains, as someone who always attacked on the final climb'. This would mean, he felt, the other contenders would regard an attack well before Pla d'Adet as a rush of impetuosity to correct the previous error. 'Once again, it was a huge bluff, but an extremely risky one bearing in mind Lucien's fragile temperament,' says Guimard, whose uneasiness grew as his leader stayed in the bunch on the early ramps of the Col du Portillon, the second of the day's four climbs. Guimard drove up alongside Gitane climber Raymond Martin and asked, 'What the fuck is he up to?'

Acting as go-between, Martin relayed to Guimard the message that Van Impe thought it was too early to attack. He shuttled back to inform Van Impe that if he didn't attack immediately, Guimard would drive him off the road. This was received with a shake of the head, provoking Guimard to press on the accelerator and his horn at the same time, the clamour catching everyone's attention.

'He accelerated as if his arse had caught fire. He went away so quickly and with such ease that no one except Zoetemelk was able to react and he was too timid to maintain his effort, which is what I had expected,' says Guimard. When Van Impe eased off once again, Guimard managed to get his car along-side his leader. 'I told him I'd manipulated rival riders and teams in order to provide this one opportunity, and he simply had to take it.'

What even Guimard couldn't count on was that when Van Impe chased up to and dropped riders from the breaka-way as he went over the Portillon and up the Peyresourde, he would end up with 1973 Tour winner Luis Ocaña near the head of that pass. The Spaniard had long held a grudge against Zoetemelk, stemming from the Dutchman hurtling into him as he was trying to get back to his feet after crashing on the descent of the Col de Menté five years earlier. The impact put Ocaña out of a Tour he was leading by seven minutes. Given the chance for revenge of sorts, the Spaniard seized it and flew down the descent and up the valley to St Lary with Van Impe glued to his wheel. When the road rose for the final time, Van Impe finally gave everything. Delisle came in more than twelve minutes after the Belgian had finished alone at Pla d'Adet, and Van Impe was confirmed as race leader once more, his lead a substantial three minutes on second-placed Zoetemelk.

Guimard's successful coup, undoubtedly one of the most outrageous in the history of the Tour de France, had been achieved. Normally, the successful partnership would have continued, but Van Impe left Gitane at the end of that season, following a disagreement over the size of his salary. 'When you're working in a team environment at any race, but especially one as long and taxing as the Tour, you need everyone to pull in the same direction, with the leader at their head. There has to be strategic coherence and agreement, and Van Impe didn't encourage that. It was far too stressful dealing with him,' says Guimard. Besides, he had Hinault waiting in the wings, a rider with huge talent who was always ready to hear what his director had to say.

While Van Impe was the cycling equivalent of a child that hangs on to its mother's apron strings and has to be coaxed and pushed into achieving its potential, Hinault was quite the opposite. Hugely strong but equally impetuous, he needed reining in. 'I wanted to win all of the time. At the start of every stage race, I lined up with the aim of being first from the opening day to the last,' he says in *Ma Vie et Mes Courses*. 'But then I realised that you can't always race at the front. You have to be patient in certain situations. To forget the desire to dominate. To lose yourself in the group. To be smart one day in order to better achieve your aims the next.'

Guimard recalls him indulging in all manner of reckless escapades – attacking when going into bends and ending up in a ditch, breaking clear right at the start of a kermesse and riding the whole thing on his own only to be caught near the finish. Hinault was a law unto himself, which Guimard relished and responded to, but he also advised: 'Stop attacking all over the place and stay calm.'

Guimard describes Hinault as 'instinctive. I would even say that he had an instinctive intelligence. It was always the same with him. He went right to the edge of the cliff, then made an about-turn at just the right moment.' Or at least he did as he got older. Initially, the Breton's huge ego and pride led to him pushing himself beyond his limits in a bid to impose his will on everyone, to dominate his rivals. 'In order to prevent his qualities becoming faults, he needed a safeguard. That's what I became,' Guimard explains.

Hinault recognises as much, acknowledging that he owed his calculating side to his team boss. 'He was the one who showed me that it is better to set precise objectives in Grand Tours and try to achieve them rather than opting for a scatter-gun approach ... From the purely sporting perspective, I have to admit that Cyrille taught me a lot. Above all, he taught me how to race. To dose my efforts. To moderate my impulses. Up until then I had a tendency to jump on the wheel of the first rider who tried to escape. I showed no discernment. I saw danger on every side. It only needed someone to show the slightest interest in attacking and I would immediately want to put them in their place.'

Hinault went nearer than anyone to emulating Merckx's *la course en tête* strategy. But he wasn't driven to the same all-conquering extent as Merckx. He began each season by marking down two stage races and three Classics that he would do everything to win, but away from these races he was happy to work for his teammates. 'Merckx, though, he never gave anybody anything,' Hinault underlined.

Thanks to Guimard's interest and investment in sports science and technology, the partnership with Hinault can also be compared with Coppi in regard to the advances it encouraged in many different areas beyond purely the racing. Renault-Gitane, as it became in 1978, was the first team to travel to races in a small bus rather than team cars, and benefited from the French car manufacturing giant's access to wind-tunnel testing and research into aerodynamics. This

led, in 1979, to Gitane producing the Profil, a bike with con-
cealed cables, the front brake hidden behind the fork and
flattened tubes. Allied to a focus on ergonomics, Hinault also
adjusted his time-trial position in the wind tunnel, Renault's
engineers calculating they had saved him two seconds per
kilometre in a time trial. Moreover, this kind of investment was made in all of the riders, not just the leaders, and
occurred thirty-odd years before Tim Kerrison advocated the
same approach at Team Sky.

Predictably, given the obduracy of both men, Guimard and
Hinault were destined to fall out. They did frequently during their mutual heyday at Renault between 1978 and 1983,
when Hinault won eight Grand Tours and most major one-day
titles. But when assessing the pair from a tactical perspective,
it is more instructive to focus on their rivalry after Laurent
Fignon emerged as Guimard's newly anointed leader, thanks
to his 1983 Tour win.

Fignon's success encouraged Hinault to leave Renault
for La Vie Claire. The result was one of the most intriguing
match-ups in racing history. On the road, it pitted the young
urbane Parisian Fignon against the more experienced man
from the provinces in Hinault. Pulling the strings – or not, as
we shall see – were Guimard, an innovator and tactical magi-
cian, versus Paul Köchli, a Swiss ex-pro who barely raised a
ripple of interest as a racer but had gone on to create a huge
stir as a coach.

'I developed a concept for cycling, how to teach it, and how
to teach coaches. I was very interested in physiology. But my
programme included everything! You cannot separate the elements – training, tactics, endurance, power, psychology, motivation,' Köchli explains in *Slaying the Badger*, Richard Moore's

excellent book on the story of the battle between Hinault and teammate Greg LeMond at the 1986 Tour.

Guimard was among those who travelled to Switzerland to study Köchli's courses. 'Paul was a technician and a brilliant boffin, the most brilliant among us by far. But he wasn't a leader of men.' Hinault, naturally, offered a different perspective. 'What you need to know is that Cyrille Guimard was Paul Köchli's pupil. So having been coached by the pupil, I switched to being coached by the teacher.'

While Guimard gave Hinault some autonomy to let him feel that he was in charge of events, Köchli allowed the Breton his head, but within a strategic plan, which he defined as 'the big picture' and would be established before a race or stage. Tactics were 'the detail', 'the micro-decisions that need to be taken quickly in the heat of battle'.

Describing cycling as 'a play sport', Köchli wanted his riders to enjoy it, telling them each morning, 'OK, today we play cycling! Let's play cycling!' As he points out in making a comparison with football, it offers no end of opportunity to do so. 'In a football game, it's very simple. There are two enemies against each other. A bicycle race is much more complicated. So many dimensions. Twenty-one teams, two hundred riders. It's hot, it's cold. Uphill, downhill. Headwind, crosswind. The wind changes. Very interesting strategically. Very, very interesting. You can be friends in a certain situation but maybe in ten minutes not friends any more. It always changes, it's dynamic.'

In the same way Sergeant describes Peter Post insisting that he didn't care which of his riders won as long as one of them did, Köchli encouraged this same ethic to take advantage of that dynamism. He highlights it most clearly in his conversation with Moore when asked about the supposed deal made between Hinault and LeMond that the former would support the latter at the 1986 Tour. Both riders maintain that it was agreed and fulfilled, but still dispute the degree of commitment on the Frenchman's side. Köchli says of such a deal, 'It goes against our strategy. It's exactly what we *don't* do.' The fundamental, he stressed, was that, 'We must win,' qualifying that by clarifying that 'we' didn't mean Hinault or LeMond, but La Vie Claire.

Sitting somewhere between Merckx's *la course en tête* and TI-Raleigh's 'all for one and one for all' ethos, Köchli went against the established grain in a number of ways. He didn't have a sprinter on his team because that would have meant one fewer rider who could attack, he didn't recognise the word '*domestique*' and didn't instruct his riders to set the pace on the front, preferring to encourage his riders into breakaways and encouraging them to act intuitively. 'We just make sure we have a rider in the next break, to force the *others* to chase. That's all. It's simple,' he tells Moore.

Yet, come the 1984 Tour, the pupil completely outwitted the teacher, as Guimard's Renault-Elf team performed imperiously, taking ten stage wins as Fignon cruised to the title. The Alpe d'Huez stage encapsulated the change in the balance of power. It followed a mountain time trial at La Ruchère won by Fignon, with Hinault thirty-three seconds down in fourth. Always counselled by his first coach, Robert Le Roux, and Guimard to strike back the day after such a setback, 'The Badger' attacked time after time as the race went over the Côte de Laffrey and towards the final climb. 'I knew every little one of his impulses by heart. I was convinced that Hinault, by turns impulsive and prone to anger, would make mistakes:

calculation, patience and messing with the strategy of his rivals wasn't his strong point,' says Guimard. This was one of those mistakes. Fignon was too strong, his dismissal of his rival's doggedness contemptuously easy.

The Parisian confessed later that he fully expected to win the Tour six or seven times, and looked entirely capable of achieving that level of success until set back by a serious Achilles injury early in 1985. Sadly, it not only meant Fignon was unable to defend his title, but also prevented a duel between the two giants of French and, at that point, world cycling when both were in peak form.

Instead, with Hinault back to his best and now supported by Guimard's former protégé LeMond, the next two Tours offered an almost flawless demonstration of the beautifully anarchic unpredictability Köchli's approach could serve up, especially with a rider at its centre like Hinault, who never appreciated being shackled. Several stages stand out in this regard, notably the Frenchman's audacious attack on the Pyrenean stage to Pau in 1986, which earned him the yellow jersey and a five-minute lead, which he followed up with another offensive through the range the next day that flew in the face of established tactical reason and all but lost him the lead at Superbagnères.

Just as notable, though, was the way that La Vie Claire continued to hound their rivals on stages that seemed to offer far less chance of making a gain. On the very next stage after Hinault almost blew his lead, a short one out of the mountains across flat countryside to Blagnac on the western edge of Toulouse, La Vie Claire placed three riders in a breakaway group, including second-placed LeMond. When that was closed down 60km from the finish, Köchli's team had Niki Rüttimann in the next escape, from which the Swiss won the stage and moved into the top eight, which already included three of his teammates. There was no question of ticking the stage off, of Hinault and LeMond simply tracking their rivals and telling the media at the end of the day, 'We're one day closer to Paris,' as is now often the case. That would have meant missing out on the chance to play. Two days later, they were at it again on a 250km stage to Gap run into a headwind, where Hinault, Rüttimann and Guido Winterberg all infiltrated a break that La Vie Claire's rivals had to chase down. Ultimately, another four-man break went clear and another one of Köchli's riders finished alone at the front, on that occasion Jean-François Bernard. They were like the two-wheeled Harlem Globetrotters, attempting what were, to almost everyone else, ridiculous tactical stunts, but ending with a slam dunk of a stage win more often than not.

It is interesting to note the perspective Köchli's riders had on his radical approach. LeMond and Bernard suggest that Hinault was actually running things and that their Swiss team director was weak and had little control over the Frenchman. LeMond also criticises Köchli for being inflexible in his planning. Hinault and Andy Hampsten, on the other hand, are full of praise, Hampsten describing him as 'brilliant because he didn't try to choreograph everything we did'. Hinault, meanwhile, insists Köchli did allow plenty of flexibility in his strategic plans and was 'ten years ahead of his time' in his approach to training and other race preparation. The fact that Köchli drove up alongside Hampsten, who was countering after Hinault had been reeled in on that stage to Superbagnères, and told him he could now win the Tour while his two teammates

THE MAKING OF MODERN TACTICS

bickered behind indicates he was very prepared to adapt, and radically so.

In offering his take on his two leaders, Köchli highlights why Hinault adjusted better at La Vie Claire than LeMond. 'Hinault, in his first career [when he rode for Cyrille Guimard], was a guy who just decided when he wanted to … *Vroom!* He was so strong he could drop everybody. But later, with me, Hinault liked the game, and he started playing the game. Greg was always there, observing … but Hinault had already taken the opportunity. I could not be against that. He was a good example for the other riders in the team, who started acting like Hinault and winning lots of other races. Greg was not familiar with that, and he could not adapt. Within the team, he was at a disadvantage.'

Reflecting on the two riders' approach to the Pyrenean stages in the 1986 Tour, Köchli says, 'The problem Greg had in the Pyrenees is that Hinault is the better rider. I make a big, big distinction between a good rider and a strong rider. Here, Greg was probably stronger than Hinault. But Hinault was clearly the better rider. The difference, most often, is better tactics. And Hinault was tactically better.'

This analysis is pertinent too for the 1987 race, when what became the Toshiba team started with Bernard as leader after Hinault had retired and LeMond had been sidelined by the injuries he sustained in a hunting accident. The Frenchman took a big lead in winning the time trial to the summit of Mont Ventoux, but then lost it the next day when Fignon, Stephen Roche and a number of other notable rivals attacked through a feed zone right after Bernard had punctured and ridden hard to rejoin the group, only for his chain to unship when he managed this. Thinking back to that day, which he finished in the yellow jersey, Roche recalls asking Bernard earlier in that stage if he felt a little bit short-handed as Toshiba had three riders up ahead in the break.

The tactic not only backfired but may well have cost the Frenchman the Tour in that instance. Yet, it also highlighted to what extent Köchli's approach hinged, like any other sporting director's, on both the physical and mental strength of their leader. Hyped by the French press as Bernard Hinault's successor, Jean-François Bernard was not able to cope with the pressure, particularly in a team governed by such a free-form strategy. 'He never showed himself tactically or psychologically to be very strong. He was a nice guy, but very nervous,' Andy Hampsten said of Bernard, who never challenged for the yellow jersey again.

By that point, the face of pro racing was changing radically as the peloton swelled. When Bernard Hinault won the first of his five Tours in 1978, the peloton had numbered just 110 riders. Five years later, when he claimed his fourth yellow jersey, the Tour field was more than 50 per cent larger. As the quest for success became increasingly competitive, new strategies emerged.

Up to the 1970s, sprinting had been a useful skill rather than a tactic around which to build a team. Fast finishers such as André Darrigade, Rik Van Looy, Freddy Maertens, Sean Kelly and Guido Bontempi were among the season's biggest winners, but they rarely depended on more than a teammate or two to set them up for a bunch finish. From the late 1980s, this began to change, as more teams focused on a marquee sprinter, a rider who was far less of an all-rounder than the likes of Maertens and Kelly, but could frequently deliver the *coup de grâce* after being delivered by a string of teammates to a point around 200 metres from the finish line.

The Superconfex and Panasonic teams managed by Jan Raas set the trend, rallying behind Dutch sprinter Jean-Paul van Poppel. But it was perfected by flamboyant Italian sprinter Mario Cipollini, who hoovered up dozens of Grand Tour victories for GB-MG, Mercatone Uno and Saeco on the back of the hard toil undertaken by a cohort of strapping *domestiques* tasked with chasing down breakaways and riding so hard into the finish that no one had a hope of jumping clear until their last man moved aside to let 'Super Mario' power away from his rivals with swaggering consistency. Where Cipollini left off, first Alessandro Petacchi and then Mark Cavendish, Marcel Kittel and André Greipel have continued. While specialist sprinters have flourished, those who thrive in breakaways have been squeezed.

Guimard has described the late 1990s as 'the end of the golden age of *directeurs sportifs*', explaining how the increasing focus on blood-boosting doping products pushed tactics and insight into your riders and their rivals down the list of qualities required for success. 'Only the doctors held the keys to success, they became the real bosses,' he said. Fignon also perceived the change. At the 1993 Tour, he jumped away from the pack on the Col de Télégraphe in the Alps. 'While I was pressing on as I used to on my best days, or so I believed at least, I saw a vast group of riders come up to me. There were at least thirty. Or forty. Not one of them seemed to be pushing it, but I couldn't stay with them.' Riders who couldn't climb over a railway bridge suddenly became untouchable in the mountains. 'All physical obstacles were blown to bits,' said

Fignon of the EPO age, which extended into the opening decade of this century.

In the last ten years or so, the balance has tipped again, as coaches and training consultants have become pre-eminent. Seventy years on from the innovations introduced by Fausto Coppi and the Bianchi team, cycling is now more specialised than ever. The argument is often made that teams now have too much control, that technology is strangling the sport, that road racing isn't as exciting as it was when the Italian and his rivals duelled with each other in what have become legendary battles. Yet that same measure of control was evident in Coppi's era, just as it was subsequently in those dominated by Anquetil, Merckx and Hinault. The strongest have always prevailed, their tactical approach adjusting to ensure this.

What is more certain is that thanks to better knowledge of training and preparation methods, allied to improved implementation of anti-doping measures, the competitive level in road racing's major events is tighter than it has ever been. It has become harder to make a difference and to win. As a consequence, strategy and tactics have become ever more important, but often more difficult to spot, understand and appreciate, nowhere more so than in the heart of pro peloton …

CHAPTER 4

INSIDE THE WASHING MACHINE - RIDING IN THE PELOTON

Perhaps the single most important element in mastering
the techniques and tactics of racing is experience.

– *Greg LeMond*

Watching a professional peloton from above is spellbinding.
It constantly ebbs and flows as riders move up and others slip
back, ripples when it sweeps around both sides of a roundabout or shimmies to avoid a piece of road furniture, the
graceful movement reminiscent of a murmuration of starlings
twirling and swooping at twilight, or a bait ball of sardines
trying to avoid becoming dinner for a school of dolphins eager
for a feast. You almost expect David Attenborough's familiar, half-whispering commentary describing the enthralling
scene, as the mass of bikes and bodies pulses together at one
moment, then unwinds and stretches the next.

As the place where professionals spend the majority of their time when racing, the peloton is to an extent their sanctuary, offering as much shelter as they're going to get from the elements, a chance to chat and perhaps even relax a little before the action kicks off. Yet any cyclist who has ridden two abreast in a group, trying to follow the wheel ahead while avoiding potholes, stones and the occasional stray water bottle is well aware of the focus and stress involved, the first time at least. Multiply the numbers of riders involved by twenty, add a competitive element that includes frequent changes of pace, as well as moments when you need to eat, put on/take off a jacket and perhaps even pee, and sanctuary seems less appropriate a description. Former pro turned sporting director Marco Pinotti puts it better: 'It's like a washing machine, where everyone's going round and round and constantly changing position.'

According to Australia's Tiffany Cromwell, 'Your level of comfort within the peloton depends to a good degree on what kind of a rider you are. I know riders who've come into the sport late who don't have a good feel for riding in the bunch. They freak out. For some riders, simply being in the peloton is a cause of a lot of stress, anxiety, and really plays on their nerves. They have trouble moving through the peloton, they can't get through gaps. There is a lot of argy bargy, and you've got to be prepared and comfortable with that,' she says. 'If you're not comfortable in the peloton it will hold you back, and you do see GC riders who are good climbers who can't find their way to the front, and looking after them can be quite a stressful task. You don't want to be using too much energy moving up through the bunch when there's a critical moment ahead because it will cost you.

'Trying to get through small gaps, being knocked as that happens, can take a toll, although I find it something that's relatively easy to do,' Cromwell continues. 'It doesn't provoke a great deal of anxiety. You do get into those situations when you almost close your eyes and hope for the best, often in sprints, but generally it feels like second nature to me, to be able to roll through from back to front, to find and get through the gaps.'

Most who have raced at the top level will be able to relate to Cromwell's words. Riding in the peloton has always been a test of character and nerve, especially when the pace ramps up approaching a crucial point in a race, particularly the finish. For most of the post-war years, the peloton had a safety valve in the shape of its *patron*, the rider, usually the unchallenged star of the era, who imposed rules on what could happen and when. Gino Bartali and Fausto Coppi fulfilled this role in Italy, imposing order in a regal manner. Eddy Merckx achieved the same, although more due to his crushing physical superiority than his desire to dominate, while Bernard Hinault bent all of his rivals to his will, intimidating them with his personality, deciding when they could attack, chasing them down when they went against his wishes, ensuring that riders who raced for up to perhaps 150 days a year didn't do so at a frantic pace at all times.

Veteran pros were often complicit in maintaining order, too. When, in 1952, the Tour organisers included summit finishes on the race for the first time, concern among riders about the damage that might be caused at Alpe d'Huez, the first ski station anointed, led to senior members of the peloton preventing riders from breaking away by brandishing their pumps, like shepherds keeping a flock together, until the foot of the final ascent. More recently, Mario Cipollini was renowned for instilling the same unanimity at the Giro d'Italia, making clear to the other members of the race's *gruppo* that there was no sense in riding at anything other than a gentle tempo until Italian TV began its daily broadcast.

When the pace did go up, stress levels went up with it, particularly just behind the team setting the pace on the front, who were usually working either for a sprinter like Cipollini or riding in defence of the leader's jersey held by one of their teammates. Clustered behind this arrowhead were the rival sprinters and general classification favourites, each with a cohort of two or three *domestiques* protecting them, with the rest of the pack sitting in behind.

A transformation came with the adoption of race radios by every professional team. First used in the mid-1990s, race radios linking riders to their sporting directors in the cars trailing behind the peloton didn't herald an immediate change, partly because only a few teams used them initially. Greater use, though, has resulted in situations when every team ends up asking its riders to do the same thing at exactly the same time, to move up towards the front of the bunch because there's a pinch point ahead or the wind is going to start blowing from the side. Something has to give, and initially it is composure.

'When I started in the late nineties the peloton was quite an organic, flowing thing. It's not that it was less stressful, it was simply a different, more independent stress. Each one of us decided how much we wanted to fight,' David Millar explains in *The Racer*. 'Nowadays it's robotic. All team *directeurs* are on the radio telling their riders to get to the front and ride as a tight unit. Fair enough, I can see what they're trying to achieve, but it ends up being counter-productive, as with so many teams trying to do the same thing it turns into a total clusterfuck.'

Yet, while radios have added to the pressure when the peloton begins to ride flat out towards the finish, the determination to be in the thick of the action has always been a fundamental part of road racing. Riders still employ the same tools and tactics as their predecessors did back in the 1920s, particularly in the northern Classics, which explains why Belgian riders are generally so adept at battling for position in the bunch and renowned for finding their way through to the front even on the narrowest of roads.

'Holding your place in the bunch does mean using your elbows a lot and asserting yourself. You do try not to be sketchy, perhaps by chopping people's wheels or pushing them onto the grass, because then you'll lose the respect of the other riders, but ultimately you have to be quite ruthless,' explains Tiffany Cromwell, who relishes races like the Tour of Flanders for precisely this reason. 'You've got to be willing to fight to stay on the wheel you're on, otherwise rivals will take advantage and move into your space because they know you're not prepared to defend that position.

'You do often need to use your body weight to assert yourself, but you would never take your hands off your handlebars and try to push someone out of the way – that's an unwritten rule. As long as your hands are on the bars, you can use your elbows to let everyone know, "Hey! I'm here! This is my spot." That said, there are certain riders in the peloton who will still try to come over you, and that's an especially key moment when you have to be strong about holding your place, about making others realise that you won't give up that easily, that you won't be bullied out of your space. If you can do that, other riders realise and it makes holding your position a little easier.'

Like Cromwell, Marco Pinotti underlines that the secret is not simply being able to ride in the middle of the bunch, which he says is easy, but of holding your position. 'The degree of difficulty depends on what part of the race you're in. If it's in the last 30k and the race is on, you have to constantly try to move up simply in order to retain your position. If you don't do that, you'll go backwards,' says the Italian. 'You want to move up but remain out of the wind, but everyone wants to do that. You have riders trying to come in on both sides of you all of the time, and they're dealing with the same thing. That's when you get the washing machine effect.'

A time-trial specialist who was prized as a *domestique* for his ability to provide a long and high-powered pull on the front of a lead-out train or tow one of his team's protected riders to the front of the peloton at a critical instant, Pinotti admits fighting for position wasn't something he enjoyed. 'Some riders find it easier to hold their position or move up than others. Sprinters go through gaps that you don't think are possible. When I had to get to the front, at 10k to go if we were setting up a sprint, I'd press the accelerator button and make a big effort to pass the bunch on one side, then do my bit as hard as I could, then "boom!" and I'd pull out of the way. It takes a real toll mentally making efforts like that in that kind of intense situation. Some riders find it comes naturally, but I wasn't one of them,' Pinotti confesses.

'You get the same kind of fight coming into a climb. It's better to be in tenth position than in twentieth, and there'll be a fight to gain that advantage. So even the climbers will fight to get on a wheel, especially when it's a [20 per cent finishing] climb like the Mur de Huy in Flèche Wallonne. There'll be a constant fight going into a climb like that, elbows everywhere,

and if you don't get involved you will end up too far back –
even being twenty metres back at the start of a climb will
make a real difference. It costs you energy to close that gap, so
it's better to learn how to defend your position, unless you're
an awful lot better on the climbs than everyone else.'

Pinotti smiles and adds with a laugh, 'That's one reason I
love time trials so much. You don't have all this pushing and
shoving, all these tactics being played out. You do have a tactic, but you don't have anyone messing around with it.'

Some pros, though, have an intuitive feel for these high-oc-
tane moments, an ability to pick their way through from back
to front with a minimum of fuss and incredible speed. Charly
Wegelius, a British pro who had a long career racing mainly in
Italy as a *domestique*, picked out his former teammates Luca
Paolini and Oscar Freire as having this innate ability 'to be in
the right place at the right time. Other guys will be fighting for
position twenty or thirty kilometres before the key point in a
race, but Luca could be coasting at the back and leave it until
the very last minute to move up. He's one of a very small number of riders who can move through the middle of a peloton
and not have to scrap in the gutter. That comes from incredible spatial awareness and confidence in his bike handling.'

For his part, Paolini credited some of this ability to the
grounding he'd had with one-day specialists such as Peter Van
Petegem, Johan Museeuw and Stefano Zanini. 'They were all
riders that you would see right at the back of the bunch but
who at the crucial moment in races were somehow in the right
place ... I tried to copy them. Now young riders will say to me,
"How come you're up here suddenly when a kilometre ago you
were at the back?" The answer is that you just sense a kind
of nervous energy in the bunch and you just feel that it's time

to move up. It's instinctive. Some have it and some don't,' he told *Procycling*.

'It's like you're a psychologist or a mind-reader and you can sense the peloton's mood. You know what certain riders are going to do, how certain teams move. You see a curve coming a few hundred metres away and you sense that there could be a crash or a split. These things stay with you regardless of course changes over the years. And some things never change: knowing how to approach the Arenberg Forest [in Paris–Roubaix], the Kwaremont [in the Tour of Flanders] ... You never stop learning because new riders come along and approach the races differently.'

It's no coincidence that all of these riders have a strong Classics or sprinting background, as these are races and situations when this intuitive ability to assess what's coming before it does, and to pick the best path through the bunch accordingly, is most essential. Koen de Kort, who spent a number of seasons as a key member in Marcel Kittel's lead-out train, is another in his mould. 'When you're in the peloton, you become aware of the guys who have a feel for what's happening and are able to react to it easily and those who find it a bit more stressful because they don't have that kind of insight, or perhaps foresight,' the Dutchman explains.

'When an obstacle is coming up, I can see the riders in front of me and who belongs to which team, and I can predict pretty well where everyone's going to go and where the space is going to be. That just comes from experience I think, but I was once told by a teammate, "It's really easy following you. It's as if there's a wake behind you, because you're flowing through." But it's down to the fact that I've done this job for fifteen years and during that time I've always had someone, a teammate, on my wheel and it's like pulling a trailer through an obstacle course. You've always got to bear in mind that you've got that trailer behind you, and you know when you can push on or when you've got to hold back. Teammates do tend to stick together, so you can usually predict where they're going to go.'

De Kort spent the back end of 2017 putting his experience at the disposal of Alberto Contador during what were the final months of the Spaniard's racing career. 'When you start to work with someone new, like Alberto, it takes a little bit of time to get used to it. We're kind of nailing it now just as he's about to retire,' says De Kort, who admits that working closely with a GC rider is a little different to the lead-out role he's principally renowned for.

'With them being sprinters, I know they can go through gaps that are quite small and they will always follow. In general, there's no time to look back. I'd just shout their name, they'd shout "Yep!" or something similar and we're off. If they lose my wheel they'll yell, so I'm just trying to listen. And there's all kinds of yelling going on, so it's noisy. There are all these trains and they're all yelling at each other. I'm yelling at the teammate in front of me and telling them what they've got to do, and then trying to communicate with whoever is behind me. It's frantic. There's so little time to think and react. There are no rear-view mirrors, and even if you did have them, you wouldn't have time to look into them. It's all happening instantly – reaction, reaction, reaction,' says De Kort.

While some riders breeze through a peloton, there are plenty who find the same process a battle that costs them much-needed energy. Interestingly, a number who do hail from outside the sport's traditional European heartlands.

American Tom Danielson, once hyped as the USA's next great stage racer after Lance Armstrong, admitted he struggled to adapt to the European peloton after racing at home in smaller fields on roads that tended to be much wider and straighter, which made for a less claustrophobic experience, and where moving up to the front was usually a case of accelerating up one side of the bunch.

Danielson, who was very much a climber, admitted to being intimidated in certain situations when he first began to race in Europe. 'When I tried to move to the front, I'd waste all this energy and come to the last climb really exhausted. I started to learn tactics and how to move through the peloton … once you begin to figure it out, it's amazing how much energy you save – and people at home often just don't understand how big of a battle it is on the road. If you start a climb ten bike lengths behind someone else … you have to make a huge acceleration up to them – it's like attacking just to get up to the front of the peloton.'

According to Wegelius, who is now a sporting director, one of the USA's new generation of climbers, Joe Dombrowski, has had similar issues. 'Joe's engine and his physiological capabilities aren't going to be his limiting factor but it's the racing environment, with lots of pace changes, that can be a bit tough for him. A rider can place himself at the correct place in a race with a big energy cost or they can do it efficiently,' Wegelius has said of his experiences of working with the American, highlighting that Dombrowski has 'struggled with the constant high-torque efforts when a peloton sprints out of corners and when the crosswinds blow'. At these points, riders often need to sprint hard to hold their place and avoid being exposed in the wind on their own.

Traditionally, Colombian riders also laboured away from the mountains where their reputation was founded. When they first raced in Europe in the early 1980s, they had little experience of long, flat stages, crosswinds and fighting for position in the peloton. The stereotype of Colombians being sensational on the climbs but out of their depth everywhere else, which was never accurate anyway, has now all but faded away, although even a contemporary star like Nairo Quintana has said he almost literally had to fight to gain respect in the peloton.

The bigger the race, the more severe the combat to get into the right position in what are often decisive locations. Each of the Monuments, the five major one-day races on the men's calendar, has them: the approach to the climb of the Cipressa in Milan–Sanremo, the foot of the Oude Kwaremont at the Tour of Flanders, the final kilometres before the first section of cobbles in Paris–Roubaix and again before the key section through the Arenberg Forest, the run-in to the steep climb of La Redoute in Liège–Bastogne–Liège, and the approach to the key climbs at the tail end of the Tour of Lombardy, the route of which currently varies from year to year.

Writing in *Procycling*, Dan Martin describes the special nature of the test presented by the Ardennes Classics, Liège and Flèche Wallonne, but his words are equally valid for the other Monuments. 'The challenge and difficulty are less obvious to the untrained eye, especially the TV viewer, where the intensity of the fight for position on the narrow twisting roads is lost.' He describes these races as 'waiting games, the winner often appearing from nowhere in the final kilometres, hidden in the shelter of the peloton, and here lies the art and beauty of these races.' With the competitive level higher than ever before and, consequently, the difference between a good result and anonymity ever smaller, Martin states that, 'It takes skill, agility and concentration, mixed with nerve and taking a few risks to be in the right place, with experience telling you when it's the right time. Notice I omitted strength, as you can't afford to use too much of your power if you want to be the strongest in the final.'

The battle for position at critical points has become so vigorously contested, he says, that it resembles a bunch sprint, with lead-out trains in drag races against each other. 'Teams are drilled to ride a hard tempo on climbs, so any attacks don't make a big gap ... As a unit a team is much stronger than even a talented group of individuals, with riders willing to sacrifice themselves. It simply doesn't make sense to attack before the final kilometres.'

Martin points out that one of the most significant reasons he finished second in Flèche Wallonne three times in four years (Alejandro Valverde claimed victory on each occasion) was because of the almost constant fight for position over 200 kilometres leading up to the final critical ascent of the Mur de Huy, where he yielded to the Spaniard in the final 'wall'. Throughout, Valverde had sat in behind his Movistar teammates setting the pace on the front.

There is nothing new in this approach. Leaders such as Eddy Merckx and Bernard Hinault invariably spent most of their time up towards the front of the peloton, rarely leaving the first twenty or thirty riders. Belgian sprinter and track star Patrick Sercu recalls trying to get Merckx to drop back a little further one day by distracting him with conversation, but as soon as they reached twentieth from the front Merckx accelerated back up again, to a position from which he could best assess his opponents and decide when to make the attack that those rivals knew was inevitably going to come.

Hinault said he rode in a similar position because 'nothing can happen without you letting it happen. You have one line of riders, a second line of riders, and you're in the third line. The riders can't go on either side of you because you'll see them, and if you have four or five teammates around you, as soon as someone attacks, your teammate pounces on them. And the race is shut down ... If you ride at the back of the peloton, you can't see what's going on.'

Hinault's description of this tactic is important because it highlights how it has been adapted over the past two decades. The Frenchman describes a situation where the riders at the front of the peloton were lined across the road rather than being lined out along it. Essentially, Merckx and Hinault were sitting at the front to impose themselves on their rivals as a way of intimidating them. They were being tactically aggressive, broadcasting their intent to attack, but at the same time giving no clue as to when this coup might occur.

Conversely, Movistar's tactic of riding in a line at the front of the peloton with Valverde sat in at the end of it and the rest of the peloton fanned out behind him is passive-aggressive. They were highlighting that Valverde was planning to attack, but every member of the team and the riders behind them knew that his thrust would only come in the final 200 metres, almost at the top of the Mur de Huy. Until that point, they were racing in a defensive mode, keeping Valverde safe from crashing, but, just as importantly, away from the stress of riding within the peloton. It came down to a simple calculation. Valverde was slightly more exposed to the wind and therefore losing energy compared to his rivals, but those rivals were losing even more by constantly having to fight for position in his wake.

To an extent, the tactic is same as that adopted by a team that holds a race leader's jersey and rides at the front all day in order to defend it, but the motivation for doing so is quite different. Inevitably, it first became apparent at the Tour de France, where the levels of competition, pace and nervousness are highest, where everyone is desperate to win because of the exposure it brings.

Writing in his autobiography *Domestique*, Charly Wegelius provides a perfect insight into this when recalling his Tour debut in 2007. On the opening stage, he goes looking for the place in the bunch that he describes as 'the office', located in most races behind the riders at the front who are fighting to get into position, a place where, Wegelius explains, there is no pushing or shoving and even the chance to chat and joke. 'The office was where I liked to spend my time on the days that I wasn't going to be in a position to do a job for anyone, or just to wait, in case my leader needed me later on,' he says. 'In the Tour, though, there was no "office" – instead it was all-out war … Bike riders will fight tooth and nail in most races for any kind of success but at the Tour that is all amplified. It is bike racing with the volume turned up.'

Expecting a chat, he instead finds riders with whom he usually passes the time of the day don't even offer a glance of recognition. 'It wasn't because they wanted to ignore me but simply because they didn't see me – they were so stressed by the race that they could only focus on what they were doing. This increasing tension and the continually rising speeds can add up to only one grim conclusion: crashes … They aren't the result of the natural hazards of the race which typically cause them – slippery descents or dangerous corners – they are senseless, caused by too much tension and too many riders trying to be in the same place at the same time,' he says, describing perfectly what makes the Tour a race apart.

Since 2007, those stress levels have increased, not only at the Tour, but at Flèche and many other races. Radios have contributed to this, but teams are also better organised, riders' objectives are more defined, and better coaching ensures they are ready to achieve them. As the competitive level between the best and the worst riders has narrowed, the number of riders who have the ability to win races has ballooned. With more bodies in the press for success, this is now most easily achieved by removing yourself from the mayhem, in the way that Movistar have done so successfully with Valverde at Flèche Wallonne.

Team Sky's head of performance support, Tim Kerrison, who came to the sport as a complete novice in 2010 after a coaching career in swimming, advised the British team to ride in precisely this way. 'It's harder than sitting fifty or sixty back in the bunch, because you get more shelter when you are hidden deep in the peloton, but what Tim says is that you can't account for the mental stress of being back there, and the mental strain adds to the physical demands,' 2012 Tour winner Bradley Wiggins has said of the tactic. Sky also noted that riding on the front instead of in the pack also has benefited its leaders by keeping them cooler, preventing the body's core temperature rising to a level that would produce an added drain on physical resources.

For the most part, its effect on racing is benign. The break goes, one team sets the pace and the rest follow, some of them perhaps lining out behind the lead team, the grouping of team colours resembling trucks rumbling along the motorway, each tucked behind the one at the front. Issues arise when more than one team wants to be in the vanguard, to keep its protected riders out of danger because there is a potential pinch point ahead or when the finish is approaching, and particularly here because the sprinters' teams want to get their leaders into a prominent position as well. As a result, several 'trains' emerge at the same time, each with its protected rider at the rear of the string, resulting in up to a hundred riders battling to set the pace.

Is there a solution? The UCI hopes that cutting Grand Tour teams from nine to eight riders and line-ups at other major events from eight to seven from 2018 will go some way to providing one. Prohibiting radios is touted as another possibility, as is restricting the provision of information disseminated in this way, only permitting the transmission of advice seen as vital to rider safety. However, teams are now so well briefed about race routes and where they need to be at particular points this may not have much impact.

There has also been talk of changing the three-kilometre rule, which lays down that any rider who loses time in the closing 3,000 metres of a stage due to a mechanical problem or a crash is given the same finishing time as the group in which they were riding at that point. Yet, this has simply changed the location of the frantic fight for position, and even after it GC riders can still be found racing elbow to elbow with sprinters and their lead-out man because the bunch can still split between that point and the finish, resulting in the loss of precious seconds.

Unless a way can be found to discourage at least some of those trains and protected riders from being at the front, which would demand a complete reversal in thought on competitive advantage, the only certain way of avoiding the intensity is by riding at the back. This is a tactic associated with some of the best-known names in the bunch, including Thomas Voeckler, Steve Cummings, Ryder Hesjedal and Thomas De Gendt.

'He cannot fathom why everybody fights so much to be at the front of the peloton, it makes no sense to him,' David Millar has said of Hesjedal, winner of the 2012 Giro title. 'In most races he'll spend the four-hour preamble that the leaders have to endure before they battle it out firmly ensconced at the rear of the peloton. I personally cannot agree with this tactic, and yet he proves over and over again that it works for him.' Voeckler and Cummings are of the same mind, consistently at the back of the Tour peloton year after year, each prepared to contribute to his team's objectives if required, but often only moving forwards when planning to attack off the front. The obvious flaw is that if there's a split in the bunch, the riders at the back are in the worst place to react to it.

There is little doubt that Marco Pinotti speaks for many when he suggests that, 'It's not riding in the peloton that's difficult, but the fact that so many teams and riders want to do so in the same place.' A sanctuary for the most part, it is also riddled with unforeseeable traps, and never more so in the prelude to a bunch sprint, when 'the washing machine' enters its fastest spin cycle …

CHAPTER 5

DIRTY DEALING

> Unseen in the background, Fate was quietly slipping
> lead into the boxing-glove.
>
> – *P. G. Wodehouse*, Very Good, Jeeves!

There always been a seedy side to cycling, with races and riders bought and sold, and dodgy deals. As one unnamed sporting director says in Richard Moore's *Étape*, 'Cycling has always
been very much a "what have you done for me lately?" kind
of sport', where an impromptu alliance agreed for strategic or
financial benefit can be much more effective in achieving a
goal than any kind of tactical coup.

In road racing's early years, riders didn't need to be covert about agreements they had cooked up. During the first
Tour's stage to Nantes, when participants were all supposed
to be competing as individuals, the four riders away at the
front were all backed by the manufacturer La Française. They
included race leader Maurice Garin, who instructed the others that he was going to win the stage. However, Fernand

Augereau wouldn't acquiesce, even after the other two riders had conspired to make him crash. After Augereau got up and bridged back up to the leading trio, Garin resorted to a more drastic measure: forcing his obstinate rival to stop before jumping up and down on his front wheel, rendering his bike useless. Garin won in Nantes.

Determined to prevent collusion between riders and teams, Tour director Henri Desgrange implemented all manner of rules and innovations, particularly in the late 1920s when Alcyon's control was so tight it made Sky's dominance of modern editions appear lackadaisical. He tried starting the race in Évian in order to split the bunch by reaching the mountains quicker and, the following year, running the race in a team time trial format. For Desgrange, the nadir arrived when Alcyon's Maurice De Waele claimed the title despite being weakened by illness. Prepared to do almost anything to keep the Belgian in the yellow jersey, Alcyon's directors paid rivals to provide him with assistance. In the Alps, De Waele's teammates blocked the width of the road to prevent attacks, and one of them, future French national team manager Marcel Bidot, hung on to the saddle of climber Benoît Faure to prevent him attacking.

Alcyon's suppression of all rivals by any means possible was typical of that era and resulted in another radical makeover by Desgrange, who introduced national teams and banned manufacturers and their sporting directors from the race. The organising newspaper, *L'Auto,* provided the bikes used by all national and regional teams. 'We had the choice between ending the Tour de France or trying this formula, under which riders will now be under our control ... and punishable if they break the rules,' declared Desgrange.

He and other race organisers were fighting a losing battle, though. In France, Belgium and Italy, racing's heartlands, hierarchies dominated. The long-established system of building a team around one star name continued into the 1970s. The 1976 Giro d'Italia offered a perfect example of how it worked. At the Tour de Romandie, which preceded Italy's national tour, Belgian climber Johan De Muynck found himself in the lead group on the stage to Leysin alongside his Brooklyn team leader Roger De Vlaeminck, Eddy Merckx, and Italian hitters Felice Gimondi, Giovanni Battaglin and Gianbattista Baronchelli. With his eyes on the win, De Vlaeminck ordered De Muynck to attack, expecting someone to chase his lieutenant down, but no one did. De Muynck won the stage to take the lead, but was quickly reminded of his place in the team's pecking order. When he came down from the victory podium, there was no one waiting for him. He had to get back on his bike clutching his bouquet and ride to the team hotel. At dinner that evening De Vlaeminck didn't utter a word to him.

On the final day, the morning leg of a split stage into Fribourg, Merckx and De Vlaeminck attempted to reassert the hierarchy, attacking De Muynck repeatedly in an attempt to weaken him before the afternoon time trial. Helped by a handsling from another of his teammates, De Vlaeminck made a final attempt eight kilometres from the finish, but the parvenu held on. That afternoon, De Vlaeminck ordered his teammate to let him win the closing time trial, but De Muynck refused and won that too to claim a decisive victory over his leader with Merckx third.

Following the dope control, the three men were put in a taxi to Geneva airport for a flight to Sicily for the start of the

Giro, with De Muynck squeezed in between the two Belgian legends. Sensing a chance to wind up his rival, Merckx leaned forward. 'Roger, he's hard this guy. He can win the Giro,' he said to De Vlaeminck, speaking across De Muynck. 'He's a *gregario* and he will remain a *gregario*,' the Brooklyn leader replied icily. 'No, Roger, you're wrong,' said Merckx, revelling in his discomfort, 'it's his moment, he's riding better than you.'

When the Giro got under way, Merckx was proved right in his assessment. De Vlaeminck took the lead in the first week, only to lose it to his teammate. De Muynck only held it for a day, but regained it from Gimondi with just three days to go. Raging once again, rather than help his team-mate De Vlaeminck attacked the next day, but ended up being caught and dropped by the other contenders including De Muynck. De Vlaeminck promptly abandoned the race, his move encouraging Brooklyn *domestique* Ronald De Witte to do the same. Struggling with the effects of a crash on the penultimate day in the final time trial, De Muynck, followed not by his Brooklyn team car but by that of a Belgian TV reporter carrying his spare wheels, lost the lead to Gimondi, who claimed the title by just nineteen seconds.

'I should have gone and talked with Giuseppe Saronni or Francesco Moser, who weren't happy seeing Gimondi win,' De Muynck later admitted, 'but I didn't realise that until too late. I lacked stature and [sporting director] Franco Cribori was too correct a man to negotiate that kind of alliance.' Presented with photos that showed Gimondi apparently being paced by a television motorbike in the race-deciding time trial, De Muynck took them to the boss of the Brooklyn chewing gum company that backed the team. But no action was taken as Brooklyn were more concerned about the impact the potential disqualification of an Italian hero of the standing of Gimondi might have on their sales. 'That was how the system worked,' De Muynck complained. 'The Italians were capable of all manner of cheating.'

There was consolation for De Muynck in the shape of an overall win at the 1978 Giro, where Gimondi was one of his willing helpers. The Belgian had also shown that the system could be beaten. Deals, though, remained very much part of racing. José De Cauwer, a professional during the 1970s and a sporting director or TV commentator throughout the period since, says that they were done on all sides, but principally among racing's big guns. 'The key thing to remember is that if you were a rider who didn't have a hope of winning a race, then there was no way you could sell it,' he says. 'If you were a favourite, it was different. You could go to a potential winner and buy their cooperation.'

There were strategic collaborations too, created for mutual benefit rather than financial gain. During the 1985 Tour, for instance, Bernard Hinault's La Vie Claire team reached an accommodation with Luis Herrera's Café de Colombia. It began when Hinault attacked with Herrera on the Morzine stage, the Colombian taking the King of the Mountains jersey and the stage win as Hinault extended his lead significantly. According to Spaniard Pedro Delgado: 'As he was intelligent, [Hinault] reached a tacit agreement with the Colombians. He would help Herrera to win the King of the Mountains and to win stages. In exchange, the Café de Colombia team would control the stages on the crucial climbs, and his riders would not carry out those mad attacks that blew the race apart.'

There's perhaps no episode that better highlights the farcical turn that bargaining for a deal can reach than Richard Virenque's abortive attempt to buy up several rivals when they had dropped race leader Jan Ullrich on the tough stage through the Vosges to Montbéliard in the 1997 Tour. Having seen the German already dropped twice, second-placed Virenque endeavoured to encourage Marco Pantani, Abraham Olano and Fernando Escartín to cooperate with the Frenchman and three of his Festina teammates to distance Ullrich. With the Tour title a possibility, Virenque made his pitch. According to his sporting director, Bruno Roussel, he offered each man 10,000 French francs, approximately £1,000, about a tenth of what would be expected in that situation. After much head-shaking and shrugging, Virenque's anger became hilariously evident, and he petulantly signalled for teammates Didier Rous and Pascal Hervé to ride off in search of the stage win.

Generally, deals are much harder to spot, though. Fearing an outsider might win Milan–Sanremo in 2003, and in doing so replicating exactly the kind of manoeuvre that Merckx and De Vlaeminck had tried to pull on De Muynck, Mario Cipollini and fellow Italian Paolo Bettini agreed to get their teams to cooperate to chase down the break. 'I know you'll attack, but I'd rather lose to you than a bunch of nobodies,' Cipollini told his rival. 'Let's set our teammates to work and race properly. After that, let the best man win.' The sprinter was spot on in his assessment, as Bettini did attack late on and finished eleven seconds clear of the bunch, led in by Cipollini.

More often, though, deals come about for strategic or face-saving reasons. During the stage out of the Pyrenees to Carcassonne in the 2006 Tour, Alessandro Ballan found himself in the breakaway with Oscar Freire and Yaroslav Popovych. By some distance the slowest of the trio, Popovych's only chance of victory was to attack and drop his two companions. The prelude to this was a brief discussion with Freire, the quickest of the little group. When Popovych jumped clear, Ballan employed the standard strategy in that situation of waiting for the faster man to chase. Freire, though, didn't budge. A deal had been done for the stage win, Popovych's Discovery Channel team effectively receiving it in exchange for assisting Freire's Rabobank teammate Denis Menchov in his quest for the yellow jersey.

There was no suggestion that money exchanged hands then, but that is very much the allegation that hangs over the result of the 2010 edition of Liège–Bastogne–Liège, when Alexandre Vinokourov beat Alexandre Kolobnev to the title. Two years on from that day, evidence emerged as part of a doping investigation in Italy that Vinokourov, who went on to become manager of the Astana team, had transferred €150,000 in two batches from his account in Monaco to Kolobnev's Swiss bank account. Vinokourov has insisted the payments were a loan, but was due to answer corruption charges in a Belgian court in 2018.

Given Vinokourov's 2007 ban for blood doping at the Tour de France, this is perhaps the moment to touch on the issue of doping to gain advantage. The Kazakh was far from the first and undoubtedly won't be the last to indulge in the practice. In the late nineteenth century, racers were already using all manner of pick-me-ups to boost performance, including life-threatening ones such as arsenic and strychnine. More recently, the use of banned substances has been employed strategically in long-term doping programmes and tactically to give a boost in certain races, and has frequently proved far more effective than any ruse or bluff. Yet its illegitimacy means doping is not a strategy or tactic, but cheating, the contemporary equivalent of pre-war racers being towed behind cars or jumping on trains with their bike.

According to UCI president David Lappartient, 'motorised' doping now presents a similar threat to racing's integrity. Elected in 2017, Lappartient promised a tougher approach to the spectre of riders boosting their wattage with hidden devices, as rumours circulated about their use in the pro peloton and criticism about the ruling body's approach to the issue grew. There has been, though, no definite proof of any professional team resorting to this chicanery. Having spent much of that same year researching a book on the issue, well-renowned *L'Équipe* journalist Philippe Brunel came up with nothing. 'The more I got into the story, the greater the impression that I wasn't learning anything, that I was simply on the outside of things. I only had indirect evidence, nothing tangible,' he said.

It is, understandably, not easy to establish the level of deal-making in contemporary racing. Off-the-record conversations suggest that there are still plenty of discussions between teams and riders and that deal-making takes place, but the buying and selling of races is not as common as it was. Agreements tend to be more ad hoc, mutual interest encouraging teams to chase behind a break or, as one team manager admitted, having an arrangement with another squad that they wouldn't chase down each other's riders. Mind you, he revealed this after one of his rider's chances of a victory had been nullified by an apparent ally and added that the accord was now at an end.

'There used to be a lot of deals, but it's not the same now. The media follows the sport so closely, the teams are so well organised, and each team is now a company and almost a national team as well. It's not so much rider against rider, as it once was, it's team against team,' says José De Cauwer. 'You don't see those deals where someone says, "You give me fifty thousand euros and your rider can win this race." That era has gone. You can't go to your sponsor now and say, "We got a good deal. We lost the race but we earned a hundred thousand dollars." Sponsors are now paying to win, to get results. They don't want pay-offs from other teams.'

De Cauwer points to the World Championships, where national loyalties conflict with trade team commitments, as the one place where deal-making is still a feature. 'You see riders from one country not riding behind a rider from another because they are on the same trade team. That's a situation that you've got to be aware of when you're in that race,' he explains, before going on to give a hypothetical example. 'If Belgium's Philippe Gilbert and France's Julian Alaphilippe are in the break, and Alaphilippe attacks in the last five kilometres, then, if you're a Belgian rider, you can't expect Gilbert to chase Alaphilippe because they are both Quick-Step riders. You can't ask him to chase his own teammate, or at least it's difficult. If you're a team manager or road captain in that kind of situation, you have to be very smart and have a rider ready who can chase after Alaphilippe.'

Matt White also believes the level of deal-making has changed significantly, but suggests other factors are responsible. 'Back in the 1980s and the 1990s, before live television, before radio communication, before social media, there were a lot of deals done between teams,' says the Australian sporting director. 'Cycling used to be very much a western European sport dominated by three or four countries, but it's very international now, and so is the makeup of the teams. There used to be a lot of Italian teams, four or five Spanish teams, alliances between countries from northern Europe, but that era's now gone. We're all now very accountable to our sponsors and the sport has a worldwide audience, so everything gets very closely scrutinised. I'm not going to ask my riders to ride for somebody else because I'm answerable to my sponsors.'

In addition, says White, a new generation of sporting directors and new ideas about how that job needs to be done have also resulted in the nefarious practices of the past being avoided. 'When I first started racing there was still bad blood between certain teams and between certain directors, but you don't see that any more. You did hear stories of directors still bearing grudges against each other from when they'd been racing fifteen years before, but that really petty attitude has also gone from our sport, which is great because the people who really lost out were the riders. Some of those directors are still around, but there's a new generation who have a very different experience of the sport now,' White insists.

The Australian adds that inter-team discussions now are generally focused on strategy and are had when there are common goals. The opening stages of the 2017 Tour saw exactly this kind of dealing between the sprinters' teams. One anonymous sporting director told *L'Équipe* that these teams continued to collaborate even as Quick-Step's Marcel Kittel was cleaning up sprint after sprint in the first half of the race because, 'It's the way things work over the season. If a sprinter's team stopped contributing towards bringing back the breakaway, it could pay for it on another race. So they prefer to avoid that kind of war and continue to set up the sprints.'

While this kind of dealing between teams has always been part of racing and is likely to remain so, there is growing concern about racing being subverted by influences outside the sport. Lappartient has voiced his fear that the sport's integrity could succumb to the threat presented by illegal sports betting. He is in favour of banning the use of race radios, partly because he believes they have the potential to facilitate race rigging motivated by illegal sports betting. Although he has admitted he has no evidence that fixing of this nature has taken place, Lappartient is adamant that the UCI has to anticipate the possibility that it might.

'Sports betting is like an iceberg. Ninety per cent of the bets are illegal and happen below the waterline. That's how it is in football, tennis and handball. I don't want to get to a day when cycling, once we've clambered out of the valley of doping and the fight against mechanical fraud has been successfully carried out, is undermined by corruption and gambling scandals,' Lappartient stated. Given the complexity of bike racing, rigging of this kind would be extremely difficult to police. Indeed, with registered gambling companies already offering match bets on riders within races, fixing the outcome of a head-to-head between two riders who roll in well behind the race winner not only appears very easy to do but almost impossible to spot. Consequently, that age-old question of whether a rider was braking at the finish to avoid the mayhem behind the line or because the fix was in doesn't appear likely to go away just yet.

CHAPTER 6

HOW TO RACE IN THE WIND

When you see an enemy lying on the ground, what's your first reaction? To help him to his feet. In road racing, you kick him to death.

— *Tim Krabbé*, The Rider

Thinking back to the tactical niceties that had to be quickly assimilated when she arrived in Europe, Tiffany Cromwell recalls one of her first World Cup races in the Netherlands. 'I noticed that about half an hour before we were due to get under way, lots of riders, including most of the top names, were making their way down to the start. It was really odd,' she says, 'and I had no idea why. As soon as the race got going, though, it struck me almost immediately. It was the wind. They knew on tight roads that it was imperative to be right at the front from the off.'

When it starts to blow, racing is less like chess or poker, more akin to a lottery. 'The wind is worse than a climb, because you know that a climb is going to finish at some point,' says

Marco Pinotti. 'The only way to get out of the wind is when you reach the finish. Windy days are always the most nervous, even if nothing ends up happening. It's one aspect of racing that television doesn't really capture.'

That edginess is never higher than when the wind starts to blow from the side. At that point, television does highlight the impact it is having, and in the most spectacular way, as echelons emerge, riders lining out in successive diagonal rows. 'On those days it's no-holds-barred – you don't think, you just do,' David Millar says. 'There's no reflection, no energy conservation, just on, on, on. A good echelon rider should have no idea what's happening behind him.'

Typically associated with the spring Classics and Tour stages run across the flatlands of northern France, echelons form in a crosswind. The rider at the front of a group or peloton continues to set the pace into the wind, but moves to the windward side of the road to allow the next rider in the line to tuck in to the side but slightly behind them, head to hip, in order to optimise shelter from the wind.

In a small group, the racer at the front will set the pace for half a minute or so, then drop back, allowing the wind to push them along the rear of the line until they can slot in at the end. At the same time, the rider second in line will move towards the wind and maintain the tempo for a similar spell, before following suit, the echelon progressing smoothly, assuming that everyone contributes to the pacemaking and nobody pushes the speed too high, thereby breaking the 'through and off' rhythm. In a much larger group, the rotation of positions has, when seen from above, a mesmerising chain-like appearance, turning constantly, with a line of riders in front moving towards the wind and another behind going away from it.

The beauty, and brutality, of the echelon is that it can only comprise a finite number of members. Once the echelon fills the road from kerb to kerb, the riders outside the chain are forced to drop back and, if they react in concert and quickly enough, form their own echelon fanning across the road. Collaboration is essential, and if not found can result in a rider falling through subsequent echelons because there is no place for them to drop into.

Millar typifies the kind of rider who tends to thrive when echelons form. A big, powerful *rouleur*, the Scot relished this kind of racing, particularly in the latter part of his career, describing the moment that you find yourself in a front echelon that is working perfectly as 'one of the joys of being a bike racer'.

But being solidly built and having a big engine are not enough on their own to enable a rider to prosper when the wind gets up. Marc Sergeant, who became one of the integral *domestiques* at Peter Post's Panasonic team and a member of Jean-Paul van Poppel's lead-out train, admits he struggled to hold his place in an echelon in his first years as a pro. 'I was quite unusual because I only started riding a bike at the age of nineteen and had to learn everything from scratch – riding in the bunch, riding in echelons, it was all new to me. It took quite a few months before I got to grips with it. I remember Eddy Planckaert once said to me, "Years ago, it was nice to sit behind you when we were in an echelon. But now it's just as a hellish as being on anyone else's wheel." What he meant by that was that he'd been able to force his way into my place in the line, but I'd improved a lot tactically and technically and after a while he could no longer do this,' Sergeant recalls.

For a rider like Cromwell, their smaller stature creates another complication when dealing with the wind. 'When I first came into the pro peloton, I quickly realised that I needed to increase my power and strength to be able to deal with conditions of that kind. It was all part of the same battle I had to learn about how to fight for position in the bunch, to hold my ground, to ensure that I was in the first echelon so that I could be competitive,' the Australian racer explains. 'I also needed to work on increasing my power in training in order to be competitive in the Classics. It's an advantage in those races to be a bigger rider, to have that innate power. I did manage to find that balance between having the power I needed to hold my position in the bunch and crosswinds, while keeping the ability I had to climb, which stems to an extent from my size. You have to tread a fine line of being strong in all areas, while being among the best at something.'

In *The Racer*, Millar offers a compelling description of why echelon racing is such a difficult skill to master. 'The beginning of it is brutal. It's a flat-out effort that continues until you blow up, unless you make it into the echelon,' he says, explaining that the riders or team that created the echelon will protect each other's positions within it while behind them chaos reigns as the other riders search desperately for temporary allies.

'If you're strong and you've been caught out you find yourself dodging the riders in front of you who can't hold the wheel and so let the gap open,' Millar continues. 'There's no point in teaming up with them because they've blown up and are slowing down, so you give everything you have to try to make it to the wheel they just got dropped from. It's double or nothing, full commitment to make it, deep into the red, in the knowledge that if you don't make it you're going to have destroyed yourself in the process. If that happens you'll have no choice but to slow down to give yourself time to recover, by which time you'll be in a group of similarly exploded guys who didn't make it, with the front of the race disappearing over the horizon ...'

There is, for the watching fan, a sadistic splendour in witnessing teams that are so well prepared being derailed by the wind. That it happens so frequently in spite of the fact that all of the major teams have staff driving ahead of the race with devices ranging from simple flags to anemometers to check the speed and direction of the wind only underlines the havoc that it can wreak. Assessing the elements in this way sounds easy, but demands experience. It's not simply a case of relaying the news that it's windy up ahead. The information communicated back to the sporting director and then passed on to the riders has to take into account how a peloton of up to 200 riders is likely to react to that wind. If there is a danger point, teams want to know in advance when they need to get into position to be ready for it.

Sky demonstrated how to do this on the 2017 Tour's stage into Romans-sur-Isère. 'Everyone knows that it often blows in the Rhône valley. You can look at the maps, the weather apps, it's not a secret. Everyone knew that it would be windy,' says Sky sporting director Nicolas Portal, who reckons that it requires a good ten kilometres of riding on an exposed road in a three-quarters crosswind, that is to say blowing at forty-five degrees from either side, to break the peloton. 'What makes the difference is a team's cohesion and having riders who know how to fight to be at the front when there's a crosswind. You just have to know the best sections to do this. We managed to do so and we knew that there were two or three zones where it could split, and on the last, just after a hill, we upped the pace in the peloton.'

The Quick-Step team managed by Patrick Lefevere is most often associated with this kind of tactical coup, essentially because it has focused on and thrived in the Classics. After becoming sporting director of his own team in 1993, Lefevere oversaw twenty-six victories in cycling's five one-day Monuments, including eleven in Paris–Roubaix and eight in the Tour of Flanders before stepping away from DS duties to focus on his team's commercial and sponsorship side.

'I was a good rider when it came to strategy and tactics. In my head, I could win any race, but my legs weren't always up to the task,' says Lefevere, who was talented enough to win a stage of the 1978 Vuelta a España. 'I wasn't a sprinter or a climber, but I was very good at assessing where the best point was to attack and always loved the tactical side of racing. I was probably one of the first directors to have radio communication, one of the first to have someone ahead of the race looking over the *parcours*. When I was a sports director I'd always be looking for places and opportunities to beat the other teams – after which roundabout or corner, by taking advantage of the wind, is there a descent where we can surprise them?'

Mulling over a quarter of a century of success, Lefevere reveals his ability to surprise when he selects a relatively insignificant stage in the 1994 edition of the sadly defunct Tour of the Mediterranean to illustrate a victory carved out thanks to his team's eye for an echelon. With team sprinter Fabio Baldato leading the race, Lefevere set them what seemed the obvious task of defending the Italian's lead, which meant riding into a block headwind.

'Guys like Wilfried Peeters were asking me, "Why have we got to pull all day? The whole bunch is laughing at us riding into a headwind." On the descents, the bunch was coming around them because they were going faster than our six or seven guys on the front,' recounts Lefevere. 'I told him, "They won't be laughing at you soon. Just give it another five kilometres." I had a big road atlas of Provence and I could see that at a roundabout the road went left and there would be a crosswind. I said to him, "Speed up at that roundabout and you'll see what happens." They sped up on what were small roads and before anyone could react the echelon had been made. Our riders ending up filling the first six places on the stage.'

Having related an echelon-related exploit at one end of his team's existence, Lefevere serves up another from the opposite end, highlighting how quick-thinking can still make a difference when the wind gets up, even though riders are now more closely matched than ever before and are so thoroughly briefed about all aspects of races they participate in. On an extremely blustery third day at the 2017 Giro d'Italia, with gusts so strong that riders were on occasion struggling to stay upright, Quick-Step forced a split that resulted in echelons forming on an open stretch of road ten kilometres from home, serving the stage up on a plate for sprinter Fernando Gaviria, who also claimed the substantial bonus of the leader's pink jersey.

'You don't want all of your riders to be intelligent from the racing point of view, because that can create problems,' Lefevere says. 'You need a mix of riders who can work and riders who can win. If you look back at Gaviria's first stage win in that Giro, we didn't have a team there that looked like it could create an echelon. That it happened was down to the quick thinking of the team. Bob Jungels did it on his own. The others, the likes of Laurens De Plus and Eros Capecchi, aren't riders noted for their ability in the wind, but they did it because it was hardwired into them by being on this team. The athletes are all so even now that sometimes only tiny details like this make a difference.'

A couple of months prior to that demonstration of how to use the elements to their advantage, Quick-Step had dished up the same treatment with the collaboration of fellow Belgians Lotto and an FDJ team packed with strong riders on the opening two stages of Paris–Nice, a race in the first half of March that is frequently visited by strong winds as it heads across the open agricultural plains to the south of the French capital. The result sheet on the opener resembled that of a race from decades earlier, riders finishing in small groups minutes apart. French star Romain Bardet was the biggest casualty, suffering the ignominy of disqualification after television images revealed he had hung on to his team car in order to regain contact with the front echelon after crashing. The next day, another of the favourites for the title, Richie Porte, saw his hopes disappear in the wind as he lost fourteen minutes.

Yet, even being aware of an upcoming weather-related ambush is not going to help on every occasion. In 2015, the Tour peloton exploded when hit by a ferocious squall on the outskirts of Rotterdam as it raced towards an unprecedented finish out on the polders built to protect the Netherlands from the North Sea. The minute or so Chris Froome gained on Nairo Quintana that day was all that separated them when the Briton claimed the title in Paris three weeks later. Hoping to repeat the unpredictability of that day, Tour boss Christian Prudhomme plotted out several stages in the opening days of the following two Tours that might similarly be affected only to be thwarted either by tranquil conditions or the peloton being well primed to react.

Recent history suggests, though, that Prudhomme may be better off reworking the race's route so that stages such as these fall in the second half of the race when fatigue has taken the edge off the peloton's physical sharpness. In 2013, Froome was among those caught out when Omega Pharma–Quick-Step (yes, them again!) and Saxo Bank sensed a shift in the wind on what had seemed like a mundane 'transition' stage to Saint-Amand-Montrond at the end of the second week. The sudden acceleration at the front of the pack provoked the formation of echelons, with Froome caught in the second. The Briton only lost a minute, in the end, but second-placed Alejandro Valverde ceded ten and lost his podium place.

Prudhomme, of course, can't plan in the wind when plotting out routes. However, by giving the elements the best chance to have an impact, clever race design can still encourage thrilling action that, on occasions, will catch out even the strongest riders in the pro peloton.

CHAPTER 7

HOW TO LEAD OUT AND WIN A SPRINT

A great sprinter doesn't need to be a great strategist.
When you're on that finishing straight, timing trumps
tactics every time.

– Mark Cavendish

As the peloton swept along the rue de Rivoli and weaved left
into the place de la Concorde, approaching the Champs-Elysées
for the final dash to the finish at the 2012 Tour de France,
two British riders at the head of the snaking line were about to
make history. Leading the way was Bradley Wiggins, wearing
the yellow jersey as Tour leader and about to become Britain's
first winner of the world's greatest race. On his wheel was Sky
teammate Edvald Boasson Hagen, readying himself to provide
the last bit of impetus for world champion Mark Cavendish.
Winner of this most high-profile of stages for the past three
seasons, the Manxman knew exactly what was required.

As Wiggins swung off to the right going through place de la Concorde, Boasson Hagen accelerated into the sweeping right-hand bend at the bottom of the drag up to the finish. The Norwegian had barely straightened up, when Cavendish went like a slingshot off his wheel, rapidly opening a gap of two bike lengths on the rival sprinters now pouring past Boasson Hagen and attempting to bridge up to the world champion. With one hundred metres left, Cavendish still maintained the advantage he'd opened with his initial injection of speed. Approaching the line, the gap finally began to close, but only thanks to the Briton taking his hands from the bars and flinging his right arm up with his fingers raised and thumb tucked to celebrate his fourth stage win on the world's most famous avenue and the twenty-third of his career.

Although little noted in the hoopla that enveloped the two Team Sky riders and the rest of the British team that afternoon in Paris, Cavendish's win was also significant because it eased him past Frenchman André Darrigade as the most successful sprinter in Tour history. Still sprightly in his mid-eighties, Darrigade wasn't able to congratulate Cavendish in Paris, but travelled from his home in the French Basque Country twelve months later to meet him in Marseille, where the Briton had just bagged up a twenty-fourth win. The two men had a warm exchange. 'He'll beat Eddy Merckx's record of thirty-four Tour victories,' Darrigade predicted later.

Darrigade had long acknowledged that his record was not going to stand for ever. Indeed, he also made the point that, based on bunch sprints alone, the Manxman had surpassed him quite some time ago. 'My strong point was the bunch sprints, but I'm different to Mark because I could win from breaks too. I'd often win from a group of four, five or ten riders,' he said. More than half of Darrigade's Tour wins came in breakaways, and even among the ten occasions Darrigade did lead in a big group it often comprised around two dozen riders rather than the 150 to 200 that generally trail in behind Cavendish.

That these weren't bunch sprints as we would now recognise them doesn't take away anything from Darrigade's achievement, but does emphasise the extent by which sprinting has changed at major events since he was in his pomp. As Cavendish closed in on his record, Darrigade, who won the opening stage of the Tour no fewer than five times, gave an insight into how both the size and the significance of sprints have changed. 'I would be picked for the French national team [when the Tour was run under this format up to 1961] basically to work for [Louison] Bobet or Jacques Anquetil; that's why I could win the first stage so often because so early in the race I didn't have to look after them. But I didn't have any backing in the sprints. No backing of any kind. In those days it was every man for himself,' he explained.

'I wouldn't pull myself out of the pack and accelerate hard like Mark,' Darrigade added. 'I'd attack from the front. I'd start accelerating three hundred metres from the line, which is a long way out, and then try and hold it all the way to the finish. Rik Van Looy would say they should never let me get near the front because then when I attacked, he knew they'd never catch me.'

Over the next three decades that every-man-for-himself approach to bunch sprints began to transform into all-for-one. It started with Van Looy who, during the late 1950s and the 1960s, introduced the more familiar sprinter's tactic of using his teammates to line him up for bunch finishes, his Flandria 'Red Guard' setting a high pace at the front of the peloton. At the finish, Van Looy would engage what was at that time an unusually large gear of 53x13 – a 53x11 gear is standard for sprinters now – and invariably unleash an unmatchable kick of acceleration to add another success to a *palmarès* that comprised a colossal 379 road victories when he retired in 1970 after eighteen professional seasons.

During the 1970s, Flandria's red colours dominated sprints once again, harnessing the bristling power of Freddy Maertens to the tactical insight of his best friend, Marc Demeyer, a stickler for discipline who made sure the rest of the team was pulling in the same direction for their sprinter. In 1976, Maertens won eight stages at the Tour, five of them bunch gallops, and he insists to this day that he gave one or two others away at the request of his well-beaten rivals. The following season, the hulking Belgian with a gentle manner claimed a baker's dozen on a high-speed romp to the Vuelta a España title, eleven of them in bunch finishes.

Yet, sprints remained chaotic in a way not often seen today. Sprinters had teammates to lead them out, but rarely enough of them to chase down the continual attacks that would come late on in a race. Consequently, late breakaways, which are rarely seen and almost never successful in the modern era, were not only frequent but often resulted in success. When bunch sprints did take place, race *commissaires* were kept busy with relegations and disqualifications thanks to jersey-pulling, elbowing and all manner of other shenanigans.

The arrival of beanpole Dutch sprinter Jean-Paul van Poppel at Jan Raas's Superconfex team in 1987 marked the start of the change to what most would now recognise as a bunch finish. 'When I joined Superconfex, Raas told the team to race for me when it was flat. When there was a chance I could win, he would go a hundred per cent behind me,' recalls van Poppel, who claimed two Tour stages plus the points title in 1987 and four the year after in Superconfex's now iconic green and grey jersey.

'However, the team didn't really work to keep the bunch together like they do now. Now you see them start working behind the break with a hundred and fifty kilometres to go and they've got lots of riders helping them in the final kilometres, but it wasn't like that for me. I'd often have just one rider working for me in the final, and it wasn't until Mario Cipollini came along that real trains appeared,' van Poppel explains. He adds that his chances were further complicated by the presence of what is now an almost extinct species of rider – the last-kilometre flyer.

'With just a handful of riders working for me, it was difficult to keep the bunch together in the final kilometres, particularly as there were a lot of punchy riders who would go on the attack in the final kilometre or two. My old teammate Jelle Nijdam was one of the best known, but there were others like Thierry Marie. It was tough keeping them reined in. It's a real shame that you don't see that kind of attack any longer because the speed of the peloton is so high over the last three kilometres,' says the Dutchman. 'In fact, compared to now, there were many more chances to break away, even in the final fifty kilometres of a stage. Breaks would go and would be able to stay away.'

Van Poppel also highlights another significant difference between Superconfex's strategy and that of sprinters' teams now. 'Even on those days that Raas would say the team would be working for me, at the start of the stage our riders could still try to get in the breakaway, and if we had a good guy in the break then he would get his chance to go for the win from the break. Nico Verhoeven managed to do exactly that at the 1987 Tour, Rolf Gölz did it twice, once that year and once the next. The team had some options and weren't simply focused on me. But it had to be the right guy in the break, someone who was fast enough to win.'

It took the arrival of a supremely confident sprinter to bring about a more complete and long-lasting change to the aspect of bunch finishes, a rider who could not only win regularly but could also convince his teammates that it was always in their best interests to sublimate their own ambitions and commit themselves to his. Mario Cipollini turned pro in 1989 with the Del Tongo team, where he joined his elder brother, Cesare, who was bringing down the curtain on his long career. A bunch sprint winner at the Giro d'Italia in that first season, the younger Cipollini quickly began to establish an impressive *palmarès*, particularly when, in 1992, he moved on to the GB-MG team that melded many of the leading Italian and Belgian stars of that era.

'Mario was immensely powerful and could develop huge top-end speed. However, he had a "long" sprint,' Cesare Cipollini said of his little brother. 'In fact, you could say that he wasn't a pure sprinter at all. Guys like Guido Bontempi could explode really quickly, whereas Mario's speed came *in progressione*. We knew, though, that nobody else was capable of riding as quickly as him, so he just had to be delivered.' Creating Cipollini's lead-out train wasn't planned, but came about gradually. At the Tour, for instance, teammates such as

Johan Museeuw recognised the Italian had the pace to beat anyone when he got up to speed, so endeavoured to make that happen.

It's no coincidence that as Cipollini and a new generation of sprinters such as Wilfried Nelissen and Erik Zabel began to dominate, that small group of lone wolves such as Nijdam and Marie were edged towards extinction. Better organisation among the sprinters' teams neutered them. It's extremely hard to escape from a peloton travelling at more than 60kph, and even if achieved it's impossible for one rider on their own to resist a large group moving at that speed for long. They'd get perhaps a few dozen metres clear before the sprinters' lead-out riders would bring them back to heel, inevitably drawing them back into the peloton.

Cipollini received more consistent support with his lead-outs when he moved to the Italian Mercatone Uno team in 1994. Not until he swapped that team's yellow colours for Saeco's red in 1996 did his train get fully up to speed. 'They were all totally focused on Cipollini, all dressed in red, all big, strong guys,' recalls Marc Sergeant, who was one of the lead-out riders at Panasonic for van Poppel and German powerhouse Olaf Ludwig, the Marcel Kittel of his day. 'The Saeco train was really impressive, and I'd say that was the first team that was completely devoted to a sprinter in that way.'

Van Poppel agrees. 'Whereas I'd have just one or two riders helping me, Cipollini managed to get six or seven riders working for him in the last three, four, five kilometres,' he says, confessing that he doesn't believe it made for a compelling spectacle. 'In Cipollini's era, he and his team were so strong that sprints were pretty boring to watch. You had just one team on the front from five kilometres out right into the finish. His successes were almost pre-programmed.'

That Saeco train mixed riders who had been schooled in the Italian tradition of team time trialling such as Eros Poli and Mario Scirea, Cipollini's closest friend in the bunch, with a final lead-out man who was a top sprinter in his own right, notably Giovanni Lombardi and, later, Guido Trenti. Given their leader's flamboyance, dressing up as Julius Caesar complete with laurels and toga at the 1999 Tour, or wearing a 'skinless' skinsuit, an anatomically correct representation of all of his muscles, sinews and bones, it was all too easy to miss the beautiful efficiency of Saeco's high-powered prep that would conclude with Cipollini engaging the turbo and surging clear to win, arms raised in a V with fingers splayed.

The most impressive demonstration of the tactic came in the 2002 World Championships, focused on and around the Zolder motor-racing circuit in Belgium. With new rival Alessandro Petacchi, another *in progressione* sprinter, working as his lead-out man, Cipollini took the rainbow jersey at a canter. 'We were a team in the truest sense, absolutely united. No one person was more important than another, not even Cipollini,' Scirea said of Italy's victory at Zolder. 'That was the real power of it, and it made you feel invincible. That team was a kind of machine, programmed to win. Unless you've been in a train like that you have no idea how beautiful it can be.'

At the Grand Tours, the organisers were quite complicit in asserting the dominance of the sudden glut of talented sprinters. The opening week of each included a number of stages almost certain to conclude in a contest between whichever combination of Cipollini, Petacchi, Zabel, Marcel Wüst, Oscar Freire, Tom Steels, Robbie McEwen and several others happened to be in the field. Such was the grip that they held that these races became formulaic and sometimes dull. It extended to other races, too. From 1997, Milan–Sanremo, perennially a hunting ground for breakaways of the strongest riders in the bunch, became the preserve of sprinters, to the point where organisers RCS investigated changes to the route to tip the balance back towards the possibility of a more unpredictable finish.

The most interesting of this cohort of speedsters from a tactical perspective was Robbie McEwen. Much smaller but more explosive than the *in progressione* stand-outs such as Cipollini and Petacchi, the Australian had lots of raw speed and talent, but struggled for several seasons to use them to his advantage because his style was quite different. Rather than sitting in behind sizeable teammates almost all the way to the line, McEwen preferred to find his own way in a sprint, sometimes sticking with a teammate but often choosing to come off a rival's wheel in the final 200 metres and use their speed as the launch pad for his final kick.

It wasn't until he joined Lotto in 2002, his seventh pro season, that he found a team that had confidence to back him and enable him to become a regular winner in the biggest races. That year, McEwen's status changed thanks to two stage wins at the Giro and two more at the Tour that helped him claim the points title. It presaged a golden period during which he took twenty-three stage wins at the Giro and Tour in Lotto colours.

'You get some wins behind you and everybody wants to ride for you. You also get more respect from other riders in the bunch,' McEwen explained at the end of that season. 'Instead of wanting to get past me to sit on Erik Zabel's wheel, they want to get on mine. Guys like Mario Cipollini and Zabel have profited from that tactic for years: they've just been sitting there behind their team, nice and easy, waiting for the final two hundred metres, by which time I've already done half a dozen sprints to get into position – fighting for a wheel, moving myself up in the wind and wasting energy. Their team pulls the sprint, everybody fights to sit on their wheel. So they've had an armchair ride to the finish. I've always had the speed, but until now I've always been coming from ninth position and finishing second or third. This year I've been starting third or fourth and winning a lot more races.'

This is a feeling that most sprinters are familiar with. A talent for speed takes them so far, but at the highest level that is no longer enough. Tom Boonen, a regular victor in the northern Classics and winner in 2005 of the Tour's points title, admitted it had taken him three or four seasons to become consistently good, with added experience and strength the keys. 'Most of the time in the first few years when you hit the final kilometre you are usually *à bloc* and it's impossible to sprint – you're in fourth, fifth, sixth position and you just stay there,' said Boonen.

McEwen's build and style mirrored that of Mark Cavendish, who also has the speed of mind and reaction to 'buzz from wheel to wheel' as he has put it. Doing so requires another quality, an astonishing memory for the sprints they've contested and for picking up the strengths and weaknesses of their rivals. Given that he tended to come from behind in sprints, McEwen needed to be particularly adept at this. 'Intelligence is certainly as important as good legs,' he reflected towards the end of his career. 'Every sprint is a lesson whether you win or lose. After a sprint, I know exactly what I've done right or wrong ... I can remember almost every sprint I've ever done, and what the others have done too. This enables me to know how I can repeat successful situations and how someone else might react in any given situation ... When you get fatigued you might not make the right decision at the right time, or you might not make it quick enough, and that's part of it too.'

Another part of that process was knowing when and to what extent to take a risk, when to lean on someone to ease them out of the way, when to aim his wheel into a gap that bigger men not blessed with the agility and handling skills he had developed racing BMX as a kid would consider. 'I've always had tunnel vision when sprinting – if I see a gap, I go through. I don't really look for riders, just for gaps. I look for where I want to go, not where I don't want to go ... The gaps don't need to be that wide, just a little bit more than the size of your handlebars,' he told *Procycling*.

He also acknowledged that, 'In my first four or five years as a pro, I got pushed out of the way more times than I pushed in, but that's what you learn from. And if that's how it has to be, then that's how it has to be, and, with time, you learn to deal with it.

'Jaan Kirsipuu, for example, had a reputation for not being pushed out of the way. You do not move him, and if you did try, you'd end up on the ground. He's a guy that I never had a run-in with. Tom Steels was the same, also Cipo, and I've never pushed with Petacchi. I'll only push someone if I believe they've got to be out of my way because I'm not going to start behind them because they're too slow.'

McEwen's last Tour stage win came on the opening stage of the 2007 race in Canterbury, coincidentally the same day when Mark Cavendish featured in the Tour peloton for the first time. The success was one of the Australian's best, highlighting the skills that brought him two dozen Grand Tour victories. He crashed twenty-one kilometres from home, banging his knee hard, his first thought that his race was over. Quickly back in the saddle, he regained the bunch with the help of his teammates, who then guided him back up to the front, where McEwen surfed from one train to the next in the final drag up to the line, taking advantage of his rivals launching their sprint too early before bursting into clear air in the final one hundred metres.

Cavendish also hit the deck towards the end of that stage, though his fall resulted in a damaged bike and ended his hopes of contesting a sprint that he was sure he would win. If that seemed bullish then for a twenty-two-year-old making his debut in the biggest race on the calendar, subsequent events suggest that he may well have pushed McEwen harder than anyone that unforgettable afternoon when an estimated two million spectators packed the verges in London and Kent. Little more than a year later, he left the 2008 Tour a week before the finish to prepare for the track events at the Olympics with four stage wins to his credit. A year on from that, he claimed six, the best bunch sprinting haul at the Tour in recent history.

A combination of the skills Cavendish had learned during so many years of track racing, his immense self-belief and drive, and a Highroad team not only completely committed but also almost unfailingly capable of putting him in exactly the right place to succeed, raised the art of bunch sprinting to a new level. The confidence of Cipollini, the verve of McEwen and the power of Saeco had been mixed to create an unprecedented winning machine.

Highroad adopted a new strategy to achieve this, putting together a train that could provide the bunch with momentum from the very first kilometres of a stage right through to the final 200 metres, where the objective was to deliver Cavendish with a clear run to the line. When it got rolling, every member of the team would have a place in it, including GC specialists such as Kim Kirchen, Tony Martin and Michael Rogers. All lent their weight to Cavendish's steamroller, designed to suppress breakaways and crush the hopes of his rivals.

Going into the 2011 Tour, by which point Cavendish had accumulated fifteen stage wins as well as another ten at the Giro and Vuelta, HTC-Highroad had become so accomplished that they expected to do this without the slightest bit of assistance from rival teams.

According to Brian Holm, HTC-Highroad sporting director during that race, which the Manxman concluded with another five victories and the points title, the tactic played out like this: firstly, the team had to ensure there were no more than five riders in the break. Allow two or three more than that and the Highroad-propelled peloton could find itself in a duel that was slightly too balanced for comfort. When the right breakaway had gone clear, the team's two 'diesels', Lars Bak and Danny Pate, would sit on the front of the bunch and set a tempo that would keep the escapees within a manageable distance of between three and five minutes, depending on how hilly the stage was.

Towards the end of the stage, emerging GC prospect Tejay van Garderen would assist Bak and Pate with their spadework, closing down the breakaway's advantage completely within the final ten kilometres. The key then was to push the tempo up steadily to discourage other riders from breaking away. With three kilometres remaining, Tony Martin, who went on to be crowned world time-trial champion a couple of months later, would add the first hard injection of pace and sustain it for a kilometre or more.

As the German pulled aside, Peter Velits, another GC hopeful, would come through and maintain that pace for the next few hundred metres, ceding his place at the front to Bernie Eisel, the 'train driver' and team captain, the most experienced rider and the *directeur sportif*'s voice in the peloton who through all this would have been shouting instructions to his teammates. The Austrian, a bunch sprinter in his early pro years, would pilot the train into the final kilometre, before passing driving duties to two Australians, firstly Matt Goss, a world-class sprinter in his own right, and then, inside the final five hundred metres, Mark Renshaw, reputed as one of the best lead-out riders the sport has seen. By the time Cavendish came out of Renshaw's slipstream with around 200 metres remaining, his speed would be above 65kph. A sudden injection of 1600 watts of power would boost him to 70kph and above.

The key to success was not so much the speed, but the organisation, the faith all nine of the Highroad riders had in each other and their ability to stay together, to avoid losing a wheel and run the risk of letting a rival rider infiltrate or disrupt the line. When they achieved this, Cavendish usually ended up collecting the winner's bouquet. Holm's colleague Rolf Aldag explained that season other teams generally couldn't find a way to derail the Highroad express. 'They tried multiple times and then gave up. There was no way to attack that train, because even if you got around Tony Martin, no other team had the strength to keep it going all the way to the line. Get past Martin and you'd find your-self up against George Hincapie,' Aldag explained, underlin-ing the pure power of every one of the locomotives in that Highroad line.

It's interesting to note Filippo Pozzato's analysis of Highroad's rivals during that period when Cavendish was bagging handfuls of victories. 'Racing as it is today plays in Cavendish's favour. There's no team like Cipollini used to have at Saeco, which would bring him onto the finishing straight at sixty-five kilo-metres per hour,' he said. 'The speed's lower in the final kilo-metre and that plays in Cavendish's favour because he's a pure sprinter. Over fifty metres, he has frightening acceleration, like no one else in the peloton ... Cavendish is most dangerous in that split second when the group starts slowing down, which is when he uses that kick.'

Cipollini offered a similar take, commenting, 'However good Cavendish may be – and I think he's exceptional – there's no doubt that he would have problems if my train were still operational. That's my belief, anyway. If you com-pared a video of the last three kilometres of one of my sprints and the last three kilometres of a flat stage now, there's cer-tainly a difference. If you take Cavendish into the last five hundred metres in the right way, he's going to be really, really hard to beat. His jump is sensational. If, however, the speed is extremely high, a bigger, heavier rider than him will be at an advantage. That's why I say he'd have struggled against my Saeco train.'

As if to prove Cipollini's point, a new train arrived, featuring 'huge, powerful guys' who looked like 'a rugby team', according to Cipo's lead-out man Giovanni Lombardi. It employed precisely that tactic, steaming along with arguably the most powerful sprinter the sport has ever seen in the box-car position.

CHAPTER 8

FROM CONTROL TO CHAOS – SPRINTING'S NEW ORDER

I think sprinting has always been underestimated. Likewise, how good you have to be to win a sprint. It's like people say, 'Oh, it was a flat, easy day, and it was a bunch sprint.' They have no idea how much energy it takes to be at the front of the bunch in the last hour doing 60km or more per hour. Then, in the finale, you have to go from 60 to 72kph to win the sprint.

– *Robbie McEwen*

Düsseldorf, 2 July 2017. The instant Tour de France director Christian Prudhomme waves his white flag adorned with the race logo to signal the start of the 203km stage linking the German city to Liège in Belgium, Laurent Pichon of the Fortuneo–Oscaro team accelerates away in textbook fashion from the side of the peloton, with Thomas Boudat of Direct Énergie on his wheel. Moments later, American

Taylor Phinney (Cannondale-Drapac) and Frenchman Yoann Offredo (Wanty-Groupe Goubert) jump across to join the two French riders at the front.

The quartet remain close-knit until the second King of the Mountains test, twenty kilometres from the finish, where Phinney outsprints Pichon to earn the right to wear the red polka-dot jersey the next day, then pushes on with the bunch little more than thirty seconds in arrears and the sprinters' teams prominent at the front. After chasing for the next two kilometres, Offredo bridges up to Phinney.

Both are supreme *rouleurs*, and for the next ten kilometres their collaboration is more than a match for the peloton, where no one team is prepared to commit riders to take up the chase. With half a dozen kilometres remaining, Phinney and Offredo's lead is still fluctuating between thirty-five and forty seconds. Is the peloton going to get mugged by these two opportunist raiders?

Five kilometres to go. The gap has been trimmed, but the peloton is still thirty-two seconds behind as it goes under the 5km banner, riders filling the road from kerb to kerb. Then a change. An arrowhead in Quick-Step's blue and white colours materialises at the front of the peloton, pushing the speed of the pursuit up to 60kph.

Two kilometres left. The gap is ten seconds. Phinney and Offredo, so smooth in their pedalling for 200 kilometres, are finally starting to rock from side to side, forcing every last watt of power out of their bodies.

Twelve hundred metres to go. Offredo glances back at the bunch and sees a quartet of Lotto riders closing rapidly, with sprinter André Greipel the last in their line, pulling the bunch along behind them. As Lotto's red and black colours lead the charge beneath the kilometre banner, staying close to the right-hand barriers, the yellow and black of LottoNL-Jumbo hurtle up the left, with Bora's black jerseys in between.

Five hundred metres to the line. As the road sweeps left, Bora win the battle for prime position on the left-hand barrier, although the red jersey of Cofidis lead-out man Christophe Laporte has infiltrated the space between Bora rival Rudi Selig and world champion Peter Sagan. Selig leads to 400 metres, then pulls tight to the barriers on the left and sits up, Laporte accelerating through to replace him as principal pacemaker, with a dozen sprinters starting to fan out across the road in his wake.

As Laporte runs out of juice and slips back along the left barrier, Sagan glides past him, still seated, and takes a look over his right shoulder. In a line stretching away from him, he can see Greipel, Arnaud Démare, Sonny Colbrelli, Ben Swift and, in space almost on his own far over to the right, Marcel Kittel, who has Mark Cavendish on his wheel.

Two hundred metres to go. Colbrelli is the first to stand on his pedals, the Italian juddering like a jackhammer as his effort sweeps him past Sagan, with Kittel the fastest to respond, coming through on Colbrelli's right. For an instant, it looks like the pair will drag race to the line, but the contest is over with the next six turns of the pedals. Unleashing 2,000 and more watts of power, Kittel opens up a bike length on the rest. When he stomps through the last of these half dozen revolutions, his lead-out man, Fabio Sabatini, is already pumping his arms in celebration from just behind the rush of sprinters, and a second later Kittel throws his arms up too. Démare is the fastest loser, half a bike length down, ahead of Greipel,

Cavendish and Groenewegen. Sagan, the first sprinter to show on the front, finishes tenth.

Ultimately, Marcel Kittel's tenth stage win at the Tour de France more or less resembled the previous nine. Powering through like a cruise liner at full throttle, the bow wave created in the air leaving his rivals reeling in his wake, Kittel looked serene and unstoppable. That he went on to claim another four victories in the next ten days underlined as much. Yet, what had happened before the final one hundred metres when Kittel's turbo kicked him clear of his rivals bore very little similarity to the rash of Tour victories he claimed riding in Argos-Shimano and Giant-Shimano colours in 2013 and 2014. Monolithic control imposed by one dominant team had been replaced by a melee. Understanding why requires an expert's eye.

There are few better placed to provide this than Greg Henderson. The Kiwi track specialist spent three seasons racing with T-Mobile/Highroad, where his stand-out result was a stage win in the 2009 Vuelta, then two seasons with Sky and, most notably, five as André Greipel's lead-out man at Lotto. Plain talking, experienced and well respected, following his retirement from racing in 2017 Henderson went on to become endurance performance director at USA Cycling, assisting their push for Olympic success at the 2020 Games in Tokyo.

'I made a conscious decision to switch to being a lead-out man,' Henderson says of his move from being a rider who mixed sprinting and lead-out duties to focusing completely on the latter. 'I knew that if I lined up against Kittel, Cavendish and Greipel on my best day I was going to get fourth unless one of them made a mistake and teams don't pay for fourth. I would have won the odd race that they weren't at, or if they'd made the odd mistake, but I was realistic. I realised if I wanted to enjoy longevity in the sport that I needed to be successful at something.

'I'd worked with Greipel in the past so when he made contact I had a think about it,' he continues. 'I'm not an idiot. I knew I wasn't some kind of sprinting superman. It was a pretty easy decision actually. What I had always been good at in my sprinting career was the positioning, and I think that came from riding for twelve or thirteen years on the track. I found that the easy part of sprinting. The one issue Greipel had was with his positioning. When he started to think too much he sometimes put himself in the wrong place or sprinted from too far back. He had the straight-up speed to win sprints, the 2,000 watts, but his lead-out needed fine-tuning, so that he had confidence in it and could focus entirely on the last two hundred metres. Once we combined, that trust developed between us and we were quite dominant for a few years.'

The Greipel–Henderson partnership came to the fore at the 2012 Tour, which, perhaps not coincidentally, was the one season Cavendish spent at Sky, where he didn't get the same support that he'd thrived on in sprints over the previous four seasons at Highroad. 'That perhaps did help us, but the amazing thing about Cav is that he's been capable of winning most sprints almost on his own,' Henderson says.

'The golden rule you have to remember when you're doing lead-outs is the "truck and trailer" rule. Wherever I go, I've got to remember that I've got a trailer behind me so I need to make sure there's enough of a gap for André to follow. Then, if there's a little bit of a crosswind and we're sitting out in it, I have to make sure I move out plus one on the wheel, so that he can sit under my wheel, in the shelter I'm providing.

'You've got to think a hundred per cent about protecting your sprinter so that he doesn't have to touch the wind and is as fresh as possible until he gets to two hundred metres to go. An integral part of the role is always thinking about how you can save the energy of the sprinter behind you.'

A degree of fearlessness is another given, but the New Zealander insists that experience counts even more. 'After so many years of racing, I could almost see crashes before they happened. Experience meant that I knew when I needed to be cautious, when we had a chance to pass. It's all about patience, which is really key, and having a feel for the surges and compressions of the bunch, for knowing exactly when they might swerve from one side of the road to the other. You just get a feel for it.'

Henderson adds, 'You also need to be calm, and the sprinter has to have that as well, which can be difficult for them because they tend to be very impatient. They want to go, go, go. That's in their genetic makeup. We'd talk about maintaining that kind of restraint in the pre-stage meetings, and Greipel would say, "I'm not thinking. I'm just following your wheel", which is precisely what I wanted to hear. The lead-out guy has to take the thinking out of it for the sprinter, so that he doesn't have to do anything but cruise through the peloton and then go to work when he is in the right place at the right time.'

In order to understand what has changed in sprinting over recent seasons, let's start by looking back at that 2012 Tour. Going into it, the Lotto-Belisol team had found a winning groove in the sprints, Greipel racking up fourteen victories. With Cavendish playing second fiddle at Sky to Bradley

Wiggins, the Belgian team aimed to show its potential right from the off, as sporting director Marc Sergeant reveals. 'The first stage was in Belgium, with an uphill finish at Seraing and I decided we ought to practise lead-outs, even though the finish of that opening stage didn't suit André. We did, though, have Jurgen Van den Broeck as our GC leader and we wanted to put him at ease on that last climb, to make sure he was in a good position with a kilometre to go.

'We went to the front with, I think, 8k to go and nobody expected that. "What are they doing? Is this for Greipel?" they were wondering. But it was just to give our rivals something to think about, to show how strong we were with Van den Broeck and Jelle Vanendert. Although we didn't win, the plan worked. We got the lead-out practice we'd been looking for and the result we wanted as our two GC riders were up at the front.'

Sergeant smiles ruefully. 'The next day we should have won in Tournai. Tactically we did everything just about perfectly, but coming into the finish there was a bit of kink in the road. We warned them beforehand that the riders ahead of André needed to swing off to the right, which was the direction the wind was coming from, and let André go down the left-hand barrier, which would have meant his rivals would have had to sprint in the wind to overtake him. But "Hendy" made a mistake and went to the left, which meant André went right and Cavendish got a little bit more shelter before coming through on his left to win. We were quite upset, to put it mildly, because the stage was in Belgium and we'd had everything planned.'

Asking Henderson to cast his mind back to that stage, it's clear that defeat still rankles. 'If we'd swung off to the right André wouldn't have been sprinting in the wind,' he responds, his upbeat demeanour disappearing for a moment. 'I think it was a question of centimetres that he lost out to Cavendish on the line, and that's going to happen. There was no question, though, that given the way we'd been leading out in the run-up to the Tour and been so dominant that we were going to win before too much longer had passed. It was just a matter of staying patient and having confidence in each other.'

The next stage, a lumpy run into Boulogne that suited Sagan and was won by him, didn't offer Lotto's sprint train an immediate chance of redemption. At the end of it, Greipel approached Sergeant and told his boss that Henderson was still unhappy about being blamed for the Tournai loss. Sergeant recalls their brief conversation. 'I asked him: "What do you want to do? Do you want to win or do you want to end up second?" He looked at me and said, "You're right." The next day, he won the stage into Rouen and ended up winning three that year. When he won that first one, Hendy was the first rider to come up and give me a big hug. André won the next day as well, so for those few days at the start of that Tour the name Lotto-Belisol was absolutely everywhere, and that made me really happy.'

For Henderson, the first of those three victories was 'the perfect team effort. We had Lars Bak start it off. He was riding at the front all day, and he had help from Francis De Greef in chasing down the breakaway. Then Adam Hansen took off at two kilometres, Marcel Sieberg took it into the last kilometre, where Jurgen Roelandts took me to five hundred metres into the final straight, and then I went down the left barriers to two hundred metres, and I knew, thanks to the speed with which Greipel came past me compared to everybody else, that he'd won it. There's a really nice photo of it, with him still sprinting and me in the background already celebrating. I knew that

Alessandro Petacchi and the rest were never going to catch him.'

Henderson's further explanation of those roles underlines how Highroad and then Lotto and others had adapted the *in progressione* tactic that had proved so effective for Mario Cipollini and Petacchi, as each member of the lead-out train added a couple of kilometres per hour to the speed at the front in the final few kilometres. 'There's a gradual progression. At two kilometres out, it's really difficult to move up. If you're stuck ten or twelve riders back and you're on your own, there's no way that you're going to get to the front because from that point it's full gas, over 60k an hour no question,' the Kiwi says. 'I'd be delivered at around sixty-five kilometres an hour and I'd sprint it up to sixty-eight, and Greipel would come past at seventy-one or seventy-two. That would be on a flat piece of road. If it was downhill or a tailwind it would be a touch quicker, into the wind and uphill a little slower. When we'd do our lead-out training that's basically what the efforts would look like in terms of speed.'

He describes a bunch sprint as being a crescendo: adrenalin and speed building steadily, then more rapidly, then insanely fast in the final kilometre. As a consequence, he says, everything takes place in slow motion. 'That might seem bananas, but it's true,' he insists. 'In high-intensity situations the body does seem to do that, to make things move a little bit slower. It's quite a weird sensation. That slow-motion effect is the same physiological adaption you get when you're in a car accident, for example, or when you crash your bike. You get the same massive adrenalin rush. The funny thing is that after the sprint you get back on the team bus and you only have a rough memory of it. You can't remember exactly what happened.'

He also confirms what Cavendish and other sprinters say about there being no time for tactics in the final 200 metres of a sprint. 'It's purely instinctive at that point. If you have the legs, the only thing you're looking for is the line – if you're boxed in, you look for a place to get out. There's not a lot going through your thoughts at that moment, basically it's just "go" time and all you've got to worry about is the line.

'In fact, the only tactic we had apart from trying to stay together was for me to make sure that we always sprinted down the barriers. That way the others can only come past you on one side. There's no point in sprinting down the middle of the road, because then the other sprinters can come past you on both sides. The key is to reduce the opportunities the other riders have to pass you.'

Henderson emphasises that limiting these opportunities did not extend to disrupting other sprinters and the riders leading them in a dangerous or underhand way. 'There's a lot of respect between sprinters and their lead-out men at WorldTour level. Our rivals would look at us and think, "There's Greg and André, we're not going to disrupt their train, they're working together." In the same way, I wouldn't try to bust Marcel Kittel off his lead-out. There's that mutual regard. If you make a dumb move one day, you know you've got to go up against them again the next day, so the top guys do tend to play very fair.'

While some sprinters and lead-out men have made it almost a badge of honour to avoid touching their brakes in the final, some even having their levers set up so that it is difficult to reach them when racing flat out, the Kiwi insists this is not a tactic he ever used or would advise. 'Of course, you have to touch the brakes sometimes,' he snorts dismissively. 'If, for instance, there's a big squeeze on the left-hand barrier and you've chosen to go down that side, then you've got to touch the brakes if you don't want to crash. But if you do have to touch the brakes in the last two hundred metres you're not going to win – and you've also picked the wrong side to sprint on. But there's definitely a time and a place to whack on the anchors because you know you've made the wrong choice, and when that happens, when someone closes the door on you, it closes really quickly.'

Henderson is adamant that sprints got no more dangerous during the decade or so he spent either contesting them or leading out Greipel. 'I know it's been said that they did when a lot of riders emerged from the track, like Cav, Mark Renshaw and myself, guys who were used to jumping from wheel to wheel in sprints, but I don't believe that. No one wants to crash, it simply comes down to riders having different skills in that environment,' he says, adding, 'but there are days when the danger levels do increase, usually because the peloton has had an easy day and everyone has got fresh legs at the finish.

'Those are the ones that are really hard to control, often in the first few days of a Grand Tour. You can end up with some cowboys in there that don't necessarily have a lead-out and get in the way,' Henderson explains. There is, he adds, a hierarchy and everyone in that elite group is well aware that there are always riders coming through who want to break into it, which can lead to tense moments.

His advice for lone rangers in that situation? 'Well, if you do happen to be sprinting on your own, getting on the back of, for instance, Marcel Kittel's wheel is not a bad position to sprint from because you know that he's going to get to the front and, assuming you've got the legs, you can use his draft to get to the front and then have a go at passing him. Obviously, not many people can do that, in the same way that it's difficult to get past Cavendish and Greipel, because they are so powerful and so fast, but it is worthwhile picking out faster wheels if you are trying to work without a lead-out.'

Just as the Lotto train had established itself as the most reliable, a new rival emerged and began to dominate. Like Mark Cavendish, Marcel Kittel had a fast start to his professional career, the German taking seventeen victories in his debut 2011 season, when he lost just two bunch sprints all year. Whereas most sprinters need time to adjust to competition at the very top level, just like the Manxman, Kittel was up to and usually beyond everyone else's pace from the off.

The mirror image of the Ivan Drago character played by Dolph Lundgren in the *Rocky* movies, thanks to his imposing physique, chiselled looks and precisely sculpted blond hair, Kittel was backed on his Argos-Shimano and Giant-Shimano teams by riders who approached sprints in the Saeco fashion, remaining in the pack for most of a race, largely content to let other teams work if they didn't need to, saving their resources for the final few kilometres. Only then would the team's mixture of Dutch and German powerhouses emerge, racing at a consistently high tempo, giving Kittel what might casually be described as an armchair passage into the final 250 metres, where he would push his speed beyond 70kph and leave his rivals contesting second.

'Giant-Shimano have replaced the gradual crescendo of race finales with a resounding cymbal crash,' wrote journalist Daniel Friebe, while French sprinter Nacer Bouhanni described the challenge of taking on Kittel and his train as like going into battle with completely the wrong weapons. 'They were coming at me with bazookas, whereas I only had a little pistol,' he said. 'Those guys have proper armadas working for them, which keeps their effort steady because they're always sheltered ... Against them, you find yourself three bike-lengths down two hundred metres from the line.'

It would be wrong, though, to depict Kittel as a one-dimensional sprinter, sitting in the wheels all day and being released right at the end. No team can get their lead-out right on every occasion, but even when his didn't, the German still maintained an extremely high success rate. He's shown he's very adaptable, that he rarely allows himself to get boxed in, that he can vary his tactics if required, holding back if he loses his lead-out men and following other wheels to ferry him towards the finish.

Key to that flexibility is his power and the length of time that he can sustain it. 'All of the sprinters I've worked with before now have been able to sustain a high power output for between twelve and fifteen seconds. With Marcel, it's from eighteen to twenty seconds,' his coach Adriaan Helmantel revealed after Kittel had ended Cavendish's four-year unbeaten run in the Tour finale on the Champs-Elysées in 2013. Helmantel also confessed he'd watched tapes of the Briton's four wins on the Champs and advised Kittel to launch his sprint ten to twenty metres before Cavendish had done. The result was a rout, with Kittel several metres clear at the line.

Analysing Kittel's hold over his rivals, FDJ coach Fred Grappe concluded that, 'There isn't a lot you can do when Kittel is delivered fast, at sixty kilometres per hour. It's basic physics: Kittel is heavier than his rivals, so if he's going at sixty-five kilometres per hour and they are too, he'll have more momentum, roll further. In other words, they have to be going considerably faster to get around him. Guys like Cavendish and Bouhanni only really have a couple of options: one, hope that Kittel gets something wrong or, two, look for sprints that aren't delivered so quickly and where the rate of acceleration is more important; they will pick up speed faster than him, and they might also be able to accelerate multiple times.'

Koen de Kort was one of Kittel's powerhouses during the period between 2012 and 2014 when the German was close to invincible. He explains that the fact that so many of the riders who were part of that train came through with Kittel, that the bond was so strong between them, was fundamental to their success. 'We had absolute faith in each other, which of course winning helps to forge,' says the Dutchman.

Asked when that strength was most evident, the moment when everything came together perfectly for Giant-Shimano and its marquee sprinter, he initially suggests that it's hard to choose. 'When you work in a sprint train you quite often have those days when everything you've discussed from a tactical point of view comes together perfectly, but you don't win simply because another sprinter is faster on the day. Conversely, I've known days the tactical plan has not worked out at all but the sprinter has still won because they're so good,' de Kort explains.

'But the one stage that sticks out for me was the 2014 Tour stage finish in London. We set the tempo from maybe five or six kilometres out going alongside the River Thames. No one came around us, everybody did their job and Marcel ended up winning the sprint. Basically, from 5k to go, Marcel didn't see any other riders apart from those on the Giant team. If you want to check out how a lead-out works, that's a good stage to look at.'

Illness meant that Kittel's final season with the Giant team in 2015 was an anti-climax that left many questioning whether he would ever reach the same heights again. Although he did soon get back into his stride at Quick-Step, who brought him in to replace Cavendish, the sprinting landscape had changed. A degree of anarchy had returned.

'It's gone from having one or two sprint trains and the other sprinters having just one or two guys to look after them to pretty much every sprinter having a train these days,' says de Kort. 'It's a lot harder to get it right now. It's become a lot more frantic. It was easier when I was on the team with Marcel as most teams tended to look to us and one or two others to lead out. Now, it's chaos.'

Henderson agrees with de Kort's assessment. 'You could argue that in terms of the number and quality of sprinters, the sport is in a bit of a golden age. There's no one train that's dominant any more. All of a sudden, there were six or seven teams that were capable of a good lead-out, which hasn't made it more dangerous, but harder to control the front and harder to win,' he reasons.

Henderson also points to another complicating factor – the presence of most of the GC riders and the trains protecting them. 'They are trying to stay up at the front, but stay out of trouble, because they don't want to get caught in a crash and lose some silly time,' he explains. 'That's another reason why it's hard for us to get into position, because these guys are super strong as well. They can ride at fifty-five kilometres an hour no problem, which means as we're setting up our lead-out they can still hang around and it's only when we go full throttle that we don't see them any more. But you have to give them respect, you don't want to accidentally knock them into the grass and have someone lose his GC chances. We're jostling for position until well inside the 3k banner.'

Returning his focus to the sprinters' teams, the New Zealander says, 'Because of the trains now, you can't open it with 5k to go like they used to back in the day because everyone can match everyone else and, as a consequence, no one can hold a lead. Instead, from five kilometres to go you're waiting and just trying to hold your position because you can actually only go flat out for the last 2k. Until that point, you've got to hang on to as many matches as possible and then light them in the last 2k when the fast guys can actually go full gas.'

It might seem paradoxical that in an era that has produced three of the sport's best all-time sprinters in Cavendish, Kittel and Greipel that lots of other teams have begun to focus more on sprints, but there are two good reasons. Firstly, the presence of any combination of those three riders all but ensures stages will end in a sprint, so other teams have brought on fast finishers of their own in order to have a presence. Secondly, they've been encouraged in this by a sudden rush of young talent, including Arnaud Démare, Fernando Gaviria, Caleb Ewan, and Dylan Groenewegen, all winners of Grand Tour stages in their early twenties.

Supporting Henderson's point, Groenewegen's team manager Richard Plugge revealed the change in strategy the Dutch team made to support their young flyer, who won the 2017 Tour's final stage on the Champs-Elysées. 'There are no trains like those we were so used to seeing any more. It's chaos,' says Plugge, using that word again (unprompted). 'Well, there are trains,' he corrects himself, 'but they're really small and usually you only put them to work between two to four kilo-metres from the finish, and at that point you rely on two or three riders at most.

'It's a better tactic than having five or six riders in front of you. I think the fact that there are a lot of good sprint-ers has something to do with it, but it's also down to the fact that there ended up being five or six trains riding next to each other, clashing with each other, with riders getting bumped off the wheel they were on, so a change came,' Plugge explains. 'If you look at the 2017 Tour, the best train was Katusha's for Alexander Kristoff and they didn't win a stage. They did have five riders in a train going into the final few kilometres a number of times, but never got the result they were looking for. The guys who did well were those who came late, with one or two teammates, and then did their own sprint. There was nothing to be gained from having five or six teammates fighting with five or six riders from other teams. Just use them and come late.'

Dimension Data made a similar adjustment when they signed Cavendish at the start of the 2016 season, team boss Doug Ryder making it clear from the off that there was no longer any point in backing a sprinter with the kind of long lead-out train that the Briton had re-popularised with HTC-Highroad several years previously. 'Times have changed. An HTC-style lead-out when you get on the front with five kilometres to go and smash it like that just isn't possible any more,' Ryder said. Cavendish responded with his best Tour performance since 2011, bagging four stages to take him to thirty in total and second on the race's all-time list of winners, just four behind Eddy Merckx.

Having got used to handing out that kind of beating to his rivals, Kittel found himself on the receiving end for the first time and set about readjusting his tactics and preparation for the 2017 season, with his focus on the Tour, the one race guaranteed to attract every one of the best sprinters in the peloton and, therefore, the ultimate judge of their ability. He instructed his Quick-Step teammates to hold off on their lead-out so that he could come from behind having assessed the right moment to move and the best wheel or line to take. He used highly detailed plans and video footage of key sections of the closing ten kilometres of road to brief his teammates on exactly where they needed to be and when. Debriefings were just as meticulous, even on the days Kittel and the riders assigned to protect him had celebrated victory.

Describing how this wait-and-move approach worked for Kittel and Quick-Step during the 2017 Tour, when sporting director Tom Steels made the point that the German was often invisible just 300 metres from the line, team boss Patrick Lefevere explains, 'He prefers to come from behind, that's his wish. He doesn't want the team to lead him out, he wants to come from the second line. He knows that there's a risk of being blocked in. It happened on the day when Sagan and Cavendish clashed [on Tour stage four in Vittel] and we missed out. But we're happy with the change in lead-out tactics. He asked for just one guy to stay with him and bring him where he wants to be with a kilometre to go. Fabio Sabatini does that.'

According to Steels, Kittel's very competitive performance in the opening fourteen-kilometre time trial, when he finished ninth, sixteen seconds down on winner Geraint Thomas, made the German realise he had the endurance to be able to employ this 'go-it-alone' strategy. But he stressed Kittel still needed to be protected from a point well before that in order to be ready for the final. 'The train starts to work thirty kilometres from the finish because it's important that he's never left alone. What happens in the final is down to his instinct,' said Steels.

Look back at that finish of the 2017 Tour's opening stage, though, and it is hard to discern any evidence of that Quick-Step train. Indeed, as Steels acknowledged, it lost its bearings well before the finish and Kittel had to look after himself for the most part, with some help from Sabatini. 'But he's realised that even if he's fifty metres from the line and still behind the others, he can still make the difference with one single acceleration. Today he employed that strategy. He was perhaps a little bit isolated in the final kilometres, having been protected by his teammates up to then, but he then burst through with a single thrust.

'Marcel always finds the best line very quickly, as we saw at Liège where he didn't let himself get boxed in by the others. It's a matter of timing, but also of lucidity. He has a very clear vision of the situation, he knows immediately what he has to do. But when you're as strong as he is, you always choose the best option.'

Pressed on what seems like a counterintuitive tactic for one of the sport's fastest-ever sprinters of coming from behind rather than leading from the front, Kittel revealed he felt more relaxed in doing so, that he was fully confident of the advantage his speed gave him to prevail even though he did have to make up ground. 'If you know you have to fight for it then maybe you panic. Now I can wait for the right moment. I have that luxury and so I'm enjoying it so much more,' he said as he moved towards a best-ever tally of five wins. 'I prefer to sprint without having to calculate ... but I've got more flexibility now, and capable of adapting to every situation, which is always easier when you've got legs as good as mine are.'

He further explained, 'I remembered the lesson from last year's Tour de France when I wasted all my matches and then Cavendish shot away off my wheel.' Having seen how the Manxman had capitalised on his explosiveness in the final metres, Kittel, who previously unleashed full power to try to distance his rivals well before the line and then hold on, opted for the same tactic.

'There are very different ways to be a successful sprinter. You can have the basics, that pure speed that every sprinter depends on, but of course you need mental strength. I think the key thing that's allied to that, though, is that you also need to have the ability to stay calm. That's very important for a sprinter. You need to be able to observe what's going on around you and be able to react to it. You have to have the right instinct, to know exactly what you have to do, and especially in a hectic final. That's a quality that I have.'

The question of who is the best sprinter of recent years, while not entirely pertinent to the question of tactics, does highlight what makes Mark Cavendish and Marcel Kittel so special. During the Tour, Norwegian sprinter Alexander Kristoff plumped for Kittel, saying, 'He's the fastest, so in order to beat him he needs to mess something up.' Elia Viviani also picked out the German. 'I think he's the strongest sprinter I've seen in the seven years I've done as a pro. When he starts sprinting I can't stay on his wheel,' said the Italian. 'If Kittel gets it all perfect, it's impossible to beat him at the moment.'

Those who have worked with both riders assess the comparison between the pair differently, though. 'Both are world class but Cav, when he puts on that Foreign Legion look, like he could kill, he can do whatever he wants. He can't do it every race but it's like he has an out-of-body experience: he has so much energy. Whereas Kittel just does his sprint, doing 400,000 watts. He's a pure powerhouse. He's like Chernobyl just before it exploded,' was Brian Holm's typically vibrant assessment.

Pressed on who's the best he's seen, Greg Henderson, without the slightest pause, goes for the Briton. 'I'd have to pick Cavendish, as much as I love Greipel,' he says. 'André's my favourite sprinter, but I think the best is Cavendish. He's won so many sprints and in so many different scenarios, sometimes with a team and sometimes on his own, and he's done that so many times and for so long. Kittel's got a few years on Cav, so maybe he will get up to Cav's strike rate. At the moment, they're pretty equally matched in terms of speed, but if you look over the past ten or twelve years you've got to go with the consistency and variety of wins that Cavendish has produced.'

Naturally, this leads to the question of who is the best lead-out man. 'That would be a guy named Greg Henderson, I think,' the Kiwi says, laughing as he does so. 'He's very reliable, very loyal. He's got very good knowledge of the sprint. He understands which side of the road to be on, when to pressure the boys and when not to. I haven't seen anyone do a better job than him.

'Seriously, though, every top sprinter has a capable lead-out man and, often, they're the reason why the sprinter thrives as well because they have a good guy in front of them, looking after them. Of course, the best lead-out guys want to work with the top sprinters, so it's a win–win situation. If you look back, Julian Dean, another Kiwi, was sensational at the job and then there's [Australia's] Mark Renshaw, obviously. It's the guys that come from the southern hemisphere and out of track racing who seem to be pretty good at it.'

CHAPTER 9

HOW TO BLUFF YOUR RIVALS

The great thing about athletics is that it's like poker sometimes: you know what's in your hand, and it may be a load of rubbish, but you've got to keep up the front.

– *Sebastian Coe*

Jean-René Bernaudeau once said that if he could have combined the tactical nous and psychological strength of Thomas Voeckler and the physiological ability of Sylvain Chavanel he would have had a world-beater at the head of his French team. While Voeckler spent his whole career racing for Bernaudeau, Chavanel moved on to become the team leader at Cofidis and Classics contender at Quick-Step, before returning to his first boss in 2017 to bring the curtain down on his career. It meant a step down from the elite-level WorldTour to a second division Pro Continental set-up, but Chavanel insisted that the move was ideal because he wanted to enjoy racing more at events where the result wasn't decided in advance or dictated by earpieces.

Events like the Four Days of Dunkirk, a six-day race that he first won for Bernaudeau in 2002 and then again in 2004.

It is held in the Pas de Calais, where huge headlands, rolling hills and the wind barrelling in off the English Channel are always likely to scatter a peloton. In 2017, the fourth stage ran from Marck-en-Calaisis, just to the east of Calais, to finish high up on the opposite side of the river to the port of Boulogne at Le Portel, where the riders had to tackle a tough final circuit that included a steep climb at Saint-Étienne-du-Mont four times.

'I didn't know the climb, it was really difficult. But instead of giving in, I watched the other riders in the break. I could see that those who made a big effort at that point then had real trouble recovering immediately afterwards on the false flat near the top. So on the last circuit, I climbed a little bit behind them but made sure that I kept grimacing like they were. In my head, I had already selected the place where I needed to attack on the false flat with the wind three-quarters from behind,' Chavanel revealed.

After several of his rivals had blown their chances with attacks on the steeper parts of the climb in Saint-Étienne-du-Mont, Chavanel made his move just before the top. Now grimacing for real, he gained enough ground to hold off the chase that eventually started behind him to win the stage and take the leader's jersey. 'I've got less "jump" at my age, but on the other hand I've got more endurance – cycling is still a difficult sport even at thirty-seven and with all my experience, but this was a perfect day,' he said. 'I'm proud of the fact that I've never done things in the way most people would predict. I always liked to spring surprises, to attack when it's least expected.'

There are few things as magnificent in cycle sport as a well-conceived and perfectly enacted bluff, a moment when a rider produces a coup that not only foxes their rivals, but leaves that rider in the position to benefit from the advantage that, for a time at least, only they are aware that they have earned. They've achieved cycling's equivalent of that rare moment in a football match when a striker feigns to shoot at the other team's goal only to run over the ball, taking the defenders with them, and leaving a teammate running in behind with a tap-in. Yet, while the perfectly judged dummy is quickly spotted by football fans, the same manner of tactical ruse can pass unnoticed in cycling. Let's face it, if those being bluffed aren't aware that they're being duped, spectators have got little chance of spotting the deceit. But being mindful of the tricks that can be pulled does help.

'Don't let anyone know your true feelings', Henri Desgrange instructed his racing novice in *La Tête et Les Jambes*, and deception has been a cornerstone of the sport ever since. The first Tour de France, which was a testing ground for all kinds of rules, some of which were introduced mid-race, provided an early example. One of those regulations allowed riders who hadn't completed a stage to line up in subsequent ones, although they were no longer eligible for the overall prize. This regulatory quirk enabled the wonderfully named Hippolyte Aucouturier to start and win the second stage into Marseille after illness – probably the result of drinking from a bottle that had been spiked with a purgative – had forced him out of the opener. Believing that riders who were no longer involved in the battle for overall honours were complicating that contest, race director

Desgrange then ruled that the stage-only riders would start the third stage between Marseille and Toulouse an hour later than the GC men.

Aucouturier was outraged. After complaining loudly that the new rule would mean he would be racing with lesser riders, thus reducing his chance of a second win, he proclaimed he wasn't going to bother going flat out on the road to Toulouse. What would be the point, he whinged? The deck had been stacked against him.

But when he set off into the sultry Midi night an hour after the GC men, Aucouturier went full bore. Unaware that he was gaining, the frontrunners reached Toulouse, where Eugène Brange celebrated victory, only to find out twenty-eight minutes later that he hadn't been the winner after all. Aucouturier had pulled a fast one, demonstrating his quickness of mind as well as of leg.

Henri Pélissier, best known now for lifting the lid on the cornucopia of doping products widely employed to cope with the physical demands of the inter-war Tour de France, was fond of more subtle ruses that might give him an edge on his rivals. The night before races he used to call the National Meteorological Office anonymously to get their forecast for the next day. Based on the details he received, he would modify the set-up of his bike accordingly and formulate a particular tactic. Astonished by his ability for being so well prepared on almost every occasion for the conditions, his adversaries endeavoured to get a covert look at his bike before the start in order to see what gear he was using and fit the same one themselves. It took them a little longer to realise that he didn't object to this, for the simple reason that he would fix the wrong gear on his rear hub and would have it changed at the last moment by a mechanic who was ready and waiting with the correct one.

Pélissier was just as cunning in his training methods. The night before a long training excursion, he would tell his riding partners to eat a hearty breakfast and what gear they needed to fit, only to turn up with a bigger gear saying his had broken and ride away from them, having had just a cup of tea and a few biscuits in preparation. At lunch stops, he would order bottles of wine and encourage drinking – 'C'est le régime Pélissier!' – but rarely indulge himself.

As the levels of organisation and competition improved in the post-war years, simple stunts like these were no longer viable, and bluffing of the sort employed by Sylvain Chavanel became a more regular feature of racing, its best exponents those racers who couldn't depend on a fast sprint or exceptional climbing prowess to guarantee them success. Tom Simpson was one such rider. The Briton's most illustrious one-day victories all depended on him marshalling his strength until the very last moment and cleverly concealing that he was doing so.

His 1961 Tour of Flanders victory over Italian Nino Defilippis was a classic of this type. On a savagely windy day, the finish-line banner had to be taken down and Defilippis later claimed that in the confusion this created he had sprinted for the wrong line. His argument was, though, undermined by the fact that he and Simpson had already been through the line three times on the finishing circuit – Defilippis suggested subsequently that the line had been moved before their final approach. More likely is that he simply got it wrong, or, more accurately, he misread Simpson, who was confident he could beat the Italian despite Defilippis being the faster of the pair.

'I started my sprint about a kilometre from the line, and as I anticipated, Defilippes [sic] took my wheel. I had worked out just what I was going to do and it went like a charm!' Simpson wrote in his autobiography, *Cycling is My Life*. 'With some three hundred metres to go I feigned that I had "blown up" and slowed slightly. Immediately the Italian took a flyer off my wheel and passed me on my right, going like a train for the line. As he went I restarted sprinting, really going flat out, and drew almost alongside him on his right. I reasoned that he would look back to see where I was, and since he had gone by me on the right, would look to his left for me. He did just that, and got the shock of his life for I was nowhere in sight! In the split second he took to turn his head to the opposite side, I went past him. He had slowed down momentarily through being taken by surprise like that, and I was over the line just a wheel in front of him!'

The ill-fated Briton produced what was almost a carbon copy of that victory when he claimed the world road title four years later, getting the better of Germany's Rudi Altig in a two-up sprint where his rival was the favourite. As had been the case with Defilippis, Altig later revealed that Simpson had told him he nothing left in the closing kilometres and almost begged his rival not to drop him as he didn't stand a chance in the sprint. As the two men came into the finish, Simpson accelerated the moment Altig moved his hand to the changer on his downtube to select the right gear for the sprint and the title was his.

Wonderful as the description of bike racing being 'chess at 150 heartbeats per minute' is, sandbagging of this type points more towards a comparison with poker. Defilippis and Altig had the best cards, but didn't play them correctly. While it was far from a case of the tortoise beating the hare, it was certainly a triumph for the head over the legs.

The most renowned example of bluffing weakness in order to force a rival to play their hand prematurely occurred in the 2001 Tour, when a whole team and indeed most of the peloton was taken in by a brazen ruse carried out by the defending champion and thought up by his sporting director. 'The Bluff', as US Postal DS Johan Bruyneel dubbed the ploy, crystallised in the wake of Lance Armstrong's second Tour win in 2000, by which point the American team had become so dominant that it couldn't rely on finding allies. Bruyneel figured that one way to get around this would be to encourage a rival squad to become an ally without them realising, but also reasoned that this would depend on said team believing that Armstrong was having a bad day.

'I knew what I was thinking was a once-in-a-lifetime tactic; I could pull it out of our bag of tricks exactly once. After that, you would never be able to surprise anyone with the move ever again. I discussed the strategy with Lance on and off. He was averse to it. He always wanted to be the best, to show his dominance, to rule the race. "If we do it," he once said, "it has to be because we have no choice." "When the opportunity is perfect," I said.'

That moment arrived during the 2001 Tour's stage to Alpe d'Huez. It was partly an effort to save Armstrong's team from having to work as the race crossed the massive Madeleine and Glandon passes. Climbing them, Armstrong slipped to the back of the group containing the favourites, pouring water over his head and doing anything else he could to give the impression he was having a bad day. Back in the team car, Bruyneel was besieged by TV motorbikes, all wanting to know whether Armstrong had a problem.

'I had a sudden realisation: if Lance really were falling apart, I would try to project confidence. If I admitted I was worried, it would be so out of character that The Bluff might be seen as being just that. I needed to pull off The Bluff Within The Bluff,' said Bruyneel. He double-bluffed, and the Telekom team of Jan Ullrich bought it. They continued to push hard on the front of the group, sensing the chance to shake Armstrong out of contention.

It helped too that Armstrong's teammates weren't in the loop either. When Spaniard Carlos Sastre rode up alongside compatriot José Luis Rubiera, one of Armstrong's key lieutenants, and asked what was wrong with him, Rubiera confessed he had no idea. Few did until the group rode onto the initial ramps of Alpe d'Huez. While Ullrich was still wondering when he should deliver the thrust that would finish Armstrong off, the American came back to life and jumped away to hand the German and his team their most demoralising defeat among many during those drug-tainted years.

Similar ruses are employed many times in every race, says Rachel Heal, a successful racer and British Olympian who went on to become the first sporting director to work on both a men's and a women's team at the highest level. 'Everybody in a race is trying to manipulate the situation so that it's in their favour. A lot of the time that will mean trying to get somebody to do the work that you want done, but don't have to use your riders to do. There is a variety of ways to get that done, to persuade a team that it's in their interest, or it's not in your best interest, or even that there's a combined interest. Nobody is going to do your work for you if they think it's going to benefit you more than them. So you are trying to bluff a lot of the time,' she says.

At the same time Heal and rival sporting directors are trying to outfox each other, those on the inside are playing similar games. 'Everybody's bluffing everybody else all the time about what cards they're holding,' Tiffany Cromwell confirms. 'So much needs to go right for you to win a bike race. A lot of the time it's not necessary to be the strongest rider. You need a little bit of luck and try to get other people to play their cards before you play yours, to leave your final bid as late as possible.

'Some people are much better at that than others, they can look like they're suffering hugely but then "recover" to win the bike race. At the same time, you see others who look like they're not even trying and they end up going backwards. This is when it helps to be able to read the other riders, to suss out what cards they are holding, to work out who's bluffing and who is simply running out of gas. The sport's about taking risks as well, which makes the analogy with poker a very good one, or even playing the financial market. You need to take a risk in order to see whether it pays out. A lot of the time, sitting back won't win you bike races.'

In women's racing, where the lack of sponsorship money and investment has resulted in the formation of teams mainly comprising riders who have to adapt their skillsets to any kind of race, to being all-rounders rather than focusing on, for instance, the Classics or hilly stage races like the men, bluffing is a tactic that even the very best racers have to resort to regularly. 'Nicole Cooke used to be very good at hiding her form. She always looked like she was suffering, but was actually very good at riding above her limit. She could suffer, suffer, suffer and still end up at the front of the bike race at the end,' says Cromwell. 'It's not just about having the tactical skillset and legs, though, it's also about having that desire to win, the belief in yourself. Bluffing is no use at all if you don't have that.'

Inevitably, given the physical toll it takes over consecutive days of competition and the consequent importance of ensuring that every attack pays off, stage racing has a particularly colourful history when it comes to bluffing. Reflecting on his head-to-head battle with Laurent Fignon at the 1989 Tour, and particularly the Alpe d'Huez stage that almost ended his push for the yellow jersey that he eventually secured by those famous eight seconds, Greg LeMond has said, 'I look back now and think, thank God there weren't radios back then. Cycling's about bluffing. It's poker. I was trying to bluff, but [rival DS Cyrille] Guimard could see me rocking and he knew.'

Even Eddy Merckx had to resort to ruses of this type on occasion, despite his apparently limitless resources. At the 1971 edition of the Critérium du Dauphiné, the Belgian only managed to follow his rivals on the Col du Granier with stalwart assistance from teammate Joseph Deschoenmaeker. Hearing the Belgian tell the waiting press at the finish in Annecy that, 'The only struggle I had today was with my derailleur,' Bernard Thévenet commented: 'I knew now what you had to say in case of a slight loss of power in the legs.' Merckx gained a reputation for hiding his form in this way, often complaining before big races that he had some kind of ailment, his complaint producing knowing guffaws among his rivals, who knew that 'The Cannibal' would soon be feasting on them.

Contemporary Grand Tour winners have suffered in the same way too. Although history now suggests that Bradley Wiggins' worst moments on his ride to Tour victory in 2012 were the 'attacks' made by teammate Chris Froome, Wiggins confessed that the hardest point of that race occurred on the medium mountain stage to Porrentruy when the event made a brief foray into Switzerland. On the fifth and final climb, none of which took the riders above a thousand metres, he almost slipped out of the small group chasing lone leader Thibaut Pinot.

'I didn't give much away when I had that brief crisis on the climb,' admitted Wiggins later, his lead just ten seconds over Cadel Evans at that point, with Vincenzo Nibali another half dozen in arrears. 'I remember as we went over the top, Nibali looked around to see if I was there; I shut my mouth as if I wasn't hurting, and then he turned to the front again. In that situation, you just try and soak up the pain, not show it. There's a lot of that in cycling. There's a lot of bluffing midway through the Tour, because you don't want to give anything away. You don't want to give anyone a reason to think, the next day, "I'm going to try and attack although I normally wouldn't." You always want to keep them thinking, "Damn, he looked strong there."'

Froome too has had to hide his weakness in the mountains at the Tour, his most notable crisis coming in 2017 on the Pyrenean stage to the Peyragudes ski station that crossed four passes beforehand. His problem was a basic one that most cyclists can relate to when they've not taken enough food and drink with them if riding for a good distance – they 'bonk' or get 'the knock' as the body's reserves dwindle to almost zero. Without the option of refuelling in a mid-ride café and knowing that even the slightest sign of weakness would trigger attacks from any number of rivals, Froome had to push himself as hard as he could without anyone realising that he was racing on empty.

Helped by the fact that his Sky teammates had also sucked plenty of juice from his rivals' tanks with their pace-setting going over the Ares, Menté and Port de Balès passes, Froome asked Mikel Nieve and Mikel Landa to ease off a touch on the Col de Peyresourde so that he could follow their wheels. 'When we were ten kilometres from the finish, my lights almost went out, and I knew that I was in danger. I started to feel really weak, I was close to blacking out, as if I'd hit a wall. I'd felt OK until then so it was a shock for me,' he admitted post-stage.

'I realised that if my rivals attacked I would have a serious problem because I wouldn't have been able to follow,' added Froome. But he managed to avoid this fate thanks to two things. Firstly, his style on the bike, like 'a spider sitting on the edge of a knife', as *L'Équipe*'s Gilles Simon so perfectly describes the Briton, with his long arms and splayed elbows. 'Then, there's that head that sways from side to side, just like those plastic toys in the back of cars, and that face stripped of all feeling, from which no emotion ever seems to emerge.' Froome's style isn't elegant, but it does make it easier for him to hide any 'tell' of discomfort.

The Sky leader also drew on his tactical intelligence, briefly moving out of his teammates' slipstream as they led him up the Peyresourde to eye his rivals from behind his sunglasses. It's a textbook tactic to employ prior to making an attack, sizing up the opposition before committing. But Froome's internal fuel light was right in the red, and this was no more than a bluff to cover that. While his rivals awaited an acceleration that never came, Froome earned himself some respite until the final sharp drag up the spec-tacularly angled mountain runway at Peyragudes, where the attacks did finally materialise, but only 300 metres from the line.

'I saved my Tour that day. I came out of it well, I managed to deal with my weakness until the final climb,' confessed Froome, who lost the yellow jersey for two days but could have seen his hopes of a fourth Tour title disappear entirely.

Froome's rivals, or perhaps the sporting directors on their teams, are likely to have spent a good deal of the off-season that followed looking back at footage of that stage, trying to decipher a 'tell' that would indicate the Briton's struggles and give them a clue to watch out for in future. Bearing in mind that riders spend so much time in close proximity to each other, any changes in pedalling action, position or expression that might signal fatigue or a *jour sans* can be difficult to hide.

Gino Bartali, for instance, had time to study his principal adversary, Fausto Coppi, in forensic detail. Racing at the Giro in the immediate post-war years, he took advantage of what he had learned from doing so. 'Up until that point, more often than not he outmanoeuvred me because he knew my weaknesses while I wasn't aware of his,' the Italian explained. 'When I started to watch him closely I discovered his flaw. What was it? A vein that was barely visible in the back of his right knee that swelled abnormally when muscular fatigue began to have an impact on him.' Aware of this, he got teammate Giovanni Corrieri to sit on Coppi's wheel with his eyes glued to the back of his knee. Late on in a hot stage, Corrieri suddenly yelled, 'The vein!' In an instant, Bartali was on the attack.

Naturally, Coppi used to study his rival just as closely. He noticed that Bartali tended to cut the hairpin bends on a mountain climb if he wasn't going well, and was just as quick to take advantage when he picked up on this.

On that day in 1989 when LeMond desperately tried to conceal the difficulties he was having, Fignon's sporting director, Cyrille Guimard, who had brought LeMond through into the pro ranks, could see the American's predicament. 'I knew Greg by heart. From the car I noticed one of his tells that signalled that he was on the verge of cracking. He moved oddly in the saddle, half standing up and then sitting back down again in a particular way. That was the moment,' Guimard explained. He told Fignon to go for it, only for the Frenchman to respond that he was cooked too. A kilometre later, Fignon summoned up all he had left to drop LeMond and gained more than a minute by the summit. Guimard remains adamant that if Fignon had been able to move when initially told, he'd have taken three and had the Tour well won before the unforgettable Versailles to Champs-Elysées time trial where the American snatched the title.

Now that racers are so evenly matched physically, noticing a tell can be priceless. Rather than make a random thrust to test out a rival, an attack can be timed at a moment when it will be felt most keenly, when it will actually stick. Later on in the 2012 Tour won by Wiggins, when Nibali had emerged as his main challenger for the title, the Briton was tracking the Italian as they ascended the Port de Balès on the road towards Peyragudes.

'I sat behind Nibali the whole way up the climb and, towards the top of it, I got a sense of his body language, the way he was pedalling. That gave me the notion that actually he might be struggling a little bit,' Wiggins revealed. 'I always watch people's pedalling action and I've learned that Nibali drops his heels when he's suffering. He doesn't give a lot away when you ride beside him. He's very good at bluffing, he's conscious of that all the time, but he does have some tells.'

Given the aggressive way that the Italian had ridden on the previous day in the Pyrenees, Wiggins was expecting another severe test, but picked up on this dropping of the heels towards the top of the Balès. 'Straight away we realised he was actually on a bad day. He just hadn't backed up the efforts he'd made the day before. That was a classic case of concentrating on someone, expecting them to do something because of how they looked the day before, when in actual fact they haven't got the legs for it.' As Wiggins admitted, Nibali is especially good at bluffing, and he acknowledged he had been for most of that day, hiding his weakness by riding on the front and presenting himself as being strong.

This knack for reading your rivals is just as vital as being able to read the race, no matter whether it's a stage of the Four Days of Dunkirk, a one-day Classic or the Tour de France that is at stake. In *The Great Bike Race*, his account of the 1976 Tour and a must-read for any bike fan looking for insight into the sport, Geoffrey Nicholson described Belgian climber Lucien Van Impe as 'playing a rather childish but more devious game than you would expect from him. On the way up the Col de Menté he has been hanging back in the bunch, rubbing his legs from time to time and calling up his teammates to help him.'

Van Impe, who had held and then lost the yellow jersey earlier in the race, is endeavouring to pull off the coup that might win him the Tour. He's undoubtedly being devious, but childish? This suggests that Van Impe is undermining the nobility of the sport, implying that he's bringing it into disrepute, that he's going against some tenet that has it that the strongest riders should always prevail.

It's a tactical sleight of hand that is fundamental to success at races as long and sapping as the Tour. It's fiendish, but brilliantly so when it works, as it did that day for Van Impe, who managed to encourage rivals Joop Zoetemelk and Raymond Poulidor to push up the pace and, thereby, expend some of their resources before he made what would prove to be his race-winning attack to Pla d'Adet. No rider can be strong every day, but every rider must pretend that they are. Success depends on it.

CHAPTER 10

SURVIVING WITH THE LAUGHING GROUP – LIFE IN THE GRUPPETTO

Being in the *gruppetto* reveals people's true nature.
— *Jimmy Casper*

Tactics aren't all about winning. When stage races, and particularly the Grand Tours, reach the mountains, for a significant portion of the peloton success is simply finishing inside the time limit and, thereby, surviving to race again the next day. This limit varies but usually means that to continue a rider has to cross the line in the winner's time plus a percentage that is decided according to the length of the stage, the difficulty of the climbs and the average speed, that figure normally being somewhere between 10 to 15 per cent. In other words, when the first rider finishes in four hours and the cut-off is 15 per cent, every other one behind has to complete the stage within the subsequent thirty-six minutes.

Introduced in the Tour de France's early years by Henri Desgrange, time limits were designed to prevent riders taking it easy one day in order to save themselves for the next. Desgrange set the limit at between 8 and 10 per cent, but managed to find loopholes if the wrong riders or simply too many of them finished outside it, notably in 1933, when only half a dozen racers arrived in Nice within the permitted time. From that point, the rule changed so that there would be no elimination if a set proportion of the field arrived beyond the allotted limit.

Riders and sporting directors also became very conversant with the race rules. In 1951, Italian national team boss Alfredo Binda unearthed a clause that enabled an ailing Fausto Coppi to remain in the race. It stated, 'When a group larger than 15 per cent of the day's starters finishes outside the 10 per cent time limit, the time limit will be extended to 15 per cent.' Binda instructed every other member of the Italian team apart from Gino Bartali to stay with Coppi, who was saved. In 1959, Brian Robinson evaded the timekeeper's axe when he fell ill and finished outside the limit in Clermont-Ferrand as another clause stipulated that any rider who held a position in the top ten on the general classification at the start of the stage couldn't be eliminated from the race. Unfortunately, this didn't apply to his teammate and friend Shay Elliott, who helped the Briton to the finish, and the Irishman's race ended.

By that point, riders who couldn't stay with the best at the front of the race had already realised the benefit of ganging together to ensure they didn't fall right off the pace at the back. They shared not only the pacemaking, but water, food and encouragement. Their group also gained a name, *l'autobus* in French and *il gruppetto* in Italian, the latter becoming the generic term in the modern era, and is also known as 'the laughing group', due to the fact that the atmosphere is more relaxed and the sense of camaraderie generally all-pervading. Prior to the advent of race radios, the 'bus' would have a driver, who was always an experienced pro who not only knew the pace that needed to be set on climbs, descents and in the valleys, but also had the respect of his peers for being able to ensure they would get home within time.

Italian sprinter Mario Cipollini was one of the best renowned in this role, as Australian sporting director Matt White recalls. 'I was with the Italian Amore e Vita team during my first pro season [in 1998] and rode a lot of the same races as Cipollini, who would control the bunch from the start of a race. I remember seeing him going to the front of the bunch on one of the opening mountain stages of the Giro and saying, "We're only going to race the last two climbs." He let riders from certain teams go in the break of the day and that was it. I was blown away by it,' says White.

'Guys like him controlled Italian racing and basically looked after each other. I saw Cipollini "helmet pop" people who tried to attack at the start, when he'd decided they weren't allowed to. He'd chase them himself. He'd bop them on the top of the head, grab them by the shirt and tell them, "You're not going anywhere." I was scared shitless of him in my first year. Cipollini ran Italian cycling in that era. There were guys like Richard Virenque and Laurent Brochard in France who did the same thing. Back then riders were racing too much. When you're racing one hundred and twenty or one hundred and thirty days a year, you can't race hard every day for one hundred and thirty days. It was self-preservation.' When the racing did get going, Cipollini's grip transferred to the riders at the rear of the field. 'Mario would call *"gruppetto!"*, and seventy blokes would sit up and we'd ride in together,' White explains.

As Cipollini never rode the Tour with the aim of finishing in Paris, the job of driver often reverted to his teammate Eros Poli. So reliable was the strapping Italian at guiding a flock through the mountains that sporting directors would tell their riders, 'Follow Eros and you will finish the stage.' In 1994, Poli turned his uncanny ability for working out how quickly to ride and when to win the stage over Mont Ventoux and down into Carpentras. Away on his own, he calculated he needed an advantage of twenty-four minutes as he started up the Provençal peak to remain out in front to the finish. He arrived there with three minutes in hand.

More recently, Bernie Eisel, a stalwart of Mark Cavendish's lead-out train and one of the best road captains around, often takes the driver's role in the mountains. Blessed with a reputation as something of a human calculator, Eisel bases his sums on a well-practised survival technique of riding 'steady on the climbs, hard on the descents'. The Austrian reckons on the *gruppetto* losing approximately a minute every kilometre on the GC riders when climbing, then recouping a minute or even two on long descents and perhaps twice that in the wet.

According to Koen de Kort, who used to spend most mountain stages in the *gruppetto* when he was working for and looking after German sprinter Marcel Kittel, the days when someone like Cipollini would shout '*gruppetto*' and attract a large band of eager adherents have gone. 'The guys who end up in the *gruppetto* are usually dropped at more or less the same time from the peloton,' says the Dutch rider. 'You get shelled out [of the main group] and as you're climbing you'll see a group forming ahead of you, so you'll sprint for two hundred metres to join them. Then more guys will come from behind and others will get dropped from the main group and they'll slowly drop back until the *gruppetto* rides up to them. Often when you get dropped, the director will come by and tell you that there's a group a couple of hundred metres behind, so you sit up and wait for them.'

Former pro and now French TV commentator Jacky Durand used to employ a clever ruse to help him in this situation, grimacing to make it look as if he was giving his all while surreptitiously asking spectators at the roadside for a push. 'Some fans refuse to push you because there's a risk of you getting a fine. I'd tell them not to worry about that and to get on with it. I wasn't going to come back and give them the bill. That's also a good reason why it's important to speak several languages,' Durand confessed.

Essentially, though, the *gruppetto* approaches the rest of the stage in the same way it always has. 'You ride tempo on the climbs, do the descents fast and ride all together on the flats, which is a good place to make up time when you've got a big group of guys all sharing the work and pulling,' de Kort confirms.

Mountain valleys favour the *gruppetto* by force of numbers. With perhaps sixty riders or more all sharing the workload, rotating at the front in between climbs, the group's speed can approach that set by the bunch heading into a sprint finish while, up ahead, the lead group of perhaps half that size tends to get pulled along perhaps 10kph slower by a handful of riders as the rest sit in to save themselves for the next climb.

The mass of the *gruppetto* can also make a difference on descents. Thanks to this, the laughing group can achieve incredible speeds, well in excess of 100kph. At the 2017 Tour of Switzerland, Frenchman Kévin Réza admitted to being frightened when his bike computer clocked him at 135.44kph coming off the Simplon Pass within a *gruppetto* in which many riders reported that they had reached 125kph and more.

'Most of the guys in the *gruppetto* are a bit crazy on the descents because they're the guys who are involved in the sprints,' says Matt White. 'They're big guys who are used to taking risks. We used to look after each other on the climbs and then they used to rail the descents. Everyone there could descend well and we'd all cooperate with each other. I can remember riding up a one-hour climb in the Giro and I put some music on, which was a way of helping myself get up the climb. Then I'd switch it off at the summit and nail it down the descent.'

The *gruppetto*'s 'band of brothers' image does come unstuck, and much more frequently now according to some experienced current and ex-pros. Often it's thanks to sprinters spotting the chance to eliminate a rival who is struggling. French galloper Jimmy Casper long held a grudge against Robbie McEwen for trying to shake him out of the Tour reckoning one year in precisely this fashion, while Mark Cavendish was on the end of the same treatment from rival Alessandro Petacchi during a 200-kilometre stage through the heart of the Pyrenees in the 2010 Tour.

Cavendish described how the Italian had approached him before the stage to suggest they cooperate in organising the *gruppetto* but had, on seeing the Briton struggling on the Peyresourde, asked his Lampre teammates to up the pace on the front of the *gruppetto* in an attempt to isolate Cavendish completely. The Manxman added that his day of suffering was further complicated by the *gruppetto*'s size being swelled by riders who rarely had to resort to riding in it. 'There's an art to pacing yourself and surviving a time cut – and these guys have never learned it. They panic, climb too fast. Ivan Basso did precisely that on the Tourmalet. Out the back we went again,' said Cavendish, who eventually made it to Pau safely in the group with the help of teammates Eisel and Bert Grabsch.

Other factors also impinge on the laughing group's sense of unity. 'Nowadays it's very different,' Matt White suggests. 'The longer the Giro and the Vuelta go, the more easily the *gruppetto* forms each day, but at the Tour guys fight it and fight it until they can't fight it any longer and they're simply forced to go into it. I think that's partly down to the fact the bunch is a lot younger nowadays and there's no one guy who controls it in that way. Riders have a lot less respect for each other, and they'll fight against falling back into the *gruppetto*. You'll see groups forming and they'll fight and fight and then eventually they'll drop back into the *gruppetto* anyway, but it's taken half an hour to form and it's taken a lot of energy out of some of those guys before it has.'

Marco Pinotti, too, senses that change. 'Some riders make mistakes when they're in the *gruppetto*. They decide that they want to set their own pace on the climbs because, perhaps, they want to get to the bus before everyone else. A rider might think if I can get there ten minutes before everyone then I can have a shower, be at the hotel twenty minutes before them, and then be massaged before them,' he says. 'Things like this often go through a rider's mind. They're important, especially on a three-week Grand Tour. If you arrive before the *gruppetto*, you might get away earlier in the car. If you're one of the last, you'll be leaving on the bus. Those five minutes you've finished ahead of the *gruppetto* might earn you thirty or forty minutes extra at the hotel.'

The Italian stresses, though, that riders need to understand that they will expend considerably less energy if they join the sizeable pack that usually gathers in the *gruppetto* than if they stay ahead of it in a group of ten or even twenty riders. 'You're simply going to do less work and that will benefit you and the team over the days ahead,' Pinotti explains. 'It's also good for the sports director to have all of the riders together. You can have one car behind it to provide assistance. If you have riders in lots of different groups, it's much more difficult to provide them with food or mechanical backup. We always tell the riders that if there's a group behind them they should wait for it. Or if there's a group thirty seconds ahead you get them to ride hard for a short time to catch up.'

Fundamentally, though, the *gruppetto* remains the sanctuary it has long been. In the end, survival is all that matters. 'The guys aren't stupid,' says Matt White. 'They just ride as hard as they have to in order to make it. They won't go one bit harder.'

CHAPTER 11

HOW TO WIN IN THE MOUNTAINS

Part of being a climber is that you can't have a bad day and just draft in. If you are bad, you are gone. There's no hiding.

– Andy Hampsten

Sky are the new Saeco and climbing is the new sprinting. As bunch sprints become ever harder to control, the nearest the sport now gets to a perfectly conceived lead-out is in the mountains, which says everything about the extent to which tactics have changed in this most challenging of racing terrains. With eight teammates lined out in front of him, Chris Froome has become the new Mario Cipollini, kept out of the wind until the moment he decides to accelerate, his rivals desperate to be on his wheel, hoping to be primed for the instant he attacks, their resources depleted by the battle to remain in Sky's slipstream.

This, cycling's decision-makers would have you believe, is the contemporary reality of racing in the mountains. Their response to it? To cut one rider from every team from the start of the 2018 season in order to reduce control, to free up strategy and liberate the peloton's born attackers, to return the sport to a more thrilling era of long-range attacks by solitary raiders and fluctuating fortunes in the high mountains, to encourage the kind of tactical anarchy that fostered the exploits of Fausto Coppi, Federico Bahamontes, Eddy Merckx and Marco Pantani, who were never hampered by such constraints.

However, if the concept of 'marginal gains' tells us one thing, it is that Sky have essentially done no more than adapt or improve established practice to gain a competitive advantage on their rivals. Nowhere is this more evident than in their strategic approach to racing in the mountains.

As with most advances that have taken place in racing during the post-war period, credit for instigating it goes to Coppi. As the peloton took on a more international and organised appearance in the early 1950s, the Italian realised that by maintaining a high tempo on climbs, he could keep pure climbers in check, neutering their sudden bursts of acceleration. Furthermore, by getting his teammates to infiltrate breakaways and attack off the front of the bunch, provoking a response from his rivals, he could sap their reserves to the extent that the mountains became a domain where he could dictate rather than defend.

What Coppi began, Jacques Anquetil continued. When climbers such as Federico Bahamontes and Raymond Poulidor jumped away from the French five-time Tour winner, he would reel them in in the same gradual manner that would be adopted later by Hinault, Miguel Indurain and Sky *domestiques* in the service of Bradley Wiggins and Chris Froome.

Merckx had been initially dismissed as a Classics specialist whose strengths in that area would not translate to Grand Tour racing because he was widely regarded as not having the ability to contain the best climbers in the high mountains. However, he also embraced Coppi's tactic to conquer his rivals in this terrain. He refined it, too, implementing his bullish and totally uncompromising strategy of *la course en tête*. Based on the premise that attack is the best form of defence, his team would begin their assault on the mountain goats on the plains, driving the peloton along in the biggest gears, undermining the potential of the specialist climbers before the mountains were even on the horizon. He not only encouraged his teammates to set a fast rhythm on these stages, but depended on the more talented among them to use the same tactic when the big climbs did appear. 'I believe in hard racing for one reason. If I do the work I am controlling the rhythm of the race and that is particularly valuable in the mountains. I wear down the others and am no more tired than they are at the finish. I avoid surprises and crashes,' he said, his explanation chiming with those trotted out now by stage race leaders.

The manner in which Merckx's team set about doing this looks very familiar to modern fans as well. Faema and Molteni devoted a significant part of their budgets to surrounding the Belgian with a core of extremely strong riders who could sustain a high pace on the flat and in the mountains, with Martin Van Den Bossche, Joseph Deschoenmaecker and Jos Bruyère among the best renowned of them. In order to counter the threat posed by Italian and, especially during that period,

Spanish climbers, such as José Manuel Fuente and Francisco Galdos, Bruyère explained that, 'We would always ride at the same steady tempo to keep them within reach then bring them back. Over the last two cols of the stage Merckx would attack and for us the race would be over then. We just had to get to the finish within the time limit.'

Managing this after racing almost to the extent of their resources well before the finish inevitably took a toll. Johan De Muynck, among the best of Belgium's climbers in the 1970s, admitted he turned down the chance to join Molteni at Merckx's personal request in 1974 because, 'with Eddy, it was work, work, work. You had to commit to a crazy programme and always ride at the front. Riding at that pace, you were finished after three years.' Yet, Merckx's *domestiques* committed to it due to the financial rewards and the satisfaction gained from playing a part in Merckx's dominance.

Recalling his Giro debut in 1973, Francesco Moser revealed how devastating the simple tactic proved to be, describing how he 'saw Bruyère and Deschoenmaecker change up a gear and everybody was dropped. Remember, it was the time when Merckx was scared of the climbers and made the Molteni team attack the climbs at fifty kilometres an hour. After that, Merckx would finish off the job.'

When Hinault succeeded Merckx as the peloton's dominant stage racer, he grasped that tactical baton. Making his Tour debut with Renault in 1978, he didn't concern himself with responding instantly to attacks by Joop Zoetemelk and Michel Pollentier in the Pyrenees, but eased back up to them. The strategy might be regarded as an acknowledgement of inferiority, but depends on the rider employing it having complete faith in their overall superiority. Like Coppi, Anquetil,

Merckx before him, and Miguel Indurain, Lance Armstrong and Froome who have followed, Hinault believed he would prevail, that reacting more instinctively was not essential. It was instead all about riding within their physical capacity until the moment arrived when they saw an advantage in pushing themselves towards their limits.

'We came into it and were really gung-ho, but we soon realised that this is a long game, and certainly when we began to look at how Bradley might win a Grand Tour, at how he could gain time in time trials and minimise his losses in the mountains, that dictated our thinking and led to us developing a style or tactical approach based around analysis of how do we win. We started with much the same philosophy when Chris became the leader, but it's changed over time because he's got an aggressive, attacking nature, and the team adapted to that.'

I'm sitting with Sky boss Dave Brailsford in the British team's mobile kitchen/dining room that's parked outside their hotel in the centre of Logroño on the 2017 Vuelta's second rest day. As is often the case when talking to Brailsford, our conversation has taken a meandering path. My intention had been to get his insight into the thinking and preparation behind Sky's approach to racing in the mountains, which has been so fundamental to their success in the Grand Tours, especially the Tour, since Bradley Wiggins took that title in 2012. So far, we've passed through game sense, the factoring and managing of risk with individual riders, the debate about salary caps and spending on riders, and the management of emotions and expectations over the course of a three-week stage race. It's typical

Brailsford, detailing almost every millimetre of ground he has covered when analysing the question of tactics. Finally, though, he's there.

'There is an art to get a team organised to work like that in the mountains. In the past there have been instances where we haven't won because another team's leader has been better. You can have the strongest team, which undoubtedly counts for a lot, but unless you've got the strongest rider you're not going to win a Grand Tour, in my experience. Alberto Contador won the Giro without the strongest team, and there have been times when we've had really strong teams and we haven't won. The bottom line is the strength and ability of your number one rider.'

In other words, Sky have simply tweaked the tactics employed by Coppi, Merckx, Hinault and others, adding their own bit of polish to keep it smart, and perhaps a bit more than most because they've achieved this with two quite different riders, one very much a *rouleur* who fitted the Anquetil mould, the other far more adept in the mountains and more adaptable in every kind of terrain, the epitome of what a modern Grand Tour champion needs to be.

Between 2010 and 2012, when Wiggins was their stage race leader, Sky developed a strategy designed to ignore accelerations made by pure climbers as soon as the road started to rise. 'I had to treat every col as if it were a time trial, thinking of getting from A to B as fast as possible without blowing up. It was not the most attractive way to ride a race, it was not riding with panache, but that was the reality of it,' Wiggins explained. 'We'd all like to be able to attack at the foot of a climb and ride Alberto Contador off our wheel but actually it's about being sensible, riding intelligently.'

As Brailsford suggests, the principal issue Wiggins had to confront was psychological as much as physical. In much the same way as Anquetil, Hinault and Indurain, he had to allow some of his rivals to ride away from him, but remain confident and calm enough to believe that he would get back on terms with them or at least limit his losses so that he could overturn them when the racing switched to his preferred terrain in time trials. Once he was comfortable with this, his confidence and proficiency in the tactic grew to the point where he would get his Sky teammates to ride on the front of the bunch with twin objectives in mind: firstly, to keep him away from the trouble that can result from sitting further back in the bunch; secondly, as a statement of intent, to let everyone know that Sky and Wiggins were riding to win.

Sky honed the tactic by repeated practice during the team's high-altitude training camps on the Teide volcano in Tenerife, where three riders would lead Wiggins onto a climb and each ride flat out for three kilometres before peeling aside and letting the next man through. At the 2012 Tour, it proved so effective that the only rider able to sustain a rhythm beyond that required by Wiggins was his teammate Froome, who had to be called back to order on two occasions having 'dropped' his leader. While this caused a furore, encouraging a rattled Wiggins to threaten to abandon the race unless his position at the top of Sky's hierarchy was assured, it did serve a very useful purpose in confirming to the British team that they had the perfect candidate to replace him when the Tour organisers ASO revealed a much more mountainous route for the following year.

The Sky-conceived adaptation of the pace-setting tactic has become more evident since Wiggins' Tour success. Not only

have the British team continued to employ it, but Astana did
so when backing Vincenzo Nibali in his successful Giro cam-
paign in 2013 and again at the 2014 Tour. It has also been
in evidence at the Ardennes Classics, where Movistar have
fielded teams strong enough to steamroller rivals to Alejandro
Valverde, a multiple winner of both Liège–Bastogne–Liège and
Flèche Wallonne. Somehow, though, the fact that other teams
and, particularly, some of the sport's greatest names, did use
their own versions of this tactic of control has been forgotten,
perhaps in the smoke screen created by marginal gains, and
Sky have been depicted as cycling Stormtroopers, emerging
from 'the Death Star', as their team bus was dubbed by rivals,
and laying waste to racing's beautifully democratic landscape.

Tejay van Garderen, who has sat on the tail of the BMC
train as their team leader, laughs dismissively at the suggestion that Sky have somehow turned racing, and particularly
racing in the mountains, into an unpalatable spectacle. 'What
Sky is doing is not a new thing, lining a team on the front,
setting the pace high, and Chris riding away at the end, or,
if someone else attacks, using the team to reel them in,' the
American climber affirms. 'This is what US Postal did back in
Lance Armstrong's era. Miguel Indurain was a very calculating
rider who rode in much the same way. He wasn't explosive and
never won a mountain stage during any of his Tour victories,
but he was always up there. The tiny climbers would attack
at the bottom and he'd just slowly reel them in. Everyone is
saying, "This is the new tactic and it's killing the sport", and
I look back and I'm thinking, "Man, we've seen this already.
This is nothing new."'

According to van Garderen, best young rider at the 2012
Tour and fifth overall in that race and again two years later, the

tactic is based on a very simple premise. 'Chris Froome has a higher threshold, higher watts per kilo than everyone else, so he can just ride away from the rest of us. When it comes down to it, he's simply the best rider.'

The American also stresses that this tried-and-tested approach is exactly the same one that every other team in the peloton would make use of given the opportunity. 'Tactics are tactics. If you're on one of the big teams, you're going to have really strong climbers who can set the pace high enough to defend a jersey,' van Garderen says, before clarifying his point. 'If you have a jersey, you're in defensive mode. It's other people's job to attack, so everyone might criticise Froome for being a boring rider – which are not my words because I think he attacks even when he is in the yellow jersey and when he attacks he really goes. It's Chris Froome's job to eliminate attacks or discourage attacks, because those attacks are on him. So if he can set the pace high enough and discourage attacks, then that's tactics.'

The employment of this tactic is, van Garderen confesses, brutal when you're on the receiving end of it but, at the same time, beautifully efficient. 'Sky line it out at the front of the bunch to make sure the pace stays at more than six watts per kilo,' he says, highlighting the magical power-to-weight figure that separates the very best climbers like Froome from the rest. 'At that point, nobody can attack. Sky are putting everyone on the limit. They also have multiple riders who can do that, and between them they can ensure that the pace remains high for a long, long time. They want to avoid that situation where someone attacks, we all chase and catch them, then it all slows down and gives people a chance to catch their breath and recover. What Sky is doing is trying to remove everyone's recovery time. So even on the sections where a climb might get a little more gradual and you're thinking that you may get a little bit of rest, they make sure they up the pace there.'

As the American makes clear, Froome's edge derives from his well-tried ability to cope with this tactic. 'You can say that having that strong team provides Chris Froome with an advantage, but the advantage he has is that he can deal with this tactic better than other people and that's why his team use it. Ultimately, Chris has got to pedal his bike in the same way that we've got to pedal our bikes. He has to follow his team the same way we have to follow his team. He just has the ability to do it better and the ability to control the pace. His team's that strong that if he's having a bad day he can tell them to dial it back a little bit, like we saw on the Peyresourde in the 2017 Tour. On the other hand, if he's feeling really good, he can get them to ratchet the pace up a notch.'

Van Garderen reveals that there are pros and cons for the riders tracking the Sky train. 'On the upside, having something like Sky's train there gives you a focal point to follow. I think that helps psychologically. On the other hand, fighting in the bunch behind them takes a toll. When Froome has his team on the front, everyone wants to be on his wheel and they're all fighting to be there, and all the while he's not fighting with anyone. It's all happening behind him. You can waste a lot of energy if you want to move up two wheels or if the rider in front of you gets dropped and you have to close that gap down. You can really pay the price for those kinds of efforts.'

In a very similar way to sprinters with their focus on the final few hundred metres of a race, climbers are conducting an exercise that is fundamentally concerned with conserving as much energy as possible until the moment when they can show how fast they can race uphill. Initially, this means sitting out of the wind on a teammate's wheel in the peloton, while ensuring that they are in the right position to be able to follow the other climbers when the surge comes that is the prelude to a crucial moment in a race, in this case the approach to a climb. Sitting too far back in the bunch at this point necessitates an acceleration to correct that error of positioning that will eat into vital resources and which could have made the difference further up the climb. Nowhere is this felt more keenly than at WorldTour level, where the margins between the riders' abilities are so narrow and each race features every one of the sport's strongest teams and is, therefore, an important objective for a significant percentage of the peloton.

When the climbing starts, drafting and holding the right position are usually just as important. 'If the gradient is around six to seven per cent, you can still get a bit of a draft,' Tejay van Garderen explains. 'Although I don't know exactly what the precise figures are, if you're going over say eighteen kilometres per hour, then you're going to be getting a bit of a draft, and sometimes on climbs we're doing twenty or twenty-two kilometres per hour, so there's definitely a benefit to be had from sitting in. If there's a headwind then you certainly get a draft. That's when you can see big differences. If you look at the Mount Etna stage at the 2017 Giro, there was a ripping headwind and nobody could attack. It was just too easy on the wheel. If anyone got out front, they would just blow up and it was really easy to tuck in there.'

British climber Simon Yates, winner of the best young rider title at the 2017 Tour, confirms the benefit of sitting in. 'On the climbs it's the same as being on the flat because we're going so fast. There is a benefit of being in the wheels,' says the Lancastrian. 'That's why people attack, because they want to get away from the rider who's sitting in behind them. They want to expose them to the wind, to prevent them sheltering and taking advantage of that further up the climb.'

Attacks are of two basic types. Those riders who prefer to ride at a set tempo rather than changing their rhythm, such as Merckx and Hinault, tend to up the pace from the front of the line, gradually increasing their power output to apply pressure on the riders tracking them. Like winding up a sprint from a long way out, which both of those supreme riders used to do in order to foil the specialists in that domain, it is the tactic of the super strong. Coppi, too, employed it, and more often and successfully than anyone. Among the most renowned are his victory in the 1946 edition of Milan–Sanremo, where his persistent pressing took him clear of Frenchman Lucien Teisseire on the Turchino pass and ultimately to a fourteen-minute winning margin, and his gradual throttling of Jean Robic during the Tour's inaugural ascent of Alpe d'Huez, where he first reeled the Frenchman in then increased the tempo, eventually realising Robic had yielded because Coppi could no longer hear him panting for breath on his wheel.

Much more common, though, is an acceleration from the heart of the group. There are some variations to this type of attack. Pure climbers such as Lucien Van Impe and, more recently, Alberto Contador deliver a series of explosive spurts of speed, these accelerations either carrying them clear instantly or after several repeats. The Spaniard would often launch them off the back of a lead-out from his teammates going full blast at the bottom of a climb. Punchier climbers such as Alejandro Valverde tend to wait longer before unleashing a burst of acceleration that is sustained for a longer period but can't be repeated with equal potency. The 2012 Giro winner Ryder Hesjedal, meanwhile, developed a more individual approach, which his former teammate David Millar described as his 'self-counter-attacking technique'. According to Millar, 'This involves him attacking, waiting for everybody to get to him, then attacking again. Once they reach him again, he rides as hard as he can until they start getting dropped, before attacking them again. He's like a four-man team.'

Pedalling technique also varies among climbers. Although it might seem counter-intuitive, smaller riders like Van Impe and, before him, Charly Gaul, dubbed 'The Angel of the Mountains', employed a relatively big gear to sweep away from their rivals. Van Impe perfected his technique training on the short but steep bergs in his native Flanders, his father often instructing him to ride several times up the Muur de Grammont in Geraardsbergen using as big a gear as possible. More recently, however, a growing number of riders have imitated the 'egg-beater' technique adopted by Lance Armstrong, studies showing that turning a smaller gear more quickly results in slower accumulation of toxins in the muscles and higher power output. Dutchman Robert Gesink, who was advised as a junior by his coach to use this technique, describes it as difficult to master because of a tendency for the upper body to move much more, lowering its efficiency, but as being ultimately worth the effort. Chris Froome has been its most high-profile adoptee, his legs whirring furiously when he attacks or responds to one.

As van Garderen indicated, when racing in the sport's biggest events, climbing and the tactics associated with it come down to psychological strength as much as anything. In an interview in *Procycling*, his compatriot Tom Danielson encapsulated this perfectly when he explained that, 'So much of climbing is about tuning out what's going on. When you are climbing, nothing feels right ... You never feel good. You have to have the ability to cancel all of the pain and chaos out.'

Another noted American climber, Joe Dombrowski, has suggested that climbing well is mostly about just turning your brain off, and not trying to rationalise is an advantage. 'A lot of great bike riders are kinda stupid. You know, having nothing going on up there, just primal instinct,' he said. I can't make the case for the switching off of one's brain being a tactic, but further investigation suggests that it is at the root of everything that goes on in any top-class race when the road starts to climb. Tiffany Cromwell, in her day one of the best climbers in the women's peloton, confirms that climbing essentially comes down to a rider's ability to suffer. 'OK, you need a good power-to-weight ratio too, but even if you've got that and you're not prepared to suffer, to go into the pain zone, then you're going to get dropped,' she insists.

'It's not like riding on the flat, where it's all about pure power. You've got to be prepared to go through that mental barrier that says that you're ready for anything that anyone throws at you. There are different kinds of climbing too. Being on a long climb and going steady at, say, four hundred watts is very different to a situation where you need to go above your threshold ten times on a climb and not blow up. If you overthink that kind of thing it can be detrimental and much harder than switching your brain off and being prepared to go deep a lot.'

Cromwell confesses that overthinking climbing has affected her form, and thinks back to a period when she used to simply deal with the suffering in a more brain-off way, recalling an attack she made in the mountains at the 2012 Giro Donne. 'On the climbs I felt so strong. I was really flying,' she says. 'It was during that period when Marianne Vos was dominating everything, and I remember thinking, "You know what? I think I could actually beat her today." I felt completely in control, that nothing could faze me, and not on the back foot, waiting for someone to attack and knowing that I would be dropped.' Unfortunately, Cromwell's chance of a famous victory went when she crashed when pushing hard on a descent.

When asked for his take on Dombrowski's 'ride without a brain' notion, van Garderen laughs. 'I think some of the best cyclists in the peloton aren't very intelligent, and I reckon that's often to their advantage because they're not getting overanalytical about looking down at their power meter and trying to overanalyse every sensation and feeling that they have,' he suggests. 'Sometimes if you turn your brain off, it almost becomes like meditating. Even if you're going easy up a climb – although there's no easy way to get to the top of Alpe d'Huez because you're going to suffer if you're going slow and you're going to suffer if you're going fast – you have to get into that mindset of suffering and sometimes that's easier to do if you don't even have a mindset.'

Alternatively, says van Garderen, you can try to pass that pain on to someone else, to make them suffer more than you are and get a lift from that. 'It doesn't feel good to have someone hurting you, you want to be the one doing the hurting. Sometimes, if you're following an uncomfortable tempo, if you simply attack, even though you were hurting before, you feel better once you're off the front because the roles just reversed. Now you're the one doing the hurting, and you're boosted by the rush of adrenalin or whatever hormone it is that makes you feel good. It boosts your morale.'

Grand Tour racing is as much about knowing the right times to hold fire as it is when to attack. Even four decades ago, when Bernard Hinault was setting about establishing himself as one of the stage racing greats, he confessed that, 'there are days when you have to know how to help your opponent, the better to beat him tomorrow.' This is very much the approach for Hinault's successors. Sky sporting director Nicolas Portal doesn't have to mull for too long before he starts to describe a moment that not only highlights Chris Froome's sangfroid, his ability to rein himself in if an opportunity is absolutely ripe for taking, but also his consummate talent as a climber. 'In the 2016 Tour there was a tough stage in the Jura mountains to Culoz. Towards the end of it they went over the Grand Colombier twice – two different ways up and the same way down, very tough,' recounts Portal.

'We had everything under control, then G [Geraint Thomas] had a puncture on the last climb so he couldn't support Froomey, which left Mikel Nieve and Wout Poels with Froomey and all the top GC guys. There was a break in front with [Jarlinson] Pantano, which was good, as they would decide the stage between them. The plan was for Froomey to stay with his teammates because there were still two summit finishes and a mountain time trial in the final week just ahead. There was no point in trying to drop someone on the climb, because then you'd have to ride hard on the tricky descent and then ride harder still on the flat run-in to the finish. You don't need to take risks when you've got two teammates with you. You just let them do their job.

'But if you look back to that point of the stage, he did make a very small attack, just as a test really. When he moved, the other GC guys moved with him, but when he stopped, they stopped. If the likes of [Romain] Bardet and [Nairo] Quintana had been in really good shape, they would have used the fact that Froomey had attacked to counter-attack. But they didn't, and why was that? Because they were full on,' Portal says.

'Two years earlier, he would probably have attacked, but the fact that he spoke to me about it showed that he probably knew himself it wasn't the right place to do it, but he was just making sure in case I said for him to go. He knew that I would probably say to hold and the fact he did, after making that little attack, showed not only that he agreed but also how smart he is. He's not a robot at all. He understands things, but he's still a bike rider who wants to race. In his mind, he would like to attack and drop everyone, perhaps a bit like Eddy Merckx used to, but you can't do that very often because it is so risky.

'That's the difference between our era and Merckx's era. Nowadays, all the bike riders are at a really high level, so you can do something like that perhaps once in a race, like he did when he attacked on the descent off the Peyresourde earlier in that Tour. But you can't do it every time an opportunity presents itself because it will cost you a lot of energy and at some point your rivals will turn that against you. You need to have the right balance between really enjoying the racing and going for it full gas, and knowing when to hold back a little bit. And I think Froomey now knows exactly when he needs to do it.'

Judging by the 2017 Tour's finish at Peyragudes, the ski station perched above the Col de Peyresourde looking down towards the slightly faded but still impressive Pyrenean spa town of Luchon, Froome's younger rivals are still acquiring that knowledge. As mentioned in the chapter on bluffing, Froome soon realised that he was running almost on empty and was relieved to lose just twenty seconds at the finish.

As it became clear that Froome had been hanging on to his team's coat-tails by his fingernails that day, his rivals defended themselves against accusations that they had been too passive and, as a result, had missed their one real chance of turning the tables on the Briton. New leader Aru was first in the firing line. 'Their tempo is so high. They are the only ones who can employ this tactic. We can't do anything else but stay in the wheels,' the Italian affirmed.

Reflecting on it some days later, Simon Yates, who finished at the back of the nine-man lead group, told me, 'That was a super-long stage, we were already well into the Tour, and you have to question how other guys apart from Froome can actually make an attack at a moment like that. I was at the front, and I couldn't move. I was just hanging on. There's a difference between having the chance to and being able to.'

Speaking on the penultimate day of the race, Bardet, one of the most tactically astute riders in the peloton, acknowledged, 'If I had realised I would certainly have tried, but Froome was very well protected. Sky were right on it. If we had seen Froome fall back, that would have given us something to think about. They rode to perfection, and he went to his limits, rode to the maximum that he could that day. They are very strong physically and have got real horsepower. And hats off to them from the tactical perspective! They don't make any errors, or at least very few. That makes the challenge of beating them even tougher.'

The UCI's decision to cut teams from nine riders to eight in the Grand Tours and from eight to seven in the Classics and most other WorldTour races, which was firmly backed by the organisers of these races, is an attempt to reduce the size of that task. When Merckx was in his pomp, he had between nine and ten teammates to support him, while contemporary stage racing leaders will have just seven.

The primary goal of the initiative is to loosen the grip any single team has on racing in the mountains, particularly at the Tour, the sport's blue riband event, with race director Christian Prudhomme saying, 'Certain team managers will be opposed but perhaps they can see it's for the general good of cycling.' Yet, many aren't convinced. Patrick Lefevere, the longest-standing of current team managers, takes a swipe at the Tour organisers ASO, insisting it's the latest instance of them thinking they are smarter than everyone else, harking back to their attempt to prohibit the use of race radios. 'But it's not the Tour de France that makes the Tour a spectacle, it's the riders. If they decide they don't want to ride, they won't. If they decide to let a group go at Kilometre Zero and then reel them in during the final kilometre, they will do it,' he says dismissively.

Nicolas Portal is more diplomatic, but is in the same camp as Lefevere. 'I think the fact that the race organisers are saying that it will make racing more exciting only underlines the fact that they don't understand racing and highlights the gap between them and the teams. A lot of the big thinkers in cycling have talked about doing this but have no evidence to back up what they're saying. They say it's not going to be as dangerous, that the racing will be more open. I don't think it will be more open,' he says, offering a persuasive argument against the move.

'In 2013, Sky finished the race with six-and-a-half bike riders. G crashed right near the start and rode the Tour with a fractured pelvis, and wasn't able to do much until the last week. We lost Kiryienka on the stage to Bagnères-de-Bigorre and we lost Edvald Boasson Hagen at the end of the second week, but we still won the race despite a really strong Quintana and Valverde. I should add that David López wasn't in his best shape at that Tour either. The year before we lost Kanstantin Siutsou on the third stage and won the race with eight. So you can win the Tour with eight guys or even fewer,' says Portal.

'Riding with eight will, I think, reduce the spectacle, because lots of riders are going to get more fatigued, so guys will be less inclined to go in the breaks, and teams are likely to race more conservatively with fewer cards to play. With one card less, you control more and attack less. You try to keep things tight. You need to be absolutely sure about playing your cards, about having your riders commit to attacks. The other aspect is that it's not economically good for the sport. What's going to happen to the rider who's dropped from those races? Will teams drop them completely and cut back their rosters?'

Tejay van Garderen confesses he's not really all that bothered by the prospect of having one fewer teammate in major events. 'My thoughts? Oh good. It's not going to be crowded on the bus,' the American quips laconically. 'Most of the time when you ride a Grand Tour you don't finish with all nine guys anyway. The cut might make a slight difference but I don't think it's gonna be earth-shattering.'

Every team, van Garderen points out, sends their very best line-up to the Tour and, he suggests, it's that rather than the size of the teams that can make for what is often perceived as a dull spectacle. He draws a comparison with American football. 'A lot of people say that college football is more exciting to watch because you get to see really long passes being thrown or running backs gaining a ton of yards, and you don't see that so much in the NFL because everybody's so good and so evenly matched. It's more strategic. I think that's the case in cycling,' he suggests, 'that you have all of these guys who are so evenly matched, you kind of do have to go to the bitter end to see real differences, especially if you have such strong teams, as it's hard to really explode the race.'

Interestingly, all those canvassed suggested there is a better way to get away from the situation where, when looking at the front of a Grand Tour peloton from an overhead camera shot, the picture reveals a long line of nine riders from Team A, followed by a long line of nine riders from Team B, and so on. 'We don't look like riders in a bunch, we look like a chain of identically coloured, perfectly ordered trucks,' as Spanish climber Joaquim Rodríguez memorably described the set-up in making the point that he'd like to see mountain stages return to a more anarchic state, where he would be chased down sixty kilometres from the finish not by one of Chris Froome's *domestiques*, but by Froome himself.

Rather than tweaking team sizes, race organisers should, according to Portal, van Garderen and many others, be looking at ways they can spice up race routes, to make them more likely to provoke all-out attacking. 'If they want to have more one-on-one duels, stages that are more hectic, they simply need to shorten the stages,' affirms Portal. 'If you've got stages of two hundred and twenty, two hundred and thirty, two hundred and forty kilometres, the guys are going to pace themselves. They know that they need to ride steady for two hundred kilometres and then there will be thirty kilometres when they'll have to play the game. If they go crazy at the beginning, they know they're going to kill themselves and they will be finished when they get to the last sixty kilometres. That's how it works.

'But with stages of a hundred kilometres, all of the sports directors at the Tour are going to be worried, because it's so hard to control a stage like that. I'd prefer to see more stages like that than for them to cut teams to eight riders. I simply think that's wrong. I think they need to find a nice balance between stages of around a hundred kilometres of length and the rest that are a bit longer.'

The Frenchman adds that there's no reason either why these short stages have to be confined to the mountains. Cut some of the flat stages to that length as well, he suggests. 'You're talking about a stage that's three hours long if it's a tough one through the mountains or perhaps two-and-a-half if it's on the flat, and on stages of that length all bike riders can maintain their highest level. There's not so much difference between the top guys like Froomey and everyone else. They're all really good over that kind of distance. Those stages will be completely flat out. I know the sprinters' teams would want to control things, but I don't think they would be able to. We certainly wouldn't be able to use the strength of our full team. We would just have to rely on three or four guys to implement a strategy.'

Italian DS Max Sciandri agrees, although he admits it pains him to say it. 'I was a guy who loved the two-hundred-and-fifty-kilometre races, the long stages and the Classics. If it was one hundred and eighty, two hundred or two hundred and ten, it was pretty open, but once you got past two hundred and twenty and up to two hundred and fifty or two hundred and sixty, there was just ten guys who could race,' he says. 'But now we need one-hundred-and-twenty-kilometre stages that offer no respite. Then you'll see real racing, the riders attacking on climbs, on descents, on a corner, anywhere. They can be more creative because they're not as afraid of the distance. They say, "I can do one hundred and ten kilometres full gas, I'm prepared to do that." That's the way to encourage more aggressive tactics, to see that kind of mythical day that we all relish.'

CHAPTER 12

IS TECHNOLOGY KILLING TACTICS?

Directeurs sportifs don't attempt to get the riders thinking any more, and that's a crime against the spirit of cycling, against man's spontaneity. More perverse still, earpieces have definitely become a sure-fire alibi for the riders.

— *Cyrille Guimard*, Dans les Secrets
du Tour de France

Once it was derailleurs, tri-bars and helmets, now it's disc brakes, radios and power meters. As in many sports, the advent of new technology has always divided opinion in cycling, but its popularisation is inevitable. While technophiles are adamant that these advances benefit bike racing, making it safer and more accessible to spectators, purists like Cyrille Guimard bemoan 'a PlayStation game', a sport where the riders are moved around like chess pieces by *directeurs sportifs* giving them orders via earpieces and are in thrall to their computers' numbers, dosing their effort and never daring to risk. The head and the legs? Not any more, they insist. But are they correct?

In Guimard's defence, it should be said that as a *directeur sportif* he was usually quick to innovate, encouraging periodisation in training and introducing aero frames into the peloton. He also points out that these advances didn't impact on the requirement on riders to think and improve as racers by doing so. But he claims radios and power meters are preventing this, and is far from alone in saying so.

These arguments are especially persuasive on days when a race has been dominated by one team setting a blistering pace on the front of the bunch and preventing all attacks on their leader, or the sprinters' teams have kept the breakaway tightly in check and gobbled it up like an hors d'oeuvre before getting their teeth into the main course at the finish. But is this steamrollering of spontaneity and unpredictability the reality of cycling in the second decade of the twenty-first century or is it more nuanced?

What can be said for sure is that road racing is different. Technology has changed it, perhaps more radically than at any point since the derailleur became widely used in the 1930s. The first step towards that was taken in 1991 when the Motorola team developed what was called the Peloton Communications System. Despite its heft, the two-way radio was initially built into the helmet of Motorola's Australian team leader Phil Anderson, until he broke it in a crash at the Tour of Switzerland and it was moved to a position under his saddle. Once fitted there, a wire wound from it along his top tube to a microphone secured at the top of the stem, the unit protected from the elements thanks to a plastic bag wrapping.

The Australian had to lean down and press a button to operate it, as if giving an announcement over a supermarket tannoy.

Gradually, the use of the technology spread, Germany's Telekom team, for instance, using mobile phones to give and receive information and instructions. The devices have become smaller and less intrusive. Contemporary receivers are the size of a credit card, the thickness of two squashed together and usually slot into a custom-made pocket on the inside of a team jersey just below the nape of the neck.

The impact they have had on racing has been as substantial as their change in aspect, according to Marc Sergeant, whose racing career was reaching its end as radio use increased. 'Before radios came in, riders had to think more about what they were going to do. Occasionally, the team car would come up and the director would tell you to do this or that, that you had to react now,' explains Sergeant, who went on to become a sporting director and manager at the Belgian Lotto team.

'But you needed clever riders on your team, guys who took decisions because sometimes you couldn't wait until the car came up. You needed guys who would look at the break's advantage and say, "We're three minutes back and we need to close that gap down." In those days, the riders had to think and respond straight away, but nowadays they often wait a little bit to hear what is said on the radio. They're not all like that, but in certain races, and especially the Tour de France, there is a tendency for riders to wait for instructions before they react.'

This pause before acting is one of the bugbears of those in the anti-radio camp, which includes three-time Tour de France winner Greg LeMond, who believes that one of the essential qualities of racing is being eroded. 'Cycling's a tactical sport, but it should be a tactical battle on the bike, not between two people watching on TV in their team cars,' LeMond has said. 'You want the people on bikes making the decisions – that's what makes cycling exciting. You don't want teams strangling a race. You want bluffing, strategy, and no one really knowing where they stand. The value of tactics has largely been lost.'

Taking much the same stance, former pro Laurent Jalabert, who is now one of the stalwarts of French television's cycling coverage, has complained, 'there's no point [for riders] even to look at the road book. You just need a bit of strength in your legs and a radio in your ear. You can't really tell who's a good rider any more, who can read a race, and who's just physically strong and knows how to listen.'

Max Sciandri, a member of that Motorola team in the mid-1990s, now a sporting director but 'never a radio guy' as a rider, agrees with this perspective. 'I came from that generation who had a feeling when the leaders would move. You'd have looked at the road book beforehand and would usually be ready for that moment and could consequently react. I would sit back behind the bunch a bit like Steve Cummings does now, and I'd sit and sit and sit, and then I'd feel the squeeze coming and move to the front,' says Sciandri.

Although he uses them at almost every race he works at, Sciandri admits that he would like to see riders regain that kind of insight and feeling that he had, to be removed from the control that sporting directors have on them, partly because, like all other directors, he often has no clear idea what is going on in the peloton up ahead and, this being the case, can't take a quick decision on tactics. 'I don't like to move them around in that robotic sense,' he says. 'I don't like radios. I'd be happy if they decided to get rid of them, and then we'd see how everyone would interpret the race.'

His is not a commonly shared view among his peers and within the peloton, however. Critics all point to the issue of safety, emphasising how quickly and efficiently details about potentially dangerous points and situations on the road ahead can be relayed to riders via radios. Removing them, they insist, could quickly lead to disaster. Patrick Lefevere highlights it in typically colourful fashion. 'Do you know any company that has a hundred and seventy-five employees and where the boss will wait five hours before going down to say that they're making mistakes, and then telling them what they should be doing? Of course not. The boss would go down straight away and put those mistakes right. A *directeur sportif* can do precisely that using a radio. Before radios, I could do exactly that, but it meant driving my car in the bunch ...'

When the UCI and the Tour de France did agree a trial in 2009, running a stage between Limoges and Issoudun with no radios allowed, fourteen of the twenty teams banded together to reject the initiative, citing rider safety as their central concern. When the stage got under way, more teams joined them and the result was a day when the bunch soft-pedalled from the start to very nearly the finish, resulting in a spectacle that was precisely the opposite of the harum-scarum action the administrators were hoping for. A plan to run a second stage without radios later in that race was dropped.

The dilemma that the UCI, the major race organisers and many expert observers such as LeMond and Sciandri face is that there is very little data relating to the impact radios have had on racing. Most of the evidence is anecdotal and often contradictory, even when it is put forward by experts. Indeed, the only research done in recent years, a 2007 study by Professor Gaël Gueguen at the Toulouse Business School entitled *Information Systems and Performance: The Case of "Tour de France" Racing Cyclists*, which compared Tour stages between 1991 and 1996 that were pre-radio, and 2000–2005 that were post-radio, revealed no significant difference between the number of stages that ended in sprints and breakaways during those two periods. The paper also suggested that breaks were more likely to finish with a bigger gap in the radio era, no doubt because a better-informed peloton knew when it was chasing a lost cause and would, as a result, sit up and roll in.

At the same time, a lot of the anecdotal evidence suggests that radios have been a boon to breakaways and the riders in them. In an open letter written in March 2011 to register his unhappiness with proposals to suppress the use of radios, Jens Voigt declared that suggestions that breakaways had a better chance of survival in pre-radio days were 'nonsense'. The German, at that time the undoubted king of the *baroudeurs*, declared: 'I am in the lucky position to talk on both sides, I was often in breakaways and I liked to have the radio, get some support from my team car, some motivating words and get exact info on what team is chasing me with how many riders, so I can plan my effort after the action in the peloton. If I won a race in a breakaway it was because I was strong, in good shape, suffered like crazy and worked hard – does anybody think the radio made me go faster?'

Marco Pinotti takes the same stance. 'Radios do help the breakaway,' the Italian insists. 'On those occasions I was in the break I'd be saying, "Easy, easy, easy!" To an extent, the break is in charge. If it slows down, the peloton will slow down. If the break goes harder, the peloton will respond.'

Pinotti adds that in races where the use of radios has not been allowed, the peloton's control of the breakaway has been much tighter than usual. Recalling a race in Ireland, he says, 'The break went but it got no more than two minutes, because the bunch didn't know what the situation was on the road as there was a delay in the communication of that information. That delay could have worked to the advantage of the break-away, but the result was that the peloton decided not to take any risks and stayed around two minutes behind the break.'

If there is a possibility for agreement, a halfway house that would ensure security would not be compromised while, at the same time, encouraging greater emphasis on tactical skills, it looks most likely to come as a result of limits being placed on who has access to race radio and the type of information that can be relayed to riders. Thomas Voeckler, a breakaway specialist who relished and thrived in situations where tacti-cal acuity came into play, is among those who have suggested the introduction of such a system. 'For me, the best solution would be a one-way radio from Radio Tour to the riders in order to tell them: "Be careful, there's a car here; there's a dan-gerous road there." I think races would be more interesting if that were the case.'

Tour director Christian Prudhomme has also mooted the introduction of a solution like this, but it does throw up the possibility of an immense change to racing because of the restriction it would almost inevitably place on the influence sporting directors would have on the action. Rather than relaying instructions instantly, they would have to depend on reverting to the traditional methods of either driving up along-side the bunch, which no one would be happy about from the perspective of safety, or having a rider drop back from the peloton into the convoy of cars to pick up orders in the same way they have to collect bottles, food or clothing.

In his open letter, Voigt suggests that such an initiative would even presage a return to 'the stone age' because riders would not be able to contact their team cars directly in case of mechanical incident. It could, claims Voigt, result in a situation where a team leader could puncture five kilometres from the finish and not be able to receive a wheel quick enough to ensure they didn't lose any time to their GC riders. Many would argue that this kind of unpredictable incident is exactly the kind of thing that we should be seeing in races because bikes aren't infallible tools. Voigt insists moments like this would disappoint team sponsors, who might review their financial backing.

As an outsider who is well aware of David Millar's dictum that 'bike racers don't like being told what to do in a bike race by somebody who has never done a bike race', it seems clear that the best way forward is for riders to agree where they stand on this issue, especially because it is their safety that is in question. Imposing a solution without them being involved is not going to work because there will almost certainly be a fatal flaw that will guarantee non-cooperation.

Over recent seasons, the debate about radios has often been extended to encompass the use of power meters within races. A more recent phenomenon, at least in terms of their entry into the pro peloton, power meters were initially used as a tool for optimising training. Over the course of the past decade, they have been employed with increasing frequency within racing, to the extent that most professionals now use some sort of measurement device that not only allows them and their coaches to analyse their power output and other informative data, but also gauge their effort during an event.

Critics, including high-profile racers such as Alberto Contador and Nairo Quintana, have condemned meters for imposing uniformity on performance and removing spontaneity from the sport, for effectively returning it to its early days when the fundamental tactic was to ride as hard as possible for as long as possible. Sky are often depicted as the team most guilty in this regard, their *domestiques* setting a pace that rivals simply have to follow, before, most often, Chris Froome clips away to finish them off.

'Sky haven't established the system, but they do now tempo the race,' says Max Sciandri. 'If you look at a Grand Tour now, it's about tempo climb one, tempo climb two, tempo and attack climb three. So, there's no real tactics. No human can ride at four hundred and fifty watts, so if they keep it at four hundred and thirty on the climbs their rivals can't even make an attack.'

Matt White, Orica-GreenEdge's chief sporting director, believes there's been a negative impact on racing because of this. 'If you've got a team like Sky riding a certain tempo on a climb with five riders on the front, it is actually pointless attacking because you'll be going nowhere. In one-day races, there is much more unpredictability, but in major stage races riders are scared to attack because they're scared to lose. It has made the racing a bit more conservative, and that's certainly the case at the Tour.'

Sky aren't the only ones, of course, to have made good use of what meters tell their riders and coaches. Breakaways can dose their effort so they preserve as much power as possible for the back end of a stage when the peloton is rolling at full speed to reel them in, while the teams leading that chase will be doing much the same thing, as Pinotti confirms. 'When I was racing, I'd organise a chase at three hundred watts. In the break they could do three hundred and fifty, but they could only do that for one hour, so we just needed to go at a steady three hundred, and then when you need to you can speed the chase up and catch them.'

Pinotti admits that when he first used a power meter in a time trial he felt like he was cheating because it enabled him to pace himself so well. But he adds that after three seasons he didn't need to refer to his meter in the same way. 'I'd look at it for confirmation, but I could have coped without it because I'd used it so much when training. After you've used a power meter for hour after hour in training, you know when you're pushing three hundred and fifty or four hundred without looking. You know from feel.'

Reflecting on the calls for use of meters to be prohibited when competing, he suggests that 'The riders who say they should be banned are the riders who don't know how to use them. They feel that they are at a disadvantage. They perhaps ride more on feel.' But he maintains that trying to reverse the impact that the devices have had on races would be futile because it cannot be reversed. 'It's a question of experience, and perhaps younger riders don't have that same feel when they come into the peloton. They might pull a little bit too hard and pay the price for that. But that experience comes quite quickly. If they do decide to ban them then we will adapt, but I think it would be a step backwards. To be honest, I don't think it would change much either. You couldn't ban their use in training, and once you practise with them in training you've got the insight you need to apply when racing.'

When asked about the possibility of a ban being introduced, Tejay van Garderen insists he doesn't care one way or another. 'If they decide to ban them, I'd kind of roll my eyes and be like, "Whatever!" It wouldn't be a big deal but it would be stupid.

'Contador should know better than anybody because he has raced with a power meter for as long as I've raced with him, and I turned pro in 2010. If he didn't want to race with one, he could have done so, but it's funny that he's waited until he's retired to say that they should get rid of them. In addition, the power meter didn't stop Contador from attacking,' notes van Garderen, who goes on to insist that their importance in races is overstated.

'I don't think the power meter is really what Chris Froome is looking at when he looks down in that way that he does. He's probably glancing at it, but I don't think that's what he's riding to because your threshold is not a set number where you say, "Put it here and let's go!" It changes every day and he's judging his own sensations and how he's feeling. I bet he's just looking at the power meter and thinking, "I wonder what it is today?" Being an analytical guy, you're going to glance at those numbers and think about them or interpret them, but they're not going to change how the race is raced.'

Van Garderen suggests that the mistake those looking on from outside a race make is believing that riders are simply riding according to their numbers. 'I do twenty-minute tests all the time in training and, depending on my fatigue levels, my threshold changes by the day. Your threshold is not just a simple number. During a stage race there's such an ebb and flow that some days I might be able to do four hundred and twenty watts for thirty minutes, while other days I might struggle to get over four hundred and sometimes it's not even that. It all depends on the fatigue in your legs, the amount of sleep you got, if it's hot or cold out, if you're under-fuelled, if you're over-fuelled – there are so many different variables.

'Sometimes you gauge your own sensations and look at your power meter and think, "I'm going to hold this for a certain amount of time", but it's not as scientific as many people assume. Sometimes you glance down at it in the same way people who are addicted to their iPhones are always glancing at Instagram. It also gives you a little bit of a focal point, but sometimes it completely screws you up. You can be feeling great, like you're on top of the world, and you're holding the pace just fine and then you look down and you're doing four hundred and forty watts and you're like, "Oh shit, I can't do this!" and really you should be trying to ignore it.'

The American re-emphasises his point that riding like Sky do in Grand Tours, setting a tempo that is intended to prevent rivals attacking and, at the same time, steadily draws energy reserves from every riders' legs, isn't a new tactic any way. Most of the sport's dominant riders have had their teams race in a similar way since the Coppi era. 'I don't think power meters really affect races in the way that people think that they do,' he concludes.

A conversation with Sky team manager Dave Brailsford the day after the British team had produced their latest display of pacemaking at Sierra Nevada to defend Froome's lead in the 2017 Vuelta supports Pinotti and van Garderen's judgement. The team's stand-out performer at the race's loftiest summit finish was Spaniard Mikel Nieve, who had steadily reeled in Vincenzo Nibali's attempt to gain some time. 'When Mikel Nieve rode for an awfully long time and gradually brought

Nibali back, his Garmin wasn't working, so he had no numbers, no data, he just did it on feel,' Brailsford reveals.

Calls for this technology to be shunned also run counter to the increasing and very popular trend towards on-screen data provision for fans. As part of a move to improve understanding of the sport, race organisers and other stakeholders such as the Velon group that comprises ten WorldTour teams have devoted considerable resources to providing stats on, for instance, heart rate, power output and speed, allied to the use of on-board cameras and GPS positioning, which will both become extremely useful tools for seeing exactly how tactics unfold – how, for instance, a team's lead-out moves their sprinter up to the front of the peloton. With applications such as Strava and Zwift also hugely popular and allowing fans to see where their favourites are riding and even compete against them remotely, cycling is reaching out to its base support like never before. Why roll that back?

Bike racing can still be as thrilling and unpredictable as it ever has been. Think of Philippe Gilbert winning the 2017 Tour of Flanders with an eighty-kilometre solo attack, Mat Hayman claiming the 2016 edition of Paris–Roubaix five weeks after breaking his arm, Tom Dumoulin triumphing in the hundredth running of the Giro d'Italia in a race that had almost everything, including the Dutchman having a Paula Radcliffe moment that required him to search out a roadside bush for some privacy. Yes, it can be dull – and almost every recent edition of Liège–Bastogne–Liège is testament to this – but no more so than it was a hundred or fifty years ago, and probably much less so than it was twenty years ago when widespread doping not only levelled the competitive playing field, but effectively flattened every hill and mountain as well.

Rather than tinkering with technology, road racing needs to adapt to it, marrying the benefits it brings in terms of safety and communication with the unpredictability and ingenuity that all sports expect from their great events and performers. To their credit, Prudhomme and his organising team at the Tour de France have been doing exactly this by making mountain stages shorter and therefore more difficult for any one team to control. This has produced the kind of frantic spectacle that challenges strategic planning and tactical responses, but also gets Cyrille Guimard smiling.

CHAPTER 13

GOING DOWNHILL FAST

Speed, it seems to me, provides the one genuinely modern pleasure.

– Aldous Huxley

As one of just half a dozen riders to have won all three Grand Tours, Vincenzo Nibali is very capable of going uphill fast, but can be absolutely astonishing heading downhill if he sees an opportunity for victory or to apply pressure on a rival. His victories in the 2015 and 2017 editions of the Giro di Lombardia owed much to his breath-taking descents off the Civiglio, the penultimate hill on the course, the narrow road dropping sharply through a series of extremely tight switchbacks in villages piled one on top of the next on its steep hillside.

The first of those successes offered a masterclass in how to open a gap on a descent. His initial attack comes in textbook fashion from the back of the lead group at a moment when his teammate Diego Rosa is on the front. Naturally, Rosa isn't going to respond, so the chase is picked up by Frenchman Thibaut Pinot, famously flaky going downhill.

As Pinot starts the pursuit, Nibali sprints into the slipstream of the TV camera bike and uses the shelter it provides to up his speed and slingshot past towards the first switchback, where the difference in the two men's skillsets is immediately apparent. Nibali sweeps around it and is quickly back up to speed, while Pinot takes it too wide, loses his momentum and his place at the front of the chasing line. It means another second gained by the Italian, maybe two.

With a knee angling out on the bends, Nibali resembles a Moto GP rider, moving his body weight from one side of his bike to the other, pushing it as far over as it will go, and he's doing this on rubber a mere two-and-a-half centimetres wide. The best measure of his speed is the rate at which he closes in on the motorbikes buzzing around the riders. Usually, a touch of the throttle fires them away from the riders in an instant. But Nibali's speed is so breakneck that they can't get away or even keep pace with him. He moves and reacts faster than they are able. It's terrifyingly exhilarating to watch. As he sweeps around the final bend and back onto the flat, his lead is twenty-five seconds with little more than ten kilometres remaining. The contest is over.

Two years later, Pinot was prepared for a repeat and made a pre-emptive strike climbing the Civiglio, going clear on his own, only to be joined by Nibali just before the summit. Approaching it, the Frenchman stuck out his right hand to grab a bottle from a team helper, and Nibali saw his chance, flashed by and, as they started down the descent, constantly applied pressure. To his credit, Pinot stuck with the Italian most of the way down, but the elastic between them stretched as Nibali kept pressing on the more technical lower sections, testing the Frenchman's nerve. Nibali came off the climb with an advantage of just five seconds, but once again it was enough.

In between, Nibali turned around his fortunes in the same intrepid manner at the Giro. Slated by the Italian press as he fell five minutes behind Steven Kruijswijk two days from the finish in Milan, Nibali went to the front of the *maglia rosa* group coming off the mighty Colle dell'Agnello pass, almost daring his rivals to see if they could stay with him. Soon after, Kruijswijk overcooked a sweeping left-hand bend and ploughed into the wall of snow at the roadside, the impact sending him and his bike cart-wheeling. By the stage's end, Nibali had almost recouped his losses. The next day, he completed the turnaround, his second Giro title essentially the result of his verve on descents.

'When we were on the Agnello, I saw something that maybe the others didn't pick up, that the *maglia rosa* was breathing quite heavily at the summit and at the same time I was feeling better, so I thought I would attack on the descent and put the pressure on,' Nibali explained. 'That's how it is in cycling, you've got to be able to attack on every kind of terrain. I realised at that moment that I could turn the whole race upside down.'

Descents, of course, have always been a part of bike racing. In the sport's early years, when bikes were either fitted with one brake that didn't provide much slowing power, or no brake at all, coming down was a haphazard experience. The most perilous sections were marked with lanterns or by flag-waving marshals. Some riders walked, while others put rocks in a bag on their back to improve stability. The most daring, though, didn't bother with caution, opting to tackle the rough, unsurfaced roads in speedway-like fashion, sticking a leg out to provide balance and a touch of control through corners, hoping that was enough.

In the post-war years, there have been plenty of instances where riders saved their hopes by being daring on descents or lost them due to nerves or pure bad luck. Certainly the most renowned occurred in the 1971 Tour when Luis Ocaña crashed out on the descent off the Col de Menté when leading the race. The Spaniard was following Eddy Merckx's recklessly frantic pace down the Pyrenean pass in a violent mountain storm that had washed debris onto the road, turning it into a rock-covered obstacle course.

The Menté is typical of the remote Couserans region of the range, not especially long, but with frequent changes of gradient as it cuts through dense woodland, with the road dropping away even more steeply at tight hairpin bends. Coming into one of them too fast, Merckx went down and the Spaniard followed him. While Merckx was quickly up on his feet and under way, Ocaña struggled for purchase. When he found it and got up, he was instantly floored by Joop Zoetemelk, his brakes rendered useless by the torrents, who hurtled into him. Too injured to continue, Ocaña lost a Tour that, with an advantage of more than seven minutes, he had all but won.

Four years later, once again defending the yellow jersey against sustained attack, on that occasion by Bernard Thévenet, Merckx repeated the same harrying tactic. Thévenet said the Belgian attacked on every descent of the Tour that year except one, and Merckx went particularly fast down the treacherous

Col d'Allos, which has a terrifying drop off one side, gaining more than a minute on the Frenchman, who was known for his weakness going downhill. For once, though, Merckx's pressing tactics rebounded on him when he ran out of gas on the subsequent climb to Pra Loup, losing the stage and the yellow jersey to Thévenet on what turned out to be the last time Merckx wore it in his career.

Like Merckx, Bernard Hinault was also ready to push to the limit on descents if he felt some advantage could be gained. He wrapped up the 1980 Giro title largely thanks to a well-planned attack over the Stelvio pass and a daredevil descent over the far side on the wheel of Renault teammate Jean-René Bernaudeau, who instructed his boss that he would shout as he led the way through a series of unlit tunnels and that Hinault should slow if the shouting stopped. Given that devotion to his leader, it was only right that Bernaudeau ended up winning the stage as Hinault took the race leader's *maglia rosa*.

Lucien Aimar was another French Tour winner with a reputation as a demon descender. Aimar claimed that he reached a speed of 140kph coming down Mont Ventoux in 1967. 'I'd been with Tom Simpson's group when he collapsed getting towards the top of the climb. I punctured soon after that, near the summit. I was two minutes thirty down on the front group going over the top, heading down towards Malaucène. So I went pretty fast, caught them, and was there at the end to contest the sprint for the stage win in Carpentras. I only found out how fast I'd been going after the stage when one of the motorbike gendarmes came up to me and told me he'd clocked me at one hundred and forty kilometres per hour,' Aimar later recalled.

Traditionally, the best descenders have been bigger riders, including most sprinters, who tend to end up riding in the *gruppetto* on mountain stages. Their rate of travel can partly be explained by the gravitational pull being greater on their larger mass, but there's a significant tactical aspect to it as well.

Former pro Sean Yates, who went on to become a DS and guided Bradley Wiggins to the Tour title in 2012 from the Sky team car, was one of those bigger riders who had a particular aptitude for descending. Realising he had a knack for it, he worked to improve it even more and often used it to his advantage in a canny way. 'Suppose there was a stage with three mountains and on the second climb the attacks start and guys start getting shredded. That was the point where I'd go as hard as I could down the other side and leave those guys behind and get back to the front group so that I'd be there to get bottles for teammates or whatever in the valley,' he explained to *Procycling*.

'Then I'd have time to just take it easy up the last climb of the day, whereas the dropped guys, somewhere behind me, are down in the valley killing themselves at fifty to sixty kilometres per hour to try to get inside the time limit. I learned it's easier to recover from the short, hard intensity that I was doing than the medium intensity that they were having to do over a longer period of time.'

Although descending has always been a skill that every top racer needs in their armoury, in recent seasons the ability to go downhill fast has become a more tested and, therefore, crucial asset. But what makes a good descender?

Tiffany Cromwell believes that more than anything it comes down to being confident. 'It's about enjoying speed and having no fear,' she says. 'Secondly, it's about getting the line right, recognising where the apex is on a corner and going through it correctly, braking before you get to the apex rather than on the corner itself, and shifting your weight at the right moment from one side to the other. This is most easily achieved when you're at the front and don't have to think about having people around you, as being in the middle of the peloton when you're going down a descent throws up some particular problems. There are a few more unknown elements when you're in that position, principally the fact that you can't control the people around you.

'Having a good bike set-up has a lot to do with it too,' Cromwell continues, 'trusting your tyres, trusting your equipment, because the moment you think there's an issue there – "Are they going to slip out from underneath me?" "Is my centre of gravity right?" – it will start to play on your mind and erode your confidence. You start to think, "Maybe I should hold back a little bit."

'It's such a mental thing, though. I went through a period when I crashed a few times on descents and it knocked my confidence completely. But I have got it back. Perhaps that comes from growing up in the hills back in Australia and training with the guys who are based around Monaco. I just love the speed. There's no better feeling than when you get a descent right and go flying down.'

The Australian admits that the only time she does hold back is when it's raining, but she adds that it's easy to overdo this, and that the most confident descenders will consequently pick up even more time in the rain. 'For me, descending is a real area of confidence. I know that I'm better than most of the peloton and I can use descents as a place to attack, especially if it's a technical descent, where you can perhaps gain more time on people than you can on a climb,' she explains.

In saying this, Cromwell lands squarely on the reason why descents have taken on growing importance in recent seasons. According to Slipstream team boss Jonathan Vaughters, 'The fitness and competitive level of all the top riders is a lot closer now than it's ever been, so it's difficult to drop anyone on the climbs. Now if you're Romain Bardet and you can't make the difference on the climb you say, "OK, well now I'm going to test their technical skills and see if they can hang with me around the corners."'

Tejay van Garderen sums it up more succinctly. 'The reason people are attacking on descents now is because they're thinking, "How do you beat Sky?" and one way is to attack on a descent. It's something that would have been totally frowned upon a few years ago, but it's another aspect to the new look of cycling. When people can see there's a potential gain, even if it's just a small advantage, they'll go after it.'

There are no hard and fast rules to what makes a good descender. According to Mikaël Cherel, the French rider who instigated the attack on the Côte de Domancy that led to his Ag2r leader Romain Bardet's stage victory at Saint Gervais in the 2016 Tour de France, 'You need vision, anticipation, to be agile because you need to be able to lean into corners, but not too much. More than anything, you need to go with the bike and not be too stiff.

'It's innate,' he adds. 'I've been able to do it since I was a kid. I take real pleasure from it. I'm never afraid on a descent. On rainy days, I don't like to ride, but I'm still happy to go down a pass. I've had real some pile-ups as well, but that's never removed my desire for risk-taking, for speed.'

Former sprinter Thor Hushovd offers much the same assessment, suggesting that sprinters tend to be good at going downhill fast because 'they have better bike control and are not so afraid of crashing'. Racers who have come from mountain biking also have a reputation for being solid performers, among them 2011 Tour winner Cadel Evans, three-time world champion Peter Sagan and Sky DS Portal, who had an off-road background before switching to the road.

While riders can work on their descending skillset when training, they can only take that so far on roads that aren't closed as they would be in a race. As Jonathan Vaughters points out, 'If you cut the apex like you should do, there could be a car coming the other way and that's a situation you certainly don't want to find yourself in. So improving is mostly a question of going as fast as you can in a closed road situation, getting used to the speed and having other riders around you.'

As descending has taken on greater significance in deciding the outcome of races, some teams have turned to experts from outside road racing to assist their riders. 'We always do some descending training in the winter, working on getting through corners as fast as possible. We work with Oscar Saiz, a former mountain bike downhiller, who comes in and teaches the guys,' says LottoNL-Jumbo team manager Richard Plugge. 'Working with him helps them pick up new things, but also reminds them of the fundamentals that are important to remember on descents.'

Saiz, who has worked with several big teams, has said of his speciality, 'It seems to me, as an outsider, that it's crazy that so much time and money is being invested in making riders better in time trials, shaving off just a few seconds, yet when riders talk about climbs they neglect fifty per cent of the mountain ... they're going down these mountains on super-light bikes, on super-thin tyres, with no protective gear and when they're already tired. You need to be prepared for that yet they do no work on it ... The first thing I talk about is how to make it safe: the consequences of a crash are too great. Then I look at how you can save energy by carrying your speed. Only lastly do I look at how to make someone faster.'

Other riders have opted for very different solutions, particularly if their confidence has been eroded. As a consequence of a crash as a fifteen-year-old that left him with both of his wrists broken, Thibaut Pinot has never been the most confident of riders on descents, often attacking just before reaching the summit of a pass simply to be able to tackle the descent at the front and on his own, as he did in that 2017 edition of Lombardy. At the Tour 2013, as pressure built on him as the home country's new favourite for the yellow jersey, the Frenchman was hit by what could perhaps be described as the cycling equivalent of the yips that can affect golfers when putting. On the first major mountain stage, which took the race over the Col de Pailhères in the Pyrenees, Pinot's confidence evaporated.

According to his brother and coach Julien, 'Thibaut's head was going in one direction and his bike in another.' Meanwhile, Bardet, his rival as France's big new hope, explained that, 'As soon as I can get past Pinot on a descent I do it. He's scared and when two or three riders are flashing past him on either side, it exacerbates his problem.' Pinot's FDJ team sent him to a motor racing school to help him regain his feel for speed, which has been rekindled, although the Frenchman is never likely to achieve Nibali's class.

Occasionally, overconfidence can prove an issue on descents. Italian team manager Gianni Savio, who has often mined talent in South America, recalls Venezuelan rider Leonardo Sierra winning a stage of the 1990 Giro for his team despite crashing twice on the same descent of the often scarily steep Mortirolo pass. 'When the Giro finished, we organised an emergency training binge in the mountains solely to work on his downhilling and realised what the problem was: it wasn't that Leonardo was a bad descender, he just didn't understand gravity. He didn't understand there was a speed limit beyond which it was pretty dangerous to ride on a mountain road. He was actually quite nifty on a bike, but he just took too many risks.'

Riders use more conventional tactics too to get an edge. For reasons Cromwell has already indicated, most pros prefer to be at the front rather than following, partly because there is usually a motorbike just ahead of them. It shouldn't be close enough for them to get any shelter from it, but watching the way the driver brakes and moves on the bike gives the rider closest behind it useful clues about when and how sharply to brake, about which way to shift their weight and turn. Rotating on the front and thereby sharing the pacemaking can also help for those in a group, especially when trying to open or close a gap. Putting on a jacket approaching the summit of a climb rather than beyond the crest can also save valuable seconds.

Over the last few seasons, Tour director Christian Prudhomme and his route-finding team headed by ex-pro

Thierry Gouvenou have increased the emphasis on descents, often testing them out in the Critérium du Dauphiné before including them in the Tour's *parcours*. Among the most notorious have been the Col de la Sarenne, included in 2013 to permit a double ascent of Alpe d'Huez, the Col d'Allos (2015) and the Mont du Chat (2017).

'Nowadays, descending is the new climbing, more or less,' LottoNL-Jumbo's Plugge said during the 2017 Tour. 'They are putting a lot of pressure on the guys. The way they designed the route this year gave riders lots of opportunities to attack, and we've seen that it's not been so easy for Sky to control the race, even though they tried to. Christian Prudhomme said at the presentation that they were attempting to make it more difficult for one team to control, and I think they've succeeded.'

Yet, as Prudhomme has been quick to point out, descents are nothing new and, ultimately, it's down to the riders to make what they will of the race route. As van Garderen suggested, some riders are being more aggressive on descents because they regard it as a way to gain vital time, and it's a viewpoint veteran Dutch pro Bauke Mollema shares. 'There did used to be kind of an agreement that when you went over the top of a climb you'd try not to kill yourselves going down the other side. But that agreement has gone now.

'If you have the skills and you know the descent very well you can gain perhaps more time than on the climbs. But if you lose just a few seconds to a group of riders in front towards the top of climb, you could end up losing three or four minutes on the downhill that follows if they go full gas.'

Mollema's point was proved as the Tour raced over the huge Galibier pass, where second-placed Fabio Aru was trailing the other race favourites by just a few seconds. By the finish down in the valley below at Serre Chevalier, he had lost more ground and dropped from a podium place to fourth overall. More dramatic, though, was the stage into Chambéry over the series of testing ups and downs in the Jura range, the last of them Mont du Chat, overlooking the finish town. Cherel, who missed the Tour after crashing on a descent while training a few weeks before, picked this out as a place where his good friend Bardet would probably make an attack or at the very least test out his rivals.

The climb caused plenty of polemic, initially because Aru launched a stinging attack an instant after race leader Froome had raised his arm to signal that he had some kind of mechanical problem and needed assistance from his team car. Within moments, the Italian had been brought to heel by a number of rivals letting him know that he had broken one of the peloton's unwritten rules by attacking the yellow jersey when he was unable to respond. Many would argue that this tactic, while perhaps underhand, is perfectly valid. Riders do, after all, depend on the good functioning of their bikes to win any race. Aru later defended himself by insisting that his strategy that day was to attack at precisely the place he did, which was his focus, so he wasn't aware of Froome having any kind of problem.

When Froome was safely back in the group, Richie Porte, once the Sky leader's key lieutenant and now rated his most serious rival, jumped away, his move triggering a flurry of further attacks that trimmed the yellow jersey group down substantially. When the favourites went over the top of the Mont du Chat, thirty-odd seconds behind lone breakaway Warren Barguil, Froome had just half a dozen riders with him, former mountain biker Jacob Fuglsang initially setting the pace ahead of the race leader.

'Everyone was flat out at the summit. I needed to recover, so I stayed behind – which is always a risk – with the aim of going hard on the descent. That's an area that I've mastered,' Bardet later explained. Two other factors were also in the elfin Frenchman's favour. As a graduate of the Chambéry Cyclisme Formation team that is a feeder squad for the Ag2r professional team, he had spent a lot of time training and racing in the surrounding mountains, including Mont du Chat. He also knew that the road had been resurfaced since the peloton had raced down it in the Dauphiné a few weeks earlier. The surface was smoother, making higher speeds more likely, and, theoretically, playing to his talent a touch more. It also helped that he was in the best form of his career, as teammate Jan Bakelants explained: 'A rider who's in top form will always be a better descender because he's fresher when he reaches the top of a col and is then more lucid in his decision-making.'

Four kilometres down the descent, as the TV motorbike tracked the yellow jersey group, Fuglsang, Froome and Aru swept around a little kink in the road, switching right, then left. Just behind, though, Porte got the corner all wrong. Out of control having got some debris caught between brake and rim, the Australian hurtled through the inside of the little chicane, his bike sliding as it went into the dirt before hitting the edge of the tarmac and catapulting the rider into the bank on the other side of the road, taking down Dan Martin as he rebounded and clipping Rigoberto Urán's rear derailleur, leaving the Colombian, who somehow avoided a direct hit, with the use of just his single biggest gear for the rest of the stage. A moment later, Bardet, who had been hanging back, picked his way through the riders, bikes and debris and began to chase those ahead.

'I often anticipate crashes. I put myself a safe distance away because I felt that that was going to happen,' Bardet explained that evening. 'Richie let himself get carried by emotion ... I didn't take any risks. I did what I planned to do. I'm not saying that Richie's crash didn't affect me because I know that could happen [to anyone].'

To suggestions that he and other riders should have halted just as others had done for Froome just a quarter of an hour before, Bardet replied: 'When a sprinter crashes, the others don't stop sprinting. They continue to do what they always do. Chris turned around, he saw that Richie wasn't there any longer, and he went flat out. I had real difficulty getting across to him, no one waited for me, just as nobody waited for Dan. It was one of those moments when you're at the very limit of your capacity. The racing is kicking off and there's a loss of lucidity on everyone's part.'

Bardet was lucky to escape with just a minor delay, but he'd given himself that chance by following rather than making attacks on the way up Mont du Chat, then taking the chance to recuperate over the first few kilometres of the descent. His subsequent attack off the front of the yellow jersey group a couple of kilometres later highlighted that his strategy had always been to use his knowledge of the drop into Chambéry and his talent in that kind of situation, which his sporting director Julien Jurdie describes as 'extraordinary', to launch an attack, to push his rivals just as Nibali had Kruijswijk on the Agnello. He was living up to the message he could see every time he looked down at his top tube: take the risk or lose the chance.

Inevitably, given the danger of this descent had been flagged up prior to the Tour, this incident provoked a furore, stoked up by Porte's condemnation of the organisers' decision to include it. 'Would they send their son or daughter down a descent like that and feel happy? I'm not sure,' he wondered. 'I think that the spectacle should be the finish on top of a mountain, not having to take unnecessary risks to get to the bottom of a stage that turned out to be a few GC guys sprinting. Is that the greatest image for cycling? I don't really know.'

Looking for an answer to this, I spoke to BMC team manager Jim Ochowicz during the last week of the race. 'These guys all know how to go downhill – you go up, you've gotta go down! – so they understand the importance of the descents and do recon them. We'd certainly looked at that particular one. They've also done them in other races during their careers, so they are familiar with them. The problem comes when the guys are tired from weeks of racing and their skill-sets aren't what they would be in a one-day or a smaller stage race,' he said.

'I would say there is a significant difference between some of the riders on descents. They can all get down the hills, otherwise they wouldn't be competitive at all, but some do manage it better. Nibali is a good example of that. Riders like him can gain an advantage, but they've got to take risks to do so. Even if you consider yourself an exceptional descender, stuff can still happen that you can't control – gravel on the road, for instance, or melting asphalt when the roads get hot.'

Sky sporting director Rod Ellingworth, who worked with Porte on the team for several seasons, was more succinct. 'I know Richie's gone down hundreds of descents and for some reason he just got that one wrong. He locked the wheel up and went down. Everybody will have their moment and try it, like Froomey did last year on the Peyresourde, but it's just bike racing in the end. I don't think it's changed in the last hundred years.'

And, just as some are quicker at going uphill, others are always going to have an edge when coming back down again.

CHAPTER 14

HOW TO WIN A TIME TRIAL

> You have to be fast on your feet and adaptive or else a
> strategy is useless.
>
> *— Charles de Gaulle*

Technique trumps tactics in time trials. 'The race of truth' pits
the individual racer against the clock, delivering an incomparable assessment on form, position, pacing, cornering and
other critical details required to maintain a consistently rapid
speed over a set distance. 'The basic approach is to start fast,
increase the speed at halfway, then sprint in the final,' says
Marco Pinotti, a six-time Italian champion in the discipline.

Yet, add up to seven more riders, as would be the case for a
team time trial at a Grand Tour, and the balance between tactics and technique is more even. Those factors remain crucial,
but are tempered by the varied strengths of each team member and the fact that a finishing time is set only when the fifth
rider crosses the line. How do you meld powerful *rouleurs* up
to two metres tall with flyweight climbers who weigh less than

sixty kilograms? Ensure that the right riders – in other words your GC contenders – finish among your leading quintet? Create an advantage over rival teams and contend for victory?

Pinotti, who has become a specialist time-trial coach with the BMC Racing team since retiring from the peloton in 2013, says the first step is to inspect the course. 'Tactics depend on the route you're facing. Some riders are quicker through corners, others faster on climbs, while the time trial specialists will thrive on wide, straight roads. I study the course very carefully beforehand, assess the riders on our team and set the strategy based on that. So I'll ask a specific rider to lead the line through certain corners because he's good at that and will maintain the highest speed, other riders will have to lead on the straights, and there will be a couple more who will lead on the climbs. You have to find a balance between all of their skills.'

Deciding on the order of riders is another key aspect of the preparations. 'If it's a straight course you have to try to find the right balance between the riders, to place them in the right position in the line,' Pinotti explains. 'For instance, you don't put a small rider in front of a big rider, because the bigger man will be in the wind when he's behind the smaller one and he will end up making two pulls and not one.'

When the riders roll down the wide ramp at the start of a team time trial, the initial task is to get up to cruising speed as soon as possible. 'It might sound obvious, but you need to start fast and not slow, but you can go out too quickly and if that happens the team will end up paying the penalty,' Pinotti continues. 'A sprinter, for instance, can guarantee a very fast start but will pay for it later, whereas a climber won't be able to produce that same power off the line. You have to use the team in the most efficient way, work out where each rider will be most useful, both in terms of their place in the string and the points on the course where their strength could be best applied.

'I tend to get an experienced rider to lead off. Normally it's Manuel Quinziato or someone who's done some team or individual pursuiting on the track because you can guarantee they will know the ideal pace at which to begin, going smoothly and quickly, but not too fast or for too long.' The day after I speak to Pinotti, Rohan Dennis is selected to fill this role in the 13.7km TTT around the French city of Nîmes that will open the 2017 Vuelta a España.

Pinotti says that the first two positions in the line are the hardest to take on because the judgement of pace in the opening few hundred metres is so critical to what happens over the rest of the course. 'The second position is particularly tough because that rider has to follow the lead man and then start to pull on the front after a few hundred metres, so it's a very big effort – Tejay van Garderen will fill that role tomorrow. He's got to establish the pace at which the whole line will travel. The first man can't do that as he's just getting the team up to a high, but not full speed from the standing start. Then the third rider comes through and normally his task is to maintain the speed that the second man has reached, and so on for the rest of the riders in the line.'

This sounds and generally looks relatively simple, but, as with team pursuiting on the track, the degree of precision and focus required is extraordinary. Frequently travelling at close to 60kph on flat, straight roads, there is little more than a couple of centimetres between a back wheel and the front wheel following it. Any loss of concentration or an unexpected encounter with debris or a pothole can lead to spectacular crashes, often taking out several members of a team at once.

Once up to speed, the single objective is to sustain the tempo, each rider drafting behind the one in front, steadily moving up the line until they reach the front and, when they've completed their effort, moving off to the side and dropping back down the line and rejoining it at the tail. The group is effectively a breakaway, each rider contributing wholeheartedly to the common cause.

A pivotal member of the Garmin team that enjoyed an extended run of team time trial success between 2008 and 2012, David Millar confirms that the simple goal is to make that pace as high as possible, which is guaranteed to push the weaker riders in a team over their limit almost immediately. This can be managed if the course isn't very challenging, as each rider will get a regular opportunity to recover. Problems arise on courses that put an onus on climbing or feature lots of corners.

'Corners involve deceleration followed by acceleration. In Grand Tours with nine-man teams that makes for quite a long line of riders, enough to make for a considerable concertina effect through tight turns.' Like a lead-out rider leading his sprinter up through the peloton, Garmin adopted the truck-and-trailer method. 'This would remind us to think about our trailer, to try to choose the smoothest line possible,' Millar says. 'Not necessarily the racing apex you'd use in an individual time trial but a line that wouldn't be so extreme as to force errors behind, which would lead to sudden braking and gaps being opened up.

'Whoever takes the team into a corner is responsible for taking the team out, so you'll often see the front rider in team time trial exiting a corner looking over his shoulder making sure everybody has made it through safely and the team is in tight formation before beginning the acceleration back up to speed.'

The natural consequence of this is that the further down the line a rider is, the bigger the acceleration they will have to make coming out of a corner because each successive rider will lose a touch more speed than the one in front due to braking. 'The lead rider won't have to brake much, if at all, the number two rider will brake a bit more, number three a bit more than number two, and so on,' says Millar, who adds that the best team time trial teams comprise riders who have spent long spells training together on the specialised aero bikes and trust each other implicitly. Ultimately, what it comes down to, Millar explains, is that 'You have to believe the guy in front of you is not going to fuck it up and cause you to crash or force you to brake abruptly.'

Pinotti explains that wastage of teammates is inevitable in any all-out effort of this kind. 'You can compare it to leading out a sprint, in a way. The aim there is to make one rider go as fast as possible. In a team time trial, the aim is to make five riders to go as fast as possible, so the other four have to do all they can to ensure that. They have to sacrifice themselves.' As a result, he never expects all of his nine riders to come across the line together.

'It's not nice at all to get dropped, but I don't regard this as a failing. When I joined this team there was a feeling that the riders who had got dropped weren't fully committed. But I think the riders who are dropped are those that should get the prize because I'm sure they've given one hundred per cent, whereas I don't always know if all of the others have, if they've gone right to their limit.'

He recalls the first occasion when he oversaw BMC's riders in a Vuelta team time trial, back in 2014. 'We finished with nine riders but in ninth place. In the bus afterwards I said to them, "The next time you ride like that I'll smash into you with the car. We'll start with nine and we'll finish with six. If it happens again be very aware that I'll accelerate and make three of you crash." It's so stupid to finish ninth and with nine riders, because you will have ridden at the speed of the ninth rider.' It's not easy to square this level of anger with someone as easy-going as Pinotti, but BMC's dominance of TTTs over the three subsequent seasons speaks volumes about the discipline he subsequently instilled.

'It's impossible to have all nine riders at the same high level. It can happen when you select riders from a large group, on a national team for example. But on a trade team, there's always a scale in terms of form. You have to mix climbers, sprinters, *rouleurs*, so if you finish with nine then something has gone wrong. I certainly don't want us to finish this team time trial with nine riders. Seven would be a good number. They need to go onto the short climb with at least seven riders and still have at least six going over the top just in case someone has a flat tyre or some other problem. Finishing with seven would be OK, but not nine.'

World team time trial champions in 2014 and 2015, victors in the discipline in all three Grand Tours across those same two seasons, and winners at several other WorldTour races, BMC followed Pinotti's script perfectly in Nîmes. Dennis led home five of his teammates in a time half a dozen seconds faster than Quick-Step and Sunweb, with Sky another three seconds back in fourth. All three of those teams, incidentally, finished with five riders.

The TTT has always been a test of togetherness and organisation. In the inter-war years, when the Tour de France occasionally featured several stages run in team formation, Alcyon steamrollered rival outfits thanks to the rigorous discipline instilled by their *directeur sportif* Ludo Feuillet. More recently, the likes of Peter Post, Manolo Saiz and Bjarne Riis all put particular focus on these stages.

'Peter Post's favourite discipline was the team time trial, and if we ended up second or third it was a big disappointment,' says Marc Sergeant. 'If we finish second or third now we're delighted. He'd say, "We blew it!"'

'I remember when we won the 1992 Tour TTT in Libourne. We had a great team with Olaf Ludwig, Maurizio Fondriest, Viatcheslav Ekimov, and at the intermediate split we were twelve seconds behind Carrera. Of course, in those days we didn't have radios, but we heard him yelling at us to go faster and we were shouting, "Speed it up! Speed it up!" Olaf Ludwig had one of those days, he could pull for a kilometre, and in a team time trial that's a long way. That makes it easier for everyone else and gives you a lot of confidence. In the end we beat Carrera by seven seconds.'

Sergeant offers support to Pinotti's belief that there is no point in finishing a TTT with a full roster of riders. 'That day, I knew I didn't have to be in the first five, so with a kilometre and a half to go I went full, and two other guys did the same. Although we weren't in the five that set the time, it might have been that effort that the three of us produced at that late point that made the difference. If we'd decided to remain in the group that finished in order to get a little bit of prestige, the team might have ended up losing. You have to throw your ego away in a situation like that.'

He smiles at the memory and adds, 'Post was very happy that night. He always was when he won. Sometimes we'd go to a race and he'd say, "We've come here with the goal of winning a stage", but when we did win one he'd always say, "Maybe we can win two ..." He was always looking for more. But it was a good way of working, it kept the riders on their toes, and that's what you want.'

Speak to almost any rider in the immediate aftermath of a team time trial and almost all will confess to it being hellish, far worse than anything they experience in an individual test. Riding alone against the clock, it is essential to avoid surpassing your threshold, apart from at those points when there is a chance to recover on a descent or until beyond the point where finishing is guaranteed. In a team TT, however, each rider exceeds their threshold every time they reach the front of the line, and, after peeling aside, are not far off it when accelerating to get onto the back of the string. It is, effectively, the ultimate breakaway, in which every member is completely committed to covering the ground as fast as possible.

'I may be putting out around four hundred and fifty watts on the flat in an individual time trial, compared to five hundred and fifty-plus watts on the flat when hitting the front in a team time trial,' Millar explains. 'The only reason this is possible is because the effort lasts approximately forty-five seconds to one minute each time. Then there is recovery time when in the slipstream of your teammates; in practice you are on the cusp of exploding when you latch onto the back of the line and only recover once in position two or three. For this reason, it's better to have a complete team for as long as possible; this allows for more recovery time until it's your turn again to hit the front and begin the horrible effort once more.'

He adds, 'People tend to think it must be easier for specialists but, in truth, it's the other way round. The specialist has to lift the team, do longer turns on the front, bring the speed back up when it's dropped, and not miss a turn; that's what's expected of them, it's their responsibility not to flake out.'

Millar believes the 2009 Tour's TTT at Montpellier was the deepest he ever went in a race, the effort leaving him unable to eat for seven hours such was the shock to his body. Garmin started it as favourites, but lost four riders before halfway, forcing Millar, Wiggins, Vande Velde and David Zabriskie to share all of the work between them, with Ryder Hesjedal hanging on for all he was worth. They finished second to Alberto Contador and Lance Armstrong's powerful Astana team, Millar describing it as one of his proudest moments during his racing career.

Pinotti, too, has similar bad memories. 'Among the worst was the 2002 Tour of Catalonia when I was with Lampre. I started third in line, and on the first corner the first, second and fourth riders crashed. I looked at the fifth rider and asked him what we should do and we waited,' he recalls. 'In fact, after the crash, we were very smooth and did a very good time trial. I think we could have won it if we hadn't waited because we lost more than thirty seconds waiting for three riders to stand up, get back on their bikes and get going again.'

With barely a pause, he corrects himself, remembering the lengthy 67.5km test from the Tour de France that same year. 'We had Raimondas Rumšas on the team, and he was extremely strong – he finished third in the Tour. I was behind him because you normally put a good time triallist behind the strongest rider as when he pulls the rider behind can follow and then still have the energy left to make an effort when the strong guy moves off the front. We reached the climb and he was going really hard and I heard from behind, *"Piano! Piano! Slow down!"* I passed on the message, but Rumšas kept riding and riding, so our sprinter, Ján Svorada, accelerated out of the line, got ahead of him and yelled: *"E ora puoi fare tutto, campione!"* – And now you can do it all, champion! – and pulled out of the line for good. He was so angry.'

There were some good days, though, he acknowledges. 'The best was with Columbia-Highroad on the opening day of the 2009 Giro d'Italia in Venice. That was close to perfection. We actually finished with nine, which is pretty rare for a winning team, and Mark Cavendish was first over the line and got the leader's jersey. We had a big rivalry with Garmin back then and were the first team to start, so we had no references at all. We were smooth, everybody was in good shape. We won by six seconds. Moments like that are when all the pain and bad memories become worth it. That's what I keep reminding our guys when I'm preparing them.'

CHAPTER 15

THE ART OF THE BREAKAWAY

> Nearly all the tactics of cycle racing are based on a simple mechanical principle: that all else being equal, two men who take it in turn to pace each other will travel further and faster than a man riding on his own.
> – *Geoffrey Nicholson*, The Great Bike Race

A lucky break. Everyone appreciates them. In cycling, though, there's a tendency for breakaway wins to be regarded, fundamentally, as fortunate, as lacking the verve of leading in the bunch at a sprint finish, and the class that is evident when a GC favourite outstrips their rivals at a mountain summit. In both cases, the bike-racing talent required for success is obvious. Breakaway winners, on the other hand, are cycling's mayflies, emerging for a day then disappearing back into the pack, anonymous once more until fortune shines on them again.

Language does them few favours either. In the Grand Tours, breakaways on the early stages are dismissed as 'kamikaze', undertaken for no other reason than to display the sponsor's brands before the TV cameras with barely a consideration of victory. Escapes are most likely to be successful on 'transition stages', those days when the race is transferring from one key battleground in the contest for the overall title to the next. The term underlines that the favourites are holding fire and are to some extent deigning to grant the peloton's water-carriers a moment in the sun.

Even on those days when the breakaway has managed to finish ahead of a hard-chasing peloton, the result, it is often said, has come about because the bunch got its calculations wrong, rarely that the escapees have outwitted it. There is the sense that the breakaway is passive rather than active, that it is attached to the main pack by an invisible thread, which the peloton can capture at any moment it chooses, like a cat pawing and pouncing on a ball of string. Occasionally, the thread snaps and the breakaway can take advantage, but for reasons that are beyond its control, because it's got lucky.

Yet, Thomas De Gendt's astute description of the craft and know-how that went into his victory in Gijón illustrates the falseness of that assumption, as does the praise lavished by the likes of Tejay van Garderen on the heightened tactical nous required by such breakaway specialists. The unfolding drama of an escape can be enthralling, although the TV coverage rarely captures this because the tactics involved are so intricate, the skills required are so difficult to pick out and illustrate. With language crucial in this area, they are breakaway artists rather than specialists, toiling, almost always in Sisyphean fashion, to create a quite remarkable feat, head and legs in perfect synergy.

French being the language of cycling, naturally there is a word to describe these breakaway artists. They are *baroudeurs*.

Derived from a southern Moroccan dialect, 'barud' was an explosive powder and the term was first used by French troops in the 1920s to describe a soldier who was quick to jump into battle. Up to and during that period, every rider was a *baroudeur*, as success depended on what were often reckless tactics, attacking early and with great determination, and no matter that there might be a few hundred kilometres to the finish. It was all or nothing, until Belgium's Classics specialists, honed in long races on rough roads, initiated a new approach, realising that great advantage could be gained by sitting in and saving themselves for the final hour of a race when their rivals were spent.

The *baroudeur*'s finest moment was Roger Walkowiak's victory in the 1956 Tour de France. A last-minute call-up to the North-East Centre regional team, Walkowiak took the yellow jersey in the first week at Angers, where he trailed in towards the back of a thirty-one-rider group that gained more than eighteen minutes on the favourites. By extremely skilful management of his own and his unfancied team's resources, the little-known Frenchman of Polish extraction allowed the lead to slip from his grasp with the aim of regaining it in the final week. He remained on the fringes of the battle for the jersey until a long stage into Grenoble, four days from Paris, when he produced the ride of his life to regain the lead, which he held to the finish.

Writing thirty-odd years later in his autobiography *L'Équipée Belle*, Tour director Jacques Goddet, who oversaw the race for half a century from 1937, said it was a 'Tour that resembled no other, constantly open, always uncertain, perpetually moving' and pronounced it his favourite. It was, essentially, an exaggerated version of the race that Christian

Prudhomme, the current Tour boss, would love to serve up. However, as teams have become more organised, the peloton more assertive in controlling the gaps, breakaways have been allowed less leeway. Although the percentage of victories taken by a lone escapee or a rider from a small group remained higher than those taken in bunch sprints until the 1990s, the balance has since tipped significantly the other way. The strong have become too strong, and *baroudeurs* have become marginalised. Leicester City's Premier League victory in 2016 showed that sporting fairy tales do still happen, but the possibility of a repeat of the Tour *à la Walko* looks like an increasingly far-fetched one.

Before looking at the how of the breakaway, it is instructive to investigate the why. Essentially, it comes down to the immutable reason advocated by Thomas De Gendt, that for riders like him there is no chance of winning unless he can escape most of the riders in the bunch. There are, though, other aspects to it, many of which emphasise the maverick nature of the best-known *baroudeurs*.

'I won't deny that I enjoy riding in the break. I can set my own pace,' says De Gendt. 'If I'm in the peloton, there are always crashes, you've got guys getting in your way, blocking you on corners, or going too fast on the descents. When I'm on the front I don't have any of that stress. I can ride as fast or as slow as I want, and I've got the team car just behind me, ready with food and water, which is a real advantage in a race like, for example, the Vuelta when it's really warm. You just put your hand up and twenty seconds later you have a fresh bottle. If you're back in the bunch and you want a bottle, you've got to get eight because your teammates all want one too. It's never easy in the bunch. It might look it, but you've got a lot to deal with. That's why I prefer being in the breakaways.'

Jacky Durand, the De Gendt of the 1990s, has acknowledged that he had a similar perspective to the Belgian. 'I had a motto: "In cycling, it's not necessarily the strongest who wins" – luckily for me, since otherwise I wouldn't have won much,' the Frenchman says in Max Leonard's *Lanterne Rouge*. 'I'm not a revolutionary of any sort, but on the bike I've always refused to come out of a mould. It astonishes me that most riders are followers, even sheep. A lot of them, the only people who know they're in the Tour are their *directeurs sportifs*. I couldn't do the job like that. They finish the Tour without having attacked once, maybe the whole of the season, even the whole of their career. I'd rather finish shattered and last having attacked a hundred times than finish twenty-fifth without having tried ... You could say that ninety-eight per cent of my attempts failed, *mais voilà*. I tried everything I had for the win.'

As Durand's career ended, his mantle was taken up by the likes of Thomas Voeckler and Jens Voigt. Voeckler, stronger mentally than he was physically, echoed Durand's philosophy, saying, 'What I like is to attack and to win, but I've never been the peloton's strongest rider. There has never been any point in me waiting to attack, you've just got to go for it and sometimes it works and at other times you simply end up wasting your energy. That's the only way I can succeed and it's the only way that I love to race.'

Voigt, who became a cult hero thanks to breakaway antics and his offbeat racing philosophy (encapsulated in the phrase 'Shut up, legs' that became the title of his autobiography) says his first coach told him at the age of twelve, '"If you attack first you already have the psychological advantage, because the others are forced to react. They're forced to play by your rules." He told me a few times and I tried it, and had success with it. Then you have a positive memory and it becomes almost automatic, like a reflex.'

De Gendt confesses he owes a debt to the German, who was very much an inspiration for him. Being in a breakaway during the 2011 edition of Paris–Nice with Voigt and Jérémy Roy, another regular in such moves, was the turning point for him. 'I'd been in a couple of smaller breaks with Voigt the year before, but this was different. This was centre stage. In the lead-up to the race, I'd actually told a Belgian newspaper that I wanted to be the next Jens Voigt, so there was a certain strangeness to be in the break with him,' he says. 'Attacking is an obsession of mine. I'm crazy for an attack. I love it and I always will.'

The best *baroudeurs* share the conviction that nothing is set in stone. The odds may be hugely loaded against them, but there is always the chance of what Durand describes rather beautifully as *un élément perturbateur*, something unforeseen happening. The Frenchman recalls an unlikely victory on a stage of the much-missed Midi Libre race, when the barrier at a level crossing came down just as the peloton was about to reach it, forcing them to wait and taking the impetus from its pursuit of him. It could equally be a change in wind direction or a crash in the peloton. The *baroudeurs*, it will be seen, have plenty of other little tricks with which they can upset the peloton's calculations when it is in chase mode.

At major stage races, there are essentially three scenarios when breakaways form. The first, and now the most common, occurs when one or more hopeful escapees are allowed a *bon de sortie*, a day pass granted by the peloton when a sprint finish is regarded as guaranteed or when the bunch wants to recuperate after several hard days of racing. The first week of the 2017 Tour featured a run of these, to the chagrin of the race organisers and France Télévisions, who had committed to broadcasting every stage in its entirety for the first time.

Tour boss Christian Prudhomme and the TV execs had been hoping that the first twenty minutes to an hour of coverage would feature a lot of frantic action as riders tried again and again to force a breakaway to form, while teams responded by nullifying all efforts until everyone was happy that the right balance of riders had escaped. According to the racers, these opening kilometres are often 'eyeballs out', a hectic whirl of riders breaking away and quickly being reeled back in until most of the peloton is happy with the makeup of the group that does eventually slip away. This maelstrom of activity also provides the first clues about the strategy teams are attempting to employ during the day.

A sprinter's team, for instance, might look to place a rider in the break to have an excuse for not committing the rest of its riders to chasing the lead group down towards the end of the stage. This would leave those riders fresher in the closing kilometres when endeavouring to lead out their sprinter for the finish. A GC rider's team might have the same strategy or, more likely, want to place a rider or two in the break who can provide support to their leader when he attacks from the peloton later in the stage, acting as stepping stones towards a stage win or a time gain on rival riders. Evidently, opposing sprint and GC teams will be determined to prevent them doing this, resulting in the constant flurry of attacks until the breakaway features the right combination of riders. In Grand Tours, they will generally be from smaller teams who don't have a top sprinter or GC contender, whose only hope of success is from a breakaway. Note, too, that the peloton won't be keen to see a *baroudeur de luxe* such as De Gendt go clear as his presence is sure to make their pursuit harder.

The 2017 Tour highlighted a variation on this, the scenario that no one outside the bunch and the team cars following it wanted to see. A small group would dash away within moments of Prudhomme waving his flag to indicate the official start of the race while the bunch tooled contentedly along behind, the riders in the front rank filling the road from kerb to kerb to prevent anyone else haring after them.

'The *barrages* when racing got under way meant that not many people could escape, and that surprised me and annoyed everyone,' confessed Tour debutant Élie Gesbert. 'As soon as three riders get clear, the sprinters' and GC leaders' teams block the road, as they don't want anyone to pass. If you are unfortunate enough to try to get clear, you get a real bollocking, and I wasn't expecting the extent of that.'

The young Frenchman explained how he managed to get through this blockade to join compatriot Yoann Offredo in the break on the stage to Bergerac. 'Yoann went clear and straight away there was a blockade at the front. I was next to Philippe Gilbert, who saw me and asked if I wanted to get away as well. He allowed me a way through and I went clear, but I felt that on that stage the sprinters' teams wanted to lock everything down.'

Jean-François Bourlart, manager of Wanty-Groupe Gobert, another of the smaller teams, admitted he was flabbergasted by the tactic given the almost total dominance of Marcel Kittel in the bunch finishes. 'Everyone knows before the stage who is going to win. I don't understand why they don't join the breaks,' said Bourlart. 'Do all of the teams think they've got a sprinter who can beat Kittel? Guys are riding on the front of the peloton and their leader is finishing twelfth every day.'

Philippe Mauduit, sporting director of the Bahrain Merida team that persisted in working for Italian sprinter Sonny Colbrelli, who had just one top ten finish in the race's opening week, defended his team's strategy during that period. 'We recognise Kittel's superiority, but you're never beaten in advance. Since teams have been organised like this, it's well known that, given this kind of profile, where it's very flat and there's no wind, that it will systematically end with a sprint. I wonder what they could do to change the scenario, because it's written in advance. In past Tours, there were always a few little difficulties that gave you a little bit of hope if you did escape,' said Mauduit.

Given that France's topography hasn't changed since the 1903 Tour and the race has always featured a good number of almost pan-flat stages, Mauduit's defence doesn't stand up. Off the record, sporting directors hinted that there was a more sinister aspect to the *barrages*, with teams being forced into participating to avoid threatened damage to their prospects in other races – deal-making, in other words.

In a Grand Tour's first week, the size of the breakaway will also affect its longevity. Generally, the break allowed its head will comprise no more than five riders. If there are any more than this, the odds tip more in the escapees' favour, and the peloton will do all it can to prevent that. Likewise, its maximum lead will be limited, with breaks allowed little more than three minutes' advantage at the 2017 Tour, which featured arguably the strongest line-up of sprinters the race had ever seen.

Returning to the breakaway scenarios, the second is much more in line with what Prudhomme and the TV directors were expecting. It comprises twenty to forty kilometres of high-intensity racing, as groups of varying sizes go clear and get reeled in until, finally, at a moment that is difficult to predict, the elastic snaps and the lucky few take flight, leaving the peloton to settle down and the organisers smiling broadly after an hour or so of hectic yo-yoing that's provided some early spice to the day's action.

'On a flat stage, you can sometimes get away on the first attempt because most guys figure that there's no chance of the break staying away so they won't be interested, but often you've got to work an awful lot harder,' De Gendt explains. 'If you really want to be in the break, you have to go full and you have to try a lot of times. Then it's just a case of being lucky. Sometimes you have to attack on a climb, because if you go hard on a climb it's a lot harder for riders to follow. I usually make my effort on a climb because it's not so easy for the bunch to follow.'

This, of course, won't work if there's no hill early in the stage or if a rider's not strong enough to take advantage of a climb if there is one. 'If you are strong then you can ride away from the group on even the smallest climb, forcing the pace,' says Voigt. 'If you're not, then you have to be clever, know when the peloton is at breaking point, and then make your move.' The German explains that as he gained experience he could almost smell when this point was about to arrive. 'I'd wait near the front, but not on it, for the moment after a series of attacks when you can tell the peloton wants to slow down … When this moment comes, you go! It's the peloton's breaking point.'

Writing in his autobiography *The Racer*, now retired British pro David Millar, whose most significant road race successes all came from breakaways, confirms this quality of being able to sense this moment, describing, 'When you feel that good, you're very lucid. You don't think, just act.' He also adds more detail to Voigt's tactic. 'There are two types of riders who make it into the long breaks: the ones who have the ability to attack many times, putting in multiple max capacity efforts until they get into the break that stays away, or ones that have to ride with their heads,' he explains, adding that he fell into the second category and further explaining that he used to look closely at stage profiles, assessing which looked best for a group staying clear and especially for those where a break would likely be able to get a gap in the opening hour of racing.

'I look for a small climb, a pinch point or a testing section where a peloton moving at full speed will be close to its breaking point,' says Millar. 'It needs to be hard for the peloton so they are urged to sit up. Then, when the peloton is at its breaking point, I make my move. I often wait until I am completely at my maximum output, then attack, going deep to get away. If you are not at your maximum then the peloton will have the ability to chase you down. You need to attack while others are on the absolute limit, so that they look at each other and are not wanting to chase you.' The Scot describes this effort as 'the hardest thing you will do in the stage and possibly all of cycling', but makes the point that breaks that gain an advantage without much effort tend to occur on stages when there is little chance of staying away until the finish.

Millar, incidentally, also highlights a factor De Gendt touched on earlier when talking about his successful Vuelta breakaway, how infiltrating the right breakaway and winning from it is often the result of several days of work. 'Getting in a break and winning a stage sounds so simple. But it is not just a case of picking a day. You have to try over several days. You need the combination of a good day, the right people, the right move. It takes a few days of warming up for. I'd say you need a good week of trying ... it's a different style of racing getting in breaks.'

When the elastic is at snapping point, it is crucial to be well placed to take advantage. Obviously, the prospective breakaway riders need to be up towards the front of the peloton, but not in the front rank, otherwise any attempt to go clear will be telegraphed to every rider behind, who will be primed to react. Ideally, the canny *baroudeur* needs to be on one side of the bunch, making it easier to assess the situation around them. Often, they'll find other breakaway hopefuls in a similar position, ready to make the same move when the moment is judged to be right, as Laurent Pichon and Yoann Offredo did on the Tour stage out of Düsseldorf.

If caught slightly out of position when the breakaway riders begin to eke out an advantage, there is still a chance of joining them. In those first seconds when the peloton begins to ease off, riders can often be seen trying to 'slingshot' after them, accelerating hard from a couple of ranks back as that slowing begins in the bunch. Bridging up to the lead group then requires an effort that Swedish pro Magnus Backstedt once described as being 'somewhere between a sprint and a track pursuit – you need to sustain it for three or four kilometres.'

De Gendt points out that 'slingshot' attacks of this type are good when they work but leave a stain on a rider's reputation when they don't. 'You have to have a certain amount of courage to be a *baroudeur* because we're not always the most popular riders in the peloton – especially if we attack at a difficult moment,' he says. 'The prime moment is when a break has gone and the pace in the peloton comes right down and guys like me attack again. In that instant we dare not fail because we've just put nearly two hundred guys on the limit again, just when they wanted to recover. If it does fail and you sink back into the peloton, the names and the insults ... well, they can fly at you ...'

The third breakaway scenario is heaven and hell – bliss for the organisers and fans, torment for those involved. The pace starts fast and never relents because the break simply won't form. This full-peloton, flat-out effort arises either when everyone is tired and no one can produce the effort required to get away and stay away, or when lots of teams are determined to put a rider into the break. It might take fifty, seventy-five or even one hundred kilometres for a group to find the right moment to escape or for the right combination of riders to coalesce so that the peloton is happy to release them. While the first week of a Grand Tour tends to feature riders from smaller teams who are keenest to 'show their jersey', breakaways of this third type typically occur in the third week of a race when many riders are running on fumes rather than with a full tank. Often, they're bigger too, as many teams are desperate for a final shot at success.

No matter which of these three scenarios has played out, as the gap widens, the riders at the front now have to commit and a new phase of the cat-and-mouse breakaway game commences. Urged on by their sporting directors, the escapees can't think too much about who the other riders in the break are, which direction the wind is coming from, or what their chances of success are. The focus now is building and sustaining the gap on the peloton, and, at a certain point, with perhaps fifty kilometres remaining, doing everything possible to hold on to at least a few seconds of that advantage going into the final kilometre, where they might discover, as Ag2r team manager Vincent Lavenu neatly put it, that the lottery ticket that they've received by joining the breakaway has been picked out as the winner.

On television and from the side of the road, watching a small group riding a few minutes ahead of an almost disinterested peloton can make for dull viewing. Yet these periods are when the comparison with chess are most apposite. Helpfully, the increasing use of data is making this easier to understand and follow, to demonstrate that the breakaway is not living completely on hope and unable to affect its fate, that the tail that is the front group is actually wagging the dog that is the peloton behind it.

'When I'm in the break, I always try to keep to a certain speed and ensure that the bunch sticks to that speed as well,' says De Gendt. 'The thinking behind that is that if I make it easy for me, then it's also easy for the bunch. The key thing, though, is that I don't use up a lot of power riding that way and should be able to keep the gap at around, say, three minutes. If I slow down, I know they will slow down as well, because they don't want to get too close to the break. If the gap fell to one minute [halfway through the stage], then guys might try to bridge across from the bunch, and they might end up with six or seven guys at the front rather than three or four. So the bunch will always try to maintain the gap at an unbridgeable distance at least until they really start to chase. So, slowing down when you're in the break isn't usually a problem, because the bunch will respond in exactly the same way. It's only when I get to the final kilometres that I go full gas. Of course, there's then a limit on how much power we've got in the break, whereas they usually have plenty to spare in the peloton and can easily chase you down, which is usually our fate.'

Durand stresses that being aware of the time gap is cru-cially important. 'You have to manage your effort differently in a break. It's not attack, attack, go all out and see where it leads. You must get a lead on the peloton but not too much, so they're not tempted to come after you. It's a game of posi-tioning – that's where my efforts went. I'd keep an eye on the board, play with the gaps a bit. It was always *les écarts, les écarts, les écarts*. If the peloton accelerated, maybe I'd acceler-ate too, to make them doubt. It was a game of hide-and-seek,' he says.

De Gendt confirms that this is exactly what it is. 'You are playing a kind of guessing game with the bunch,' he explains. 'You have to know when to speed up. Usually, the bunch will speed up on a climb because they think that the break-away's speed won't pick up there. But if I go full, if I go at four hundred and fifty watts for the climb – well, if it's a small one at least – then the bunch might speed up but get to the top of the climb and find rather than coming down the gap has actually gone out by a minute. I know that will provide a little bit of stress for them because they won't have been expecting it. They'll have sped up, probably suffered a bit because of that, and lost a minute.

'You have to play those kind of mind games with the bunch, to wrong-foot them a touch, to make sure it's not easy as they might have been expecting. If they do get a bit stressed, they sometimes make stupid mistakes, like riding a bit too fast and gaining ninety seconds on you very quickly, which might look impressive on TV, but can mean they're using their power too quickly. That can give the break more of a chance, as it will then speed up and the peloton might not be able to respond as it needs to.'

De Gendt continues his illuminating insight by revealing other tactics that the breakaway can employ to bamboozle the bunch. 'Riding fast through the feeding zone is a good way to gain time. We've got a team car behind us so we don't have to slow down to pick up a *musette*, but the bunch has got to do that. So if you speed up in the feed zone you'll easily gain thirty or forty seconds,' he discloses. 'You've also got to look at the profile and say, "I'll accelerate there, and there, and there", and, of course, they don't know what you're planning so that gives them something else to chew on. Most of the time, none of this works out, but occasionally it does, and that's why I keep trying again and again.'

That the same names are often heard again and again suggests a degree of complicity between the riders involved in breakaways. While this can work in scenario one, there is little chance of it occurring in the other two situations when the battle to get into the break is much more drawn-out and unpredictable. 'It's not as if the *baroudeurs* band together,' De Gendt affirms. 'There's no fraternity between us, we don't go looking for each other in the peloton. But we do respect each other's work and we know what kind of riders we need in the break. For example, if I see Jérémy Roy in the break, or Julien Fouchard or Thomas Voeckler, I know they will go full gas all the way. When you get guys from smaller teams in the break, you can be pretty sure they will collapse in the last twenty kilometres.'

For his part, Durand says, 'I didn't have a favourite rider. Let's say I'd calculate a little who I went with. Sometimes I'd say "Let's have a go" in the peloton. I'd look for someone in good shape, who was riding well, who was someone I could beat in the end!'

De Gendt also explains that there is often not much chat exchanged between the members of the breakaway, that everyone knows the job they have to do and gets on with it. 'Especially when it's a big group, there's not a lot of talking. I just tend to focus on myself,' he says. 'When it's down to four or five guys, then you tend to talk a little bit about what the tactics should be. If you're in a group of twenty-odd riders you don't need to talk because you just go full. You don't have to make so much of an effort to create a big gap. If there's twenty-odd guys and everyone does his share of the work then it's really easy, but if you're only with four other guys it's a bit more difficult to get a gap and to stay fresh until the finish. It's a bit more tactical. In that case, you might be saying to each other, "What's your take on what we should do? Should we go full? If we go full should we do it from fifty kilometres?"

'When it's a big break, I just let everyone else do what they want to do and keep my opinion to myself. The only time that would change is if I had a teammate or two in the break with me and then you have to decide on what's the best tactic for your team. There are other aspects you have to factor in too over the final fifty kilometres. What's the profile like? Is it all flat? Are there any hills? Is it into a headwind? A headwind is always the worst thing to deal with because the bunch will always go much faster than the break when you're racing into the wind. Of course, you also need to be looking at the strengths of the riders you've been with all day, assessing where they might attack or where you might have an edge on them.'

This sizing-up of their fellow escapees is an ongoing and essential process of analysing where a collaborator's weakness might lie. Do they pull a little softer on the hills? Hold their head in a funny way when struggling? Look over one shoulder to check on their rivals and not the other? Watching how fast a rider accelerates out of a corner late on in a stage might give an idea of how strong they will be in a sprint. Do they open a slight gap or is it easy to stay on their wheel? Could they be bluffing? The permutations are endless. It is chess on wheels.

Unpredictable to the last, Thomas De Gendt doesn't select any of his three Grand Tour stage wins as his best from a tactical perspective. Of his first, on the mythical ascent of the Stelvio during the 2012 Giro d'Italia, he insists, 'That one was actually easy. It was just a case of staying in the bunch and trying to survive on the Mortirolo. Then near the top of the Mortirolo I jumped away to join the breakaway, or at least what was left of it. When we got to the foot of the Stelvio, we had an advantage of three minutes and I just went as hard as possible. It was a stage of two hundred and twenty kilometres with almost six thousand metres of vertical gain, so it was a hard day.'

He plays down the difficulty and tactical significance of his success in the 2016 Tour on Mont Ventoux, a victory overshadowed by a crash into a motorbike that resulted in yellow jersey Chris Froome running up in the mountain without a bike. 'The Ventoux stage was quite easy too. The only tough bit was finishing up the Ventoux,' says De Gendt. 'It was just one hundred and seventy kilometres and then ten kilometres up the Ventoux. The break went from the start. There were thirteen guys and we had a lead of eighteen minutes. I think we were still all together coming onto the Ventoux and then it was just a case of going full on the climb.'

Surprisingly, he selects his win on the opening stage of the 2017 Critérium du Dauphiné as his best. 'If I had to pick out one win that I really liked from a tactical perspective, that would be it. I got into the break with six other riders that day purely with the aim of getting into the mountains jersey. I went at my own speed on every climb, picking up the points I was after,' he recalls. 'At the end, we had to do three laps of a finishing circuit in Saint-Étienne with the climb of Col de Rochetaillée on it. We did a lap, which meant I knew precisely what lay ahead, and our lead was still more than three minutes with two more circuits to go. I pushed hard the second time up the climb and Axel Domont was the only rider who could stay with me. We shared the work until the last climb, then I went hard again about a kilometre from the top. Everything that I planned to do worked out perfectly – well, almost. I'd planned to end the stage in the polka-dot jersey but instead pulled on the yellow.'

Once touted as a Grand Tour contender, particularly after that Giro stage win that pushed him up to third overall at the finish in Milan, De Gendt insists he won't go looking for GC success unless it happens to come his way thanks to a breakaway victory. 'I can assure you there's no possibility of me changing the way that I race now. I'll definitely keep getting into the breakaways. It's the only way that I can win races. If I go in the break twenty times, then I've got twenty chances of winning,' he says, very much in the spirit of the likes of Durand, Voigt and Voeckler. As was the case with this trio, racing in this let's-give-it-a-go manner has made De Gendt one of the peloton's most popular performers, both with fans and race organisers, the modern-day epitome of Henri Desgrange's model rider.

CHAPTER 16

HOW TO WIN A CLASSIC

In preparing for battle I have always found that plans are useless, but planning is indispensable.

— *Dwight D. Eisenhower*

The first time I reported on one of the Classics was in 1994 at the Tour of Flanders. Sharing a car with three Belgian journalists, we drove from the start in the small town of Sint-Niklaas along a warren of roads, eventually weaving through narrow lanes until we reached a small crossroads. 'Up that way is the Oude Kwaremont, and that climb is the first big test in this race,' one of the Belgians said, noticing my bewilderment as to why we were standing in what appeared like the middle of nowhere as far as the race was concerned. 'If you're not in the front twenty riders when you come around this corner, then you've got almost no chance of winning this race. So we come here to see who is at the front.'

By the time the race came through, there were plenty of others standing on the junction, waiting for the bunch to reach the sharp right-hander that led towards the Oude Kwaremont's steeply rising cobbles. First came the break, a few minutes ahead of the main pack. 'Nobodies, they'll soon be caught,' I was told. A handful of minutes later, the peloton arrived, bowling along the narrow road, travelling so fast there seemed little chance of any of the riders negotiating the right-angle turn. Almost as startling was the frenzied noise of bellows and shouts, brakes squealing, the clattering of gears engaging, the whoosh of air being shifted by 200 riders travelling at perilous speed on a lane where cars would struggle to pass each other. I couldn't pick out a single individual from the blurred mass. Amid a rush of thoughts, one stood out: why on earth are they sprinting with eighty kilometres still left to the finish?

There are several answers to that question, each of them highlighting a fundamental difference between the strategy applied to one-day races such as Flanders and stage races. David Millar sums them up particularly well, explaining, 'A stage racer is always trying to control the variables – if risks are taken, they are calculated – whereas a one-day racer essentially knows they can't control the variables, so they reduce them by racing aggressively ... The closer to the front they are the fewer riders they have to deal with – for a one-day racer the biggest variable is the number of racers in front of them. Classics turn into a war of attrition, they become elimination races. It doesn't matter how strong you are, if you're not in the right place all the time you won't win.'

What then are the keys to being in the right place when racing in one of the Monuments? The first, says Millar's former sporting director Matt White, is to watch specific teams, generally those regarded as the favourites based both on their history and line-up. 'For Flanders, for instance, you do focus on Quick-Step because they're always strong in that race. They're the best team in the northern Classics, and they often control them, so we will usually ask our *domestiques* to mark their riders, to follow them if they move. I think at Orica we've had a strong team for the Ardennes for the last few years, and people have often looked to us in those races.

'There are clearly key points too. The Ardennes races don't change much so the guys know beforehand at exactly which points they need to be at the front, and those races are a bit predictable from that point of view. Flanders and Roubaix have a different level of chaos, though, with a great deal depending on the weather and the conditions of the roads.'

From a tactical perspective, these two cobbled Classics are the most intriguing because the approach required for them is quite different from what is required for the other three Monuments and the individual stages of a multi-day race, where success most often depends on saving resources for as long as possible. While endurance does matter enormously at both races, Roubaix and Flanders don't follow a predictable pattern and, therefore, encourage boldness, even from the best teams and riders. They and other cobbled Classics are the races that hark back most closely to the sport in its early days, when being at the front was the sole strategy on roads where racers had to be ready for the unexpected, especially in bad weather.

Since its inception in 1913, the Flanders route has been given frequent makeovers to maintain its legitimacy as one of the sport's outstanding racing challenges and to accommodate the practicalities of racing on public roads. As its Flemish title De Ronde van Vlaanderen suggests, it began as a tour around Dutch-speaking Flanders, passing through most of the major towns and cities in that region on a route that extended to 324 kilometres but was primarily flat. The first climbs in the Flemish Ardennes, the Kwaremont and Tiegemberg, were added in 1919, with more added gradually over the next eighty years to ensure the race remained selective. The race usually features around eighteen of these *hellingen* nowadays. In 2012, Flanders underwent another extensive overhaul to tackle the issue of increasing traffic and spectator chaos along the meandering route, with the organisers introducing a finishing circuit featuring a number of the toughest climbs including the Oude Kwaremont, that has to be covered three times.

The beauty of the pre-2012 route, say three-time winners Tom Boonen and Fabian Cancellara, was that winning was not simply about power and being the strongest. According to Cancellara, it was a much more tactical race than Roubaix and, therefore, much harder to win, Boonen adding that the victor could make his move on any one of the closing climbs. 'You always had to be watchful,' said the Belgian. 'It's the hardest race to read. The Tour of Flanders challenges you. It wants you to start racing ... you have this big fight to get into each climb. Then everybody sits up and goes up the climb easy. Then you get it all over again. Every time you do this, you reach the bottom of the climb full of adrenalin.'

Confirming what my Belgian colleagues informed me on my first visit in 1994, success at Flanders is about being very close to the front of the group of favourites once the race is into its final eighty kilometres, with the Oude Kwaremont the first important marker of form and position. Experience, technique and tactical nous are essential at this point. Speed is vital not only for positioning but also because carrying momentum into these relatively short but often very steep climbs enables riders to power up them, often remaining in the same gear.

'The run-up to this climb is a race within a race. It's nervous, and elbows and shoulders are the order of the day to secure the best spot at the front,' two-time Flanders winner Peter Van Petegem confirms. 'You really need to be a nasty bastard to defend and keep your position, but I had no problem with that … It's important to be in the first two rows in order to get in the right position. What's more it's important because from this moment on hills feature regularly in the race … If you have to chase from the foot of the Oude Kwaremont, you've lost already. That's why the Oude Kwaremont is so crucial. You can be sure that one of the first ten riders to the top will win the race.'

Van Petegem, who was born on and still lives on the race route, says that when he was racing he knew it 'like I know my own wife'. The Belgian trained regularly with German Classics specialist turned *directeur sportif* Andreas Klier, who realised that knowing the sections in between the climbs was often more crucial to success in Flanders as a result of these excursions with Van Petegem. Having this insight, says Klier, enables a rider to work out which way the wind will be blowing from at every moment, making positioning easier on a course that switches back and forth continually along the sharp ridge of the Flemish Ardennes.

'We always met at the same point of the Ronde – he had the same tactics as me, and I knew exactly where he would go – but I couldn't always follow him,' Klier recalls of his racing days at Flanders. 'You didn't see Van Petegem for two hundred and twenty kilometres, then all of a sudden he was there. You don't see anyone do that now; he had a better eye than anyone else.' Yet, while Klier was looking for Van Petegem, rival riders would track the German knowing that he was a good rider to watch, even if victory always eluded him.

The radical revamp in 2012 shifted the emphasis for success away from tactical prowess and towards brute strength. In Boonen, Cancellara twice and Alexander Kristoff, the route still produced victors of the highest quality, but it made Flanders more of a waiting game. It also stripped the race of its most iconic climb, the Muur at Geraardsbergen, which winds up from the heart of the town to the chapel at the crest that gives the ascent its alternative title, Kapelmuur.

However, the move in 2017 of the Ronde's start from Gent to Antwerp presented the organisers with the opportunity to reinsert the Muur. Although it now featured a hundred kilometres from the finish rather than in the final thirty as had previously been the case, it nevertheless played a decisive role in the outcome of the race, suggesting that the scales had tipped back towards brain from brawn.

Going into the redesigned race, the favourites were world champion Peter Sagan and the in-form Greg Van Avermaet. Sitting at home in Italy watching the race on TV, Marco Pinotti, one of the sporting directors on Van Avermaet's BMC Racing team, tuned in for the second half of the action and soon noticed a gaggle of blue Quick-Step jerseys had begun to gather near the front of the peloton approaching Geraardsbergen. 'I could see that they were planning something and also that there weren't many BMC riders up there ready for whatever it was,' says Pinotti. 'Mind you, no one could have expected an attack with a hundred kilometres still left to race. It seemed too far out to try anything, even though the Muur has such a reputation.'

Quick-Step boss Patrick Lefevere and his management staff had been counting on this. 'In one-day races, sometimes it comes down to the tactic of the strongest prevailing, but at Flanders we managed to get around that,' he reveals. 'We knew going into that race that it was going to be very difficult to beat Van Avermaet and Sagan given the form they were in at the start of the season. You can't beat them in the last thirty kilometres as it's impossible to drop them then and they are faster in a sprint, so we made another plan, thinking that no one would expect us to open up the race a hundred kilometres from the finish. Every rider has respect for the Muur van Geraardsbergen, but they're not afraid of it when it's so far out from the finish. It was just another climb to be negotiated before getting onto the final circuit, although it's always special wherever it features.'

Boonen, riding his final Flanders before retirement, said after the race he had been expecting Sky 'to go full gas on the Muur. There was another race, I cannot remember when, but they tried some old cyclo-cross trick, when you have many guys go hard to the base, then pedal at three kilometres an hour, and then everyone behind you has to step out of the pedals, and then those at the front accelerate again. But then [Luke] Rowe asked me if we were going to attack and I realised they were more afraid of us. So I said, "Screw it", and decided to go for it.'

As well as getting the home fans in a frenzy, Boonen's acceleration carried fourteen riders clear of the peloton, including teammates Matteo Trentin and Philippe Gilbert, with a breakaway of eight riders almost six minutes ahead of them. Over the next twenty kilometres, this group pushed its lead over the bunch out to more than a minute. By the time it had reached the second ascent of the Oude Kwaremont, with fifty-five kilometres left, the Boonen group had reeled in the escapees, but now looked likely to suffer the same fate with the peloton less than thirty seconds behind.

Lefevere explains that the plan had indeed been for three or four Quick-Step riders to get away, but now the plan was unravelling with the favourites almost back on terms. The veteran team boss could see this, but admits he had no inkling of what would happen next, that it wasn't part of his team's plan.

Realising they weren't going to stay clear, Gilbert opted to attack the Oude Kwaremont in the same aggressive way that Boonen had the Muur, aiming to keep the initiative by having one or more Quick-Step riders at the front. With climbs coming every few kilometres in the final section of the race, it was a canny move. He guessed rightly that the bunch would be slimmed down dramatically by the Kwaremont and the Paterberg almost immediately after and that the regular ups and downs would disrupt the chase behind him. What he hadn't figured on was that not a single rider from the lead group would be able to go with him. Having reached the top of the Paterberg with his lead beyond thirty seconds, he called up his team car to get some instructions. Keep going, he was told.

Gilbert did precisely that, all the way to the finish, to claim his first Flanders title and give Lefevere his eighth as a team manager. Luck played a very significant role in this success, most particularly when Sagan clipped the roadside barrier the final time up the Oude Kwaremont and crashed, taking Van Avermaet and Oliver Naesen with him just as the trio were making inroads into the lone leader's advantage. However, by making himself the hare, Gilbert was using the fundamental ploy required in cobbled Classics by making his rivals chase. They are, as Millar says, elimination races. You have to be in the right place at the right time to win. Even from fifty-five kilometres and with no one for company, the front can be the right place if you're one of the strongest.

'Gilbert is from the old school. He goes when he feels it's the right moment, and when he goes there's no stopping him,' says José De Cauwer, who rates his compatriot as one of the ultimate tacticians of recent years and believes his Flanders victory was his best yet, a coup of true sporting beauty. 'His move might have seemed to be unsound tactically, but when no one could follow and then they all looked at each other to chase, it turned out to be quite the opposite. Yes, you do need a bit of luck, like he had with the crash involving Van Avermaet, Sagan and Naesen. But don't forget that he was in the right place to take advantage of that bit of fortune. By being ahead, he was putting pressure on Sagan and the others to chase, and that helped him win the race.'

It was, even after so many before, a special moment for Lefevere too, especially given some of the flak he'd received for taking on Gilbert when his best years appeared to be behind him. 'I remember people thought I was a bit foolish to take on an old horse, but even old horses can become young again. This is what happened with Philippe when he got the right team around him and became part of the team spirit we have here. A character like Philippe's thrives in a team like ours, an aggressive team. Setting up an attack a hundred kilometres from the finish on the Kapelmuur was in the eyes of many like committing hara-kiri, but our aggressive mentality landed the win.'

Lefevere compared Gilbert's triumph to the solo victories claimed in Paris–Roubaix by Johan Museeuw and Tom Boonen in 2002 and 2012, respectively. Like Flanders, Roubaix demands a particular set of skills and tactics. Like Flanders, there are key sections where good positioning towards the front of the main group is vital. Yet, in almost every other aspect, Roubaix is a race apart, almost demanding the heroic, never likely to serve up mundane fare. It is a race where absolutely any tactic can result in the ultimate prize, from joining the early break two hundred kilometres and more from the finish to a sprint at the velodrome finish, and that adds to its ageless quirkiness.

This distinctiveness derives, of course, from its fifty-odd kilometres of *pavé*, more than two dozen sections of the kind of cobbled roads that would have been found in every part of France even in the post-war period, but are now maintained by dedicated volunteers and preserved as part of the country's heritage. Negotiating them at speeds of up to 50kph and more demands smart use of tactics, technique and experience.

In his autobiography, Laurent Fignon underlines the difficulty that *pavé* novices face. 'I had absolutely no idea how to ride on the cobbles,' he says of his first encounter with Roubaix's roads during the opening week of the 1983 Tour de France. 'No one told me one elementary principle: you must never grip the handlebars with all your strength. That was what I did and it was perfectly understandable, because of the fear of losing control and falling off. In fact, you keep the bike stable not by the tightness of your hold on the bars but from general balance and natural pedalling rhythm.'

Other aspects of coping with the cobbles are equally counterintuitive. While speed is important, the correct cadence is even more so. 'If you have too high a cadence, you jump. If you have too low a cadence, you blow. If you have the right cadence, you float,' explains three-time Roubaix winner Fabian Cancellara. The key, say the specialists, is to tackle the cobbles in a big gear, but not a huge one. Logic would also suggest avoiding the crown of the road, where the cobbles stand proudest, and opting instead to stay on the edges that are often coated by mud or dust, but the specialists also insist this is the wrong line to take. 'The best way is to ride straight down the middle of the road. It's the hardest, but it's the best,' says 2007 winner Stuart O'Grady. 'When riders start getting a bit tired or a bit desperate they dive off into the sides or into the dirt because it's a little bit easier to ride there, but that's where the rocks end up and where all the punctures are going to happen.'

If it's wet, it is even more important to stick to the centre of the road as the puddles at the side can hide the perils lurking underneath, cobbles that are missing or displaced, stones large enough to send a tiring or unwise rider tumbling. In these conditions, the expert and strongest performers will tend to be seen right at the front of the group or peloton rather than sitting a little further back and drafting as they would when it's dry. *Domestiques* also have to ride differently, sitting behind rather than in front of their leaders to allow these protected riders to pick the best line they can and also to be ready to hand over a wheel in case of a puncture.

It goes without saying that the favourites need to be in peak physical condition. 'If you're not, the cobblestones will ride you and your bike rather than the other way around,' says Stijn Devolder, a two-time Flanders champion and a key *domestique* for the likes of Boonen and Cancellara at Roubaix. 'In fact, racing on cobbles has some similarities with climbing in the mountains. When you arrive with the bunch at the final climb, you need to be in a good spot at the beginning of the climb, and it's the same when you approach a section of cobbles ... In both situations, if someone's attacking off the front and you can't bridge the gap, then it's game over.' Cancellara used to stress that one of the keys to his victories was not simply his strength on the cobbles, although that was vital, but to sustaining that power when he came off them, because that is when a rider is most likely to blow up having expended so much energy coping with the *pavé*.

Because there is no one well-established way to win Roubaix, no one set of cobbles that traditionally provides a launch pad to victory in the way that the climb of the Poggio can in Milan–Sanremo or the final drag up to the finish of Liège–Bastogne–Liège does with routine monotony, the race known as 'The Queen of the Classics' guarantees a very different spectacle each year. In 1996, for instance, the Mapei-GB team managed by Lefevere made its initial thrust a hundred kilometres from the finish, in much the same way its Quick-Step successor did in Flanders twenty-one years later.

Lefevere explains that the foundation to a victory that begins with an attack so far from the finish is the riders having belief that their sporting director's tactic is going to work. 'Sometimes they would say, "Why are we attacking so far out?" And I'd reply, "Why? Because we're the strongest and nobody expects us to attack." It's like in boxing, where the guy who strikes first may not knock out his opponent completely, but that blow will be important further into the contest,' he says.

'The plan that day in 1996 was to blow up the group a hundred kilometres from the finish. I told them to take the race into their hands, to accelerate and be away with twenty-five riders with maybe six from our team, but it ended up that there were just three of our riders at the front. I went up to them in the car and said, "What are you doing? Are you ready to move? OK then, let's go!" Every time one of them had a flat I made the other two wait because Mapei's slogan was "Winning Together" – *per vincere insieme*.'

The finale was controversial, not because Mapei finished with Museeuw winning, Gianluca Bortolami second and Andrea Tafi third, with the rest two minutes and more behind, but because their finishing positions were decided not by a final sprint on the velodrome, but, it has often been suggested, by Mapei boss Giorgio Squinzi. 'Of course, everyone wants to win Paris–Roubaix, but I told them, "This is how it will be. You will be first, you will be second, you will be third. If you don't agree, you can change to another team tomorrow,"' Lefevere insists. 'Squinzi used to ring before every race, but just to say good luck. He did ring me during that Roubaix and told me about Mapei's slogan and added that it was his wedding anniversary that day and that we'd be doing him a huge favour if we could finish with three Mapei riders on the track in Roubaix.'

Mat Hayman's Roubaix victory in 2016 could hardly have been more different. A hard-riding and very experienced road captain for whom the race is one of the very few opportunities he has to play his own card each season, Hayman didn't even look likely to start when he broke his arm at Het Nieuwsblad, just five weeks before Roubaix. 'His preparation was naturally badly disrupted, so he only raced again the weekend before Roubaix and had just two races in seven weeks leading up to it,' explains Matt White, his sporting director.

'He trained in a very different way, a lot of it on a home trainer where he did specific top-end power stuff, and he came into the race very relaxed because there was no pressure on him to do anything. We didn't know how far he'd go, so we gave him a free role. He's a very intense guy who puts a lot of pressure on himself, especially at Roubaix, which is a race that he loves, but he went into it with a different mindset. He made one move after seventy kilometres and that put him in the break of the day. The fact that he had a teammate with him helped, as did the fact that he didn't puncture or crash all day, which is always going to be an advantage at Roubaix. Because he didn't have that pressure to do something, he rode a very relaxed final, but he also had the knowledge of how to win Roubaix. Everything lined up for him,' says White.

When the lead group was reeled in with more than sixty kilometres to the finish, it appeared that Hayman's very slim hopes of success had disappeared completely. Yet, the Australian still dosed his effort very carefully and had no problem joining what proved to be the winning move with forty-five kilometres to go. Coming towards the finish, the lead group was just five-strong, comprising Ian Stannard, Tom Boonen, Sep Vanmarcke, Edvald Boasson Hagen and Hayman. Everyone, including the first four named, assumed Hayman was simply pleased to be there given his recent injury. Yet the Australian looked as strong as any of them as attacks went and came back in the final few kilometres before the five leaders rode into the velodrome. There, employing a version of the tactic that brought Bernard Hinault victory in 1981, Hayman went to the front with a lap to go and kept winding the pace up higher and higher. The odds were on someone, probably Boonen, the quickest sprinter of the quintet and going for a record-breaking fifth win, coming by, but the disbelieving Hayman hung on to win it by a bike length.

'In terms of his preparation, which was very unorthodox, it just shows that you can do things that seem a big stretch, particularly if you have years of experience,' White says. 'He'd also had a very good winter, and he took very little time off the bike between December and March, and I think people get very stuck on ideas, that you have to ride this race in order to win that race. That's a perfect example that you don't.'

As Hayman's win proved yet again, one of the perennial beauties of the Classics is that a rider regarded as a complete outsider can win given the right combination of strength, luck and tactical nous. Unlike the Grand Tours, where only a handful of riders have a realistic chance of success, the Classics can make a winner out of almost any of the riders who start them. Join the break and there's that slight possibility of emulating Jacky Durand (1992 Flanders), Dirk Demol (1988 Roubaix) or Marc Gomez (1982 Sanremo) as an escapee who was never brought back, or sit in the pack and there's the chance of upsetting the odds with a winning sprint as Frédéric Guesdon (1997 Roubaix) and Gerald Ciolek (2013 Sanremo) did.

José De Cauwer reveals he used to use this possibility of a dream becoming a reality as a means of motivating his riders. 'Every winter I'd ask all of them which one race they would like to win the next season. I felt it was important for every rider to aim for a victory, even if they didn't get one, because winning is fundamental to being a racer, or at least the prospect of it is. It's so important to have the feeling, "I am still a bike rider",' he says, adding that the Classics offer an especially potent attraction because they're one-offs.

'So Demol came to my room and I asked him what race did he dream of winning the following season … Paris–Roubaix! I didn't say anything for a few minutes. In the end, I said to him, "You realise there's no guarantee that you will start." He said he did. "I realise that, but it's my dream, and you asked what my dream is", he told me.'

Demol, runner-up to Stephen Roche in the 1980 amateur edition of Roubaix, did manage to earn selection, and then surprised De Cauwer again by asking for a protected role along with team leader Eddy Planckaert, who had won Flanders the previous weekend. 'I was really taken aback. Work for Dirk Demol? I said to him, "How will the race pan out if you're going to win Roubaix?" He shrugged. "To win this race you've got to be in the main break. When you get in the breakaway you can tell the others that you can't ride on the front because Eddy Planckaert won the Tour of Flanders last weekend and he is my leader. I can't work because I've got to wait for him when he comes across later in the race." That was his chance, and it was a very small one,' explains De Cauwer, who told Demol and teammate Luc Colijn that one of them needed to be in any break of more than seven riders.

When the race got under way, two breaks went without Demol featuring in either of them, leaving De Cauwer bewildered and angry. 'Then it happened a third time, so I asked the *commissaire* if I could go up and talk to my rider. I went up alongside the peloton, which was riding at thirty to thirty-five kilometres per hour, and I could see Dirk was still weighing up what to do, knowing that it would take a big effort to get across to the break. I went up to him and said, "If you don't go now, I'll run you over with the car. Get going!" I dropped back, and five minutes later I heard, "*Quinze coureurs échappés.*"

Dirk Demol was one of them. Now he was in the right place to help his leader, but also to help himself.'

De Cauwer had told Demol and Colijn that if they did get into the right breakaway then they had to ration their resources in case that moment arrived when the favourites, including Planckaert, came back up to them. 'So I always took my pulls, but I made them short and saved myself as much as I could,' Demol recalls. 'With somewhere around forty kilometres to go, there were still five of us at the front and cars were going past us taking journalists to the finish. One of them slowed down. It was Roger De Vlaeminck, "Mr Paris–Roubaix" who had won the race four times and was driving with some journalists from *Sports 80* magazine. He shouted across, "Hey, Dirk. The gap's still three minutes. You're going to stay away. They're all dead back there. They've killed each other off. This is the chance of your life." And off he went. I thought, "This is insane."'

Demol has two regrets about that day. The first is that his victory came in one of the years when the race finished outside the Roubaix headquarters of race sponsor La Redoute and not on the illustrious velodrome. The second is that a handful of kilometres from the line, his final breakaway companion, Thomas Wegmüller, got a plastic bag caught in his derailleur, although Demol insists the battle to tug the bag free didn't affect the final result.

'They called Thomas "The Terminator" because he just rode really hard. He never used to think. If you were on his wheel, he didn't care. The funny thing is that he did the same thing four years later with Jacky Durand at Flanders. He was strong that day too, but did too much work before the finish,' says Demol, who adds: 'Just recently I went to a cancer benefit in Belgium with quite a few current and former riders, and they showed some highlights from our careers, and during mine they showed this interview of me that day that I'd never seen. The interviewer asked me about Wegmüller looking so strong, and I said to him, "Yes, he was strong, but I was the smartest and I won, and there's nothing wrong with that." That can happen in the Classics. That's why we all love them so much.'

CHAPTER 17

CONDUCTING THE CHAOS – *DIRECTEURS SPORTIFS* AND ROAD CAPTAINS

A good horse is not a good jockey.

– Co Adriaanse

This was Dutch football manager Co Adriaanse's take when the Netherlands' legendary striker Marco van Basten moved into team management at the end of his playing career. To apply a cycling spin to it, great riders don't necessarily make waves as sporting directors. José De Cauwer chuckles when I put this to him. 'I think that's a hundred per cent correct,' says the Belgian who guided Greg LeMond to the Tour de France title in 1989 and Tom Boonen to the world title in 2005.

'When a champion becomes a director and tells a rider, "You've got to do this, you've got to do that", they assume that what they are asking is normal, that any rider can do it. But what they're asking might not be at all possible for the rider concerned. I remember being at the Tour of Austria with a team managed by Lucien Van Impe and he had his riders' bikes fitted with a twenty-five rear sprocket in order to tackle the Kitzbüheler Horn. He said, "That's more than enough." Everybody in the peloton was saying that it wasn't possible to climb that mountain with a twenty-five, but Van Impe only weighed fifty kilos and he could manage it fine. His problem was that none of his team could. What seems normal for a great champion is often not normal for a normal rider.'

De Cauwer's compatriot Dirk Demol, who has directed many of the best riders over the last two decades, including Fabian Cancellara and Alberto Contador, has a similar story. 'I think if you were a good rider, you can't be a good DS. You have to be able to understand what suffering on the bike is all about, what it takes to work for a leader, every aspect of racing. I know how it feels for a rider to do everything he can to be good, but ends up going nowhere,' says Demol, who was good enough to win Paris–Roubaix but spent most of his years working for others and was doing so even that day he triumphed in the cobbled Classic. 'A top rider can't understand that. They can't understand how it is possible that a rider gets dropped in a certain situation, when it would never have happened to them. I remember I worked with Roger De Vlaeminck when he was a DS and he couldn't handle the fact that our riders were in trouble.'

Much like Cyrille Guimard, José De Cauwer realised very quickly that his ability to analyse what other riders were likely to do far surpassed the extent of his ability in any other aspect of racing. 'Once I'd been racing for a couple of years, my directors started to come to me to ask what I thought would happen the next day,' De Cauwer recounts. 'They realised I could see what was likely to happen and who was strong. It was often little things, like seeing a rider stop for a pee when I was struggling to stay in the bunch and then seeing him come back with no problem at all. I'd say, "Keep an eye on that guy because he's looking really good."

'You might be working your way back up through the convoy of cars towards the back of the peloton, moving from behind one car to the next, trying to get some shelter and save some energy, and you notice a guy riding two metres away from the cars and making his way up with no problem. There are lots of little things like this that can tell you which riders are in good shape and need to be watched – a rider going up a climb in what seems a ridiculously big gear but making easy work of it. You need to have a feeling for these little things in order to spot them. You can't simply say to a rider to look for something like that if they don't have the feel for it. It's quite possibly innate.'

Speaking to the likes of De Cauwer and Demol, it's very apparent that the ideal place to start analysing the qualities required to become a sporting director is by examining the role of the road captain. Essentially, their job is to be the sporting director's eyes and ears in the bunch, making sure orders are carried out, leading by example, making tactical decisions when the DS is not able to do so, and reporting back to them in the post-race debrief. Often, the road captain will also be responsible for tactical negotiation with other teams, reaching agreements to share the workload when, for instance, setting the pace on the bunch or chasing a break. Underpinning all of this, it is vital that the road captain has the respect of their teammates, both as a personality and as a decision-maker, that they appreciate their captain is very capable of reading a race and making the right decisions.

The role demands experience, and David Millar is one rider who switched into it in the latter part of his career. In *The Racer*, his account of his final season in the pro peloton, which he spent as road captain for Garmin, the Scot offers his take on the job, explaining, 'I have such a depth of knowledge that I can read races better than anyone in the team and have never been afraid to make decisions and call the shots on the road. More importantly, at this point, I am still strong enough to be at the front of the race in key moments when the most important decisions have to be made ... It's always good to have a leader whom you can count upon to get the result and a captain to manage plan A and create plan B if necessary. Those decisions have to be made on the bike rather than from the following car because, more often than not, they unfold at key moments in the race, to the degree that the *directeur sportif* in the following car is unaware of what's happening.'

There is also, Millar reveals, a motivational aspect to the role, which includes giving teammates jobs to do in order to maintain their focus. 'Simply being sent back for bottles can sometimes give a new lease of life, but more often than not riding on the front is the best solution because, psychologically, it's ten times better being at the front of the peloton – riding in the wind, controlling the effort and dishing out the suffering – than being back in the wheels feeling like you're being pummelled by everybody else, while listening to your internal monologue telling you repeatedly how much you suck and how it's just a matter of time before you're dropped like a stone,' he says.

Dutchman Koen de Kort, who has spent almost the entirety of his career working for others, notably Marcel Kittel and Alberto Contador, agrees with Millar's take, stressing that the role is very much about taking decisions quickly. 'We start with a plan but there are things that need to be done on the spot and it's usually down to the road captain to make that decision. I don't necessarily make the right decision, but it's better to take the wrong decision than no decision at all,' de Kort admits.

'In that sense, I always try to understand what's going on in the race, to view things with the performance of the rider who's our clear leader in mind. In Alberto Contador's case, that would mean organising basic things like keeping him out of the wind, making sure that we're all together at key points, such as on the approach to a climb. There might be another train coming around us and you have to decide whether you should pull back and come around them, or do you push on and hold the position you've got on the road. It's the kind of stuff that you can't see from the car. You've got to make those decisions from the bike.

'It's not a computer game, and often the sporting directors can't even see what's going on,' de Kort continues. 'They can see a lot less in the car than people watching the race at home and are almost guessing most of the time. Even I don't know precisely what's going on as I can only see what's happening right in front of me. It's probably quite different to what most people would expect, in terms of what we're being told on the radio. Most of what we're getting is information, and is not about tactics. They're telling us where there's going to be some wind and its direction, when a climb is coming up, when there's a roundabout, when there's an important point on the *parcours*. But, from a tactical perspective, the sporting directors can't decide all that much.'

Given the responsibility that road captains carry, it is no surprise that many make the switch to the role of sporting director. Rachel Heal says she fell into both positions without expecting to, but admits it was perhaps inevitable that she made the transition from team leader to road captain and then to DS. 'During my last couple of years, tactics weren't the problem, it was having the strength to carry them out. I knew how to attack, how to win a race, but I just didn't have the legs to be able to,' says Heal, who, at the 2014 edition of Milan–Sanremo became the first woman to direct a men's team in a WorldTour race. 'Perhaps as a result of having that experience and knowledge, you can instruct a teammate because you know what either you should be doing or somebody else on your team should be doing.'

Heal thrived in the role, which she found much easier than being the protected rider. 'I think that's because you're asking your teammates, "I need you to help me do this so that such and such a rider can win", rather than, "I need you to do this to help me win." It's easier to motivate other people when you're asking them to join you in the effort you're making. You're presenting that idea of you all being in it together, rather than simply trying to get someone to do something just to suit your own objectives.'

Heal's move into the director's seat came, she says, partly at the suggestion of British compatriot Emma Pooley. 'I was guest riding on a team with her and ended up helping some of the other girls with tactics. Emma made an off-the-cuff comment along the lines of, "You know, you'd really make a good director one day", and the idea stuck with me. A couple of years later, the Colavita team I was on was going to lose its director and I was getting older and slower and ready to retire from racing. Having already been in the real world, as it were, I knew I didn't want to go straight back into a nine-to-five job, so the idea of staying in the sport but not racing any more was appealing. It seemed like a relatively natural progression.'

While not all sporting directors have stepped into that role after getting a grounding in race strategy and tactics in the road captain's role, even those who haven't need to develop a deep understanding of these aspects of racing and, just as vitally, an insight into how to encourage, motivate and instruct their teammates. Nicolas Portal, the sporting director at Sky, explains he learned this from watching and listening to the experienced riders when he was racing as a pro. He suggests, indeed, that as a rider who came to the road from mountain biking, he had to listen or he would never have been able to adapt to the change in mindset that the switch requires.

'I didn't really like the road initially, the fact that you had to shave your legs and all that stuff. I found it a little bit boring, riding on a bike with tiny tyres and nothing happening for three or four hours, and where the downhills are pretty short,' the Frenchman confesses. 'The first time I raced I didn't know anything about tactics and I attacked on every climb and descent. On the flat, I wasn't in the wheels and in crosswinds I really suffered. I was surprised that I didn't win because I'd gone in thinking I was one of the best. Not only did I finish totally empty, but I was much more tired than if I'd done a mountain bike race.'

Portal picked up quickly on the fact that if he rode smartly he could win. As a mountain biker, he had needed to focus on being really good technically, particularly on descents, but he realised other tactics were more important on the road and, by grasping them, he could beat riders who were stronger than him. 'That's what really appealed to me about road racing, the fact that you can use your head to beat someone who is better than you,' he says.

Portal's mentors during his four seasons at Ag2r were, in one-day races, Estonian sprinter Jaan Kirsipuu and French stalwart Christophe Capelle, and, in stage races, Frenchmen Laurent Brochard and Stéphane Goubert. 'I would always watch how they rode and I was very vocal in the race, although not over the microphone. I loved talking with them and trying to understand what was happening around me,' he says. 'Jaan Kirsipuu, for instance, who won about a hundred and twenty races, didn't always win in a sprint. Sometimes he'd attacked with 20k to go, or fifty, or five. He was always trying to figure out whether he needed to wait for a sprint, or if he could move with a few other guys and beat them. He knew, though, that if he attacked with 15k to go and the bunch got back up to him that he would have no chance because he'd be too tired, but he'd make that decision quickly and once he'd done so he wouldn't be concerned about it. He would just focus on trying to win, and only if he didn't win would he then look back and consider why.

'I could relate to that from my time in mountain biking, when you're thinking, "Should I attack on the descent? On the climb?" You reach your decision and go. And I still think like that now at times, making a split decision but always having a plan B in the back of my mind. You've got to be confident in yourself. The simple philosophy is, "If we lose, we go down with all guns blazing."'

He highlights Brochard as a particularly strong influence, acknowledging that he didn't know what to expect of the 1997 world champion who rode for Festina and was tossed out of the 1998 Tour and banned for doping. 'I expected him to fit some kind of stereotype, that he was an ex-doper, blah, blah, blah ... But I don't like to pre-judge people and I thought I should make an effort to talk to him, to find out some more about him and we got on well, we became good friends and I ended up being his roommate all the time, at the Tour de France and all the big races, and I learned so much from him,' Portal recalls. 'He taught me about keeping calm in races, because when I was with Ag2r I liked the strategy but I also liked to have a bit of freedom, that impulsive side that comes from mountain biking. I could see that Laurent was calm even when he was in difficult situations. When a member of the public was having a go at him for what he'd done, he would always listen politely to what they had to say, and accept it. As a bike rider, he was just as calm, but also super smart. I know he was clean and he was, for me, an example. I wanted to be like him, to be in difficult situations in races and finding the right solution to them, not freezing because I was panicking about what was best to do.'

Over the last two decades, the role of the sporting director has changed, and as a result so have the qualities required for the job. From the mid-1970s, the descriptions team manager and *directeur sportif* were interchangeable. Team bosses such as Cyrille Guimard, Peter Post and, later, Jan Raas, José Miguel Echavarri and Manolo Saiz combined both tasks, running the administrative side of the team as well as directing its strategy on the road. Managers kept a close eye on every part of their riders' lives, setting their training programmes, checking their diet, pushing for results. They insisted the riders on their roster race and behave in a certain way. Often great motivators and, in some cases, equally talented as innovators, most had a reputation for inflexibility. ONCE boss Pablo Antón, whose company backed Spanish team boss Saiz for fifteen seasons, could have been describing any one of many directors from the 1980s and 1990s when he said of Saiz, 'He plans absolutely everything for each of his riders. But sometimes he could be more sensitive to people's feelings.' When ONCE's star rider, Laurent Jalabert, left the team at the end of 2000, he confessed, 'With Saiz I felt tense the whole time.'

Since the mid-2000s, the one-man-band team model has all but disappeared, as the business, financial and sponsorship aspects of management have become increasingly specialised and vital to survival. Coaching has become ever more specific too and teams have invested heavily in this, and, as a consequence the sporting director's role has been much more focused on strategy within individual races and across the season.

'It's tricky working out a strategy, but it's one of the roles that I love most about the job, partly because it changes so much,' Matt White says of the main focus of his position at the Mitchelton-backed GreenEdge team. 'You need a very different mindset for a one-day race than for a three-week race, and within that it's different again if you're focusing on GC or on the sprints. One key is getting to know your rivals well, getting to know how different directors work, how different teams work. That takes a little bit of time and I'll readily admit that the first couple of years were a bit of a shock for me, going straight from being a rider to being a director in January and taking a team to the Giro and the Tour that season. It certainly accelerated my development.'

White, lauded by David Millar as one of the few sporting directors who has remained empathetic to the lot of the racer, explains that a significant part of his job involves reconnaissance of race routes and planning how his team will tackle them. He admits that he picked up a lot of his knowledge in this area when he was riding under Johan Bruyneel at US Postal.

'That was a bad era and a lot of people will deride me for saying this, but Bruyneel was brilliant when it came to tactics, and one of the areas where he stood out was in recons and knowing the courses,' says White. 'Every team does it now, but I think that was something that teams didn't do much of back then. It's pretty simple stuff, but it makes a difference. Back then, we were all racing a hundred-plus days a year and there was no time for recons, resources were always stretched. US Postal were just about the first team to spend a lot of time doing recons like that, which was why they caught a lot of teams out.'

Picking out an instance when this kind of legwork worked for him and his team, White recalls the third stage of the 2013 Tour, when the race started in Corsica. 'I'd been out there earlier in the year with another DS to check out the route and we'd decided that one stage into Calvi suited our characteristics. We had a guy in the break in Simon Clarke, and we had the guys really well prepped for the sprint, which was a bit of an awkward one, and I don't think many people had looked at it because Calvi was quite a hard place to get to.

'Daryl Impey and Michael Albasini did a great job of controlling the sprint in the last 5k. Impey did an incredible lead-out for Simon Gerrans, and Simon timed his sprint perfectly and managed to hold off Peter Sagan. The work that went into that stage started four months before when we first saw the course. Moments like those when you identify a target and the team manages to achieve it, especially at a race like the Tour, give you a fabulous feeling.'

And the flip side? 'The worst moments are when you think your riders can do something that they can't, and it backfires on you,' White continues. 'You lose time when you can't, or you put the team under undue pressure and it doesn't work. You try to avoid those moments as much as possible. I've got selective memory, so I can't remember any of those!'

White and Sky's Nicolas Portal typify the new breed of sporting director, decent riders blessed with extremely quick-thinking and insightful tactical minds. Yet, while White always looked likely to make the move from saddle to team car driving seat, the Frenchman hadn't considered it until he received a surprising offer from Sky boss Dave Brailsford. Effervescent and very engaging, Portal laughs when he thinks back to that moment. 'There was no way I ever thought I'd become a sports director and I'm sure that anyone else who knew me would have said, "Nicolas Portal, a sports director? No way, that's a big mistake."'

For a start, says the Frenchman, he was only thirty-one when he moved into the role. 'I was the same age as most of the riders on the team and, because I didn't need to be a road captain when I joined Sky, I felt pretty free. I'd had some experience at Caisse d'Epargne as the road captain, and I was quite prepared to move into that role with Sky if they'd wanted me to. But Dave asking me to become a sports director was something I wasn't expecting at all. Initially I said, "No, it's not for me. I don't want to do it at all." But then Dave explained a bit more, and I'll admit that I'd already been very impressed by the directors at Sky.'

Brailsford acknowledges it did seem to be one of his more left-field ideas when it came to him, developing over the course of the 2010 season, Sky's first in the pro peloton. 'He's got a great way of handling people. He's very good at relationships, very personable and, obviously, he knew racing. It just seemed to me that he'd got the ingredients to be able to develop with us,' says Brailsford. 'We had Sean Yates, who was absolutely fantastic, but there weren't too many other people who didn't come with very set ideas, and what I was interested in was getting a younger group together to see whether they could all develop together. Because he came originally from mountain biking, he had a very open mind, and he really invests time with each rider as well as with the group.'

Brailsford had sounded out the mechanics, *soigneurs*, the other riders and even the media, and all had confirmed his impression that Portal had a rare gift for communication, for being sociable. He told Portal that this was the quality he needed above any other in order to manage people. 'You've got it,' Brailsford kept insisting.

Crucial, though, was Portal's general demeanour when put under pressure. 'He's calm, doesn't panic, he's not a screamer and shouter, and that aspect of him has grown over the last few years,' he continues. 'He's such a key part of what we do. He knows when it's right for the riders to go all in and when to hold them back. He's got a really good feel for what's going on in a race, for reading the situation. It's chaotic most of the time, they haven't got full information on what's happening, but he feels it very much like the riders do. His decision-making is so good. That's not taught, it's there and gets better as he gets more confident.'

Sky's performance manager Rod Ellingworth offers an example of the Frenchman's unflappability. 'I was in the car on that day at the 2017 Tour into Le Puy-en-Velay when Chris [Froome] had to stop to swap his wheel right at the bottom of the final climb just as the speed in the bunch had rocketed and it was really impressive to see how Nico kept everyone cool. Froomey just laid it down and waited pretty calmly,' he recounts. 'All of the time, Nico was telling him what the gaps are, all of the riders knew exactly where Chris was and what was happening, and that's all down to the DS. If he's shouting and bawling into the radio, it just doesn't work.'

Portal admits to all manner of reservations about taking up the role. He didn't speak much English and, more than anything, didn't see himself as being the right fit for a management position at a team with such a sharp corporate image. In Yates, though, he saw both a kindred spirit and an example of how to do the job in his own way. 'Sean changed my perspective on the job of a sports director. He had tattoos, he still loved riding his bike, he was cool, he talked in French slang, he didn't wear a shirt and tie. He didn't represent at all the idea of a sports director being all of the things I hated. He was like a surfer or a skateboarder. He didn't look like an ex-roadie and that was exactly why I liked him.

'I thought about it for three weeks. Initially I was sceptical, but as I thought more about Sean and what Dave had said I decided, "Actually it would be cool to do something different." In the end I said, "OK, let's do it." I felt I could help the group and would be able to contribute to the team's success.'

Portal, who counts mountain bike legends Ned Overend, John Tomac and Rune Høydahl as his sporting heroes, believes his calmness stems largely from his background in the MTB world. 'The riders tend to be quite calm, but it's a calm that's hiding what's going on inside, all the constant thinking. There are so many things to consider when you're racing mountain bikes that you need to be calm, otherwise you'd burn up all of your nervous energy before you'd started. That starts the week before when you're thinking about the weather and your choice of tyres, the pressure in the tyres, the oil level in your forks, the type of circuit you're racing and how well it will suit you. If it does suit you, you consider who your rivals will be. You have to learn how to deal with all that, how to control that stress, so that you're completely ready to go when the race starts.'

Having called a premature end to his racing career, Portal spent 2011 and 2012 as an assistant sporting director, as Yates's apprentice. 'During races, he'd talk to me on the radio and ask, "Nico, what would you do now?" I'd tell him, "I think I'd do this and that, then this ..." and he'd respond in that laidback way of his, "Nah, you'd do this ..." I began to learn from that and he could see that I was improving, and after six months the relationship changed. I'd be asking him what we should do, and he'd ask me what I thought. I'd lay out my plan and he'd listen and say, "Goood jooobbbb, Niiicoooo."

'Sometimes when I was talking to him my stress levels were really high, but he'd tell me that everyone was looking at me to take a decision, that was my job. He explained that if I spoke on the radio and I wasn't sure of what I was planning to do, the riders would quickly pick up on that in my voice, and that would stress them and wouldn't be good for the atmosphere in the group. He told me that whenever I gave an instruction that I should ensure the riders had confidence in what I was telling them, even if I wasn't sure it was the right thing to do.'

With twenty-odd teams racing each other for supremacy on the day and, at the same time, over a week or even three, every sporting director is bound to make mistakes, even if they do have the best riders in their colours. Portal admits he has made plenty, that this is part of a learning process that never ends. It's vital, says the Frenchman, that if it becomes clear that you've made a mistake, you have to be honest about it with the riders. 'You've got to underline that both you and they have learned a lesson and that you'll be ready the next time you're in that situation. You don't want the riders to be frustrated and for the DS to feel the same way as well,' he says.

'The key thing when you're making a fifty-fifty decision is to be aware of the fact that sometimes it is going to go wrong, and that will be the same for everybody because no one gets every decision right all the time. When mistakes happen, Sean told me you have to say, "Sorry, guys, I got that decision wrong, but I had to go one way or the other at the time." He told me that if they're smart, they'll say, "Hey, Nico, no worries, because we know what a difficult job you've got to do. We could have made the same mistake too and next time we will all be better prepared for it." Then they will be confident in you, and that's what you want, that confidence, as well as an understanding about who's making the decisions. If it's not the road captain, then it will be you, and when you do have to do it make sure it's with real confidence even if you're not completely sure.'

Whether racing or directing, accumulating this knowledge is vital for achieving success when competing in 'chess at 150 heartbeats a minute', or bluffing poker-style about the cards that you hold or the strategy you are planning. 'There are so many things going on at once. It's a battle within a battle sometimes,' says British climber Simon

Yates. 'Some days you're wondering what's going on with the sprinters – Why's this guy riding? Why's this guy trying to get away? It's not just about the GC, even if your focus is the GC. It's about everything that's going on in the race. You have to be aware of all of it, wise to all of it.' Matt White agrees that the poker and chess analogies are very fitting. 'But what happens is that some people are playing chess and some are playing poker on the same day,' says the Australian DS.

Always a good talker, Portal becomes even more enthused when considering this assessment of road racing. 'I really like the idea of using chess as a way of describing racing, no matter whether it's Froomey I'm talking to or anyone else. In chess, you know you've got strong pieces and good tactics, and based on that you know you can beat your opponent. At Sky we've certainly got some strong riders. I do look at other teams, though, and think that they've got some really strong riders, but they're playing poker. When you play poker, you can lose everything on a single hunch.

'I prefer to play chess. It may not be so cool, but I prefer to play this way because I want to make sure that the likes of Sergio Henao, Geraint Thomas, Vasil Kiryienka or Christian Knees – who spend six months getting ready for the Tour de France and will spend so much time away from their families, who will work so hard, who'll crash and fight their way back – don't get wasted in a game of poker. I prefer to play chess, so that when I get them to move and expend their energy, there is some thought behind that, a tactical plan. If they get tired, then I'll move to plan B. I don't want to play poker with them and risk the strategic plan for the whole team. That would only frustrate them and me. Instead, I tell the guys to focus on our plan, that if they stick to it and achieve what we're aiming for then we're going to be in a good place at the end of the day.'

Portal gives the example of Sky riding on the front of the bunch day after day at the Tour to support what he is saying. 'Taking control like that is better than saying to them, "I know no one is going to ride with us today, so we're not going to ride and control the race", because that's playing poker. I would perhaps do it if we had a team that wasn't so strong and we didn't want to ride with the others just sitting in behind us. But that's a different scenario.'

The Frenchman pulls out an example from his racing career with the Caisse d'Epargne team of having to do exactly this because they weren't strong enough to take control of the bunch for extended periods. 'Even though we had Valverde as our leader, we had to be a little bit riskier in our approach, to play a little poker, thinking, "OK, we've got Valverde, but if we ride for him now then we're probably not going to be able to support him at the end and he's going to end up isolated and there'll be no chance that he can win. So, don't control the bunch, let the other strong teams take control, and then at the end we can help him." At Sky we don't have to do that and it would be a shame to do so, because we're happy carrying out the role we've taken on because it's part of a winning strategy.'

Portal's ready for the obvious next question even before it can be asked. 'People always say that it must be easy to play the way we do, with nine guys who are so supremely talented, but I don't really agree because even though you've got a strong team at the start of a race, you've got twenty-one other teams riding against you and you know full well that you're not going to get any help from them. That's completely normal. As a DS in that situation, you're really under pressure, all of the other teams are trying to outwit you, and the guys are expecting a lot from you. You're in the car trying to understand what's happening up ahead in the bunch, which is pretty demanding. But when it works well I get the same feeling I used to have on the bike when we achieved what we were aiming for, that same sensation of exhilaration mixed with relief because you've won the battle or the war. That's an amazing feeling.'

One particular Tour de France stage illustrates the importance of Portal's role and his ability in this position. It occurred during the 2013 race, where Froome had replaced Wiggins as Sky's leader and Portal had taken over from Yates as directeur sportif. *Portal describes how they survived it ...*

The Bagnères-de-Bigorre stage of the 2013 Tour is one of my clearest memories as a *directeur sportif*, in fact, it's probably the clearest. The build-up to that began at the Vuelta in 2012. Dave Brailsford told me, 'You're going to lead the team there and Froomey will also begin his transition to leading the team on the road. He was clearly super strong in the Tour. He helped Bradley a lot and now we're going to try to develop him as a leader. You're going to learn with him.' So I started with Chris at that race and then we continued into 2013, me working as the DS at the races where Froomey led the team.

The day before that Bagnères-de-Bigorre stage, Chris had won the stage at Ax 3 Domaines. The plan that day had been for the team to ride as hard as they could until that climb, and for Chris to try to gain as much time as he could. Even I couldn't believe how well it went for us. I was delighted, largely because whenever I said something on the radio that day, the guys did it. It was clear they believed in me, so if we fucked it up, it was clearly going to be my fault because the guys were so strong. Happily, Froomey won the stage, finishing almost a minute ahead of Richie Porte, a little over a minute up on Alejandro Valverde and one minute forty-five on Alberto Contador and Nairo Quintana. We absolutely smashed it.

The next day we had this tricky stage, with the Portet d'Aspet and the Menté at the beginning, then the Peyresourde, Val Louron and the Hourquette d'Ancizan one after another. We were hit by an accumulation of small setbacks. Pete Kennaugh crashed at the bottom of the first climb, we had some mechanical issues for some of the riders, some punctures, and, perhaps most crucially, Richie had a bad day and it began right at the start of the stage. Because the racing was full on right from the off as they went over the Portet d'Aspet, after forty kilometres there was no one with Froomey when they started up the Col de Menté. To add to our difficulties, we were in the Couserans area of the Ariège, which is pretty remote, and there was no TV coverage at all. Because we had no riders with Chris, it was hard for me to work out what the situation was, where all of our riders were, and give everyone instructions on what they should do. I did know there were a couple of groups behind Froomey, but we had no split times from Race Radio, so I didn't know how close Richie was to him. Chris was telling me that there were guys attacking, so I had to work out quickly what to do.

I knew Sean [Yates] was commentating on the race for TV, and luckily my phone was working. I tried to remain calm and thought the best thing to do was to get another perspective on the situation, so I called Sean. He actually didn't have much more information than me in terms of the time gaps. All he knew was that Quintana, Valverde and Contador were up at the front and he gave some other names. I thought for a few moments and then got on the radio to Froomey. I told him to follow the main GC contenders but not to go crazy. By the time I got up behind the group, I knew that the whole Movistar team were on the front working for Quintana and Valverde.

They did the Portet d'Aspet and then the Menté, and after that they had fifteen kilometres or so of valley road to reach Bagnères-de-Luchon and the foot of the Peyresourde. I told Froomey, 'The most dangerous place for you is that section on the flat. On the climbs, it's easy. If someone pushes, you push as well. If a guy is pushing four hundred watts, you're going to do four hundred watts as well. Everyone is equal on the climb. It's not a big deal. But on the flat, with no team around you, you're very vulnerable.'

I wanted to make the situation as simple as possible for him, so I told him, 'Froomey, it's very easy. You're changing colours. Your new team is Movistar. You just follow them and stick with Quintana and Valverde. Don't try to follow Dan Martin, or Contador or anyone else. Just follow those two guys. They've got numbers at the front and the situation is good for them because Richie has been dropped, so they're going to race to ensure he can't get back on so that they can take second place. If Contador attacks, they will use their numbers to catch him or anyone else who's a threat to them taking second place. But, at the same time, you cannot let Quintana or Valverde attack on the flat. If Movistar play that card and Quintana goes on the attack in the valley, there's no point in chasing because it's too hard. You're going to take too much out of yourself if you do that and they will attack you on the climb. If they do attack on the flat, you need to go straight away with them or not at all.'

I remember when I told Froomey that his new team was Movistar, Dave was in the car with me and he gave me a look as if to say, 'Fucking hell! What are you telling him?' I didn't have time to go into all the detail I'm laying out now. All I could basically tell Froomey was, 'Your new team is Movistar. I'll explain it all to you later. In the meantime, we'll see if Richie or some of the other guys can come back to you, but we'll be lucky if they do.' He was pretty surprised, to say the least.

Then I explained my thinking to Dave, and eventually when we got onto the Peyresourde I was able to tell Froomey a little bit more. On the flat, Valverde did try to attack, but Froomey was straight on his wheel, with Quintana right on his. I wasn't so concerned about Quintana getting clear because I didn't think he could stay away on his own on the flat. The key thing was, though, that Froomey was really strong and quick to follow my instructions.

We had another problem, though, as I explained to Dave. We now had no one to give Chris food or bottles. Our solution to that was to ask him to drift towards the back of the group on sections of the climb where we could get up alongside him and give him what he needed before Movistar fully realised what was going on. I stressed that it needed to be done very quickly, though, otherwise Movistar might notice that he was slightly out of position and attack. There was a feed zone in Luchon, so Chris picked up a *musette* there no problem, but after that we told him that if he needed anything else we would have to hand it to him on the climbs and definitely not on any flat roads where Movistar could attack.

I know the Peyresourde like the back of my hand and I knew that there was a good place halfway up the climb to hand over some food, so I told Froomey, 'Let's see how Movistar ride on the first half of the Peyresourde and then we'll decide. If they're happy setting a good tempo, we should be able to give you some food and bottles halfway up.' Coming to that point, I told him to drift back quite quickly and we'd hand him the food, stressing that the distance between him and Quintana and Valverde would only be twenty metres or so. It was so intense. Small things that you'd normally do in a race almost without thinking about it became a real challenge because he had no teammates. We had another issue too, as normally we'd stop the car somewhere so we could take a leak, and I told Dave and the mechanic that there was no chance of us doing that. If we'd stopped even for a minute and Chris had some kind of issue then we would have lost the Tour.

All this time I was doing everything I could to seem calm, even though underneath it all I felt anything but serene. I also had to give instructions to the guys behind. I told Richie that some of the other guys were in a group behind him and not to kill himself trying to get back up to the yellow jersey group, and especially not in the valley as it would take too much out of him. If he wanted to try he had to do it on the Peyresourde. Kiry and G [Geraint Thomas] were not so far behind and managed to catch Richie's group and helped him in the valley across the Peyresourde. Then Richie went hard on the Peyresourde. He did a really long pull and got back to within forty seconds or so of Froomey's group on the Col d'Azet. But he totally emptied himself. In the end I told him, 'Don't worry, Richie, no stress. We're going to deal with the situation. Now there's only one climb to go for Froomey, it's all about climbing so everything will be OK.'

When they got on the descent, there was a headwind, which helped Froomey, as it made it harder to attack. He just had to follow Quintana and Valverde. I felt that Movistar wouldn't want to play poker at that point, that they'd be satisfied with their day. Contador was probably the only one who might take some risks, but I was fairly certain that if he did Movistar would probably close him down. I figured that Movistar would stick to a chess strategy, feeling that they'd made some gains and might still benefit from Froomey having a bad day further into the race. That's effectively what Movistar did, and Froomey ended up finishing in the group that came in twenty seconds behind Dan Martin, who won the stage. It could have been an awful lot worse.

I was helped enormously by having a very strong rider in Froomey, but in that situation it's really easy to make the wrong decision because of the stress. I had Dave with me and he was good at keeping me calm, at letting me do what I thought was the best thing to do without trying to complicate the issue by suggesting that Froomey should wait for his teammates. Sometimes there are moments when you do need to wait for your team, but on occasions that's not going to work. You have to get your rider to stay where he is and explain that you're trying to find a way to get some support back up to him. I think we did exactly the right thing, and I learned a lot that day.

I should say 'chapeau' to Froomey as well because, even though I'm pretty much the same age as him and many of the other riders on the team, he believed in me and that helped me gain even more confidence within the group. I didn't have a history behind me like Sean, of being a DS with Contador, with Armstrong. I'd just done the first half of that season in the lead role. I guess you'd call it a baptism of fire. It was one of those days when you cross the line and everybody's happy, even the guys in the *gruppetto*. We realised we had a good group and also that we'd all done the right thing in the most testing of circumstances. That day was a shock, but it made us stronger.

Personally, I felt like I wasn't fully confident in what I was doing prior to that day, but that stage really boosted me, it gave me such self-belief, which is hard to gain when you're in a totally new situation. It gave me a bit more maturity too, and every year that process has continued, I get calmer, more experienced. If there's one day when I felt that I really helped my leader, that was it.

CHAPTER 18

A TACTICAL SHOWCASE – THE RISE OF WOMEN'S CYCLING

I hope I'm not alone in thinking the Pro Women's race in #Bergen2017 was the most exciting of the whole week. Perfect way to showcase.

– *@MarkCavendish*

Finally, let's turn to women's racing. Rather than being an afterthought, the positioning of this chapter is deliberate – designed to encourage a focus on races where the full range of tactics is most often and clearly on display at a professional level, where the action tends towards unpredictable rather than controlled, where, as Mark Cavendish suggested in his tweet during the 2017 World Championships, there is often plenty to excite.

Before the why, the how. Few are better placed to assess this than Rachel Heal. 'I think men's racing is a little more predictable in terms of how the races will unfold. You can say at the beginning of the race, "You, you and you look to get in the early break", because you know that, perhaps not on every stage, but on a lot of them, there will be an early break, and depending on the type of stage, the sprinters' teams or the GC teams will chase it down. You can predict far more easily what will happen, but that's not so easy to do in women's racing. There are more possibilities that can play out.

'Sometimes you have that style of race, where a break goes and it gets brought back, but sometimes the break has a selection of the stronger riders so sometimes it doesn't come back. It's a little more difficult to work out how a women's race is going to unfold and that makes it tougher as a director to work out who on your team you should be telling to get into the break if they can. When you can pretty much guarantee that the break's going to come back, you can simply tell your riders who aren't going to be in the mix at the finish to join it. But if you don't know, then you're thinking, "Do I risk one of my top riders?" It's much harder to know which cards to play when.'

With that Mark Cavendish Tweet in mind, Heal offers the example of the 2017 Worlds to support her argument. 'If you'd asked people to predict the winners of the men's and women's races at the Worlds, I'd suspect a lot would have gone for Peter Sagan as the men's winner but very few would have gone for Chantal Blaak as the women's winner. You'd probably have had a lot going for a Dutch rider, but not necessarily her.'

When it comes to the why, the fundamental reason is the lack of investment and resources in women's racing, resulting in smaller teams and fewer opportunities for talent to emerge and to be nurtured in the right way when it does. 'There are perhaps twenty to twenty-five girls, maybe a few more, who are right at the top level, whereas in the men's peloton there are a lot, lot more,' says Ellen van Dijk, the world time-trial champion in 2013 and winner of the Tour of Flanders a year later. 'There's not the same depth in women's racing, so races can be harder to control. As a consequence, many of the girls want to race, they want to attack. There's more variation than in the men's races, more surprises, which can make it very exciting.'

Australian pro Tiffany Cromwell agrees with van Dijk's assessment. 'There isn't the same control imposed on the peloton. Sometimes it can be a bit frustrating because there are so many attacks, there's almost no sense to the racing. But that does show that more riders are willing to have a go, that the races aren't as selective, that there's more opportunity,' she says.

Traditionally, racing has tended to be dominated by a few very outstanding athletes, including, over the last decade or so, Britain's 2008 Olympic champion Nicole Cooke and her successor at the 2012 London Games, Marianne Vos, of the Netherlands. Both had a Merckx-like hold over their rivals, Vos equally capable of dominating in the mountains, Classics and time trials, as well as in cyclo-cross and track racing, while Cooke had almost peerless will power.

'I always thought that physically and athletically, pure strength wasn't her biggest asset. I think her head was her biggest strength,' Heal says of Cooke, with whom she raced as both teammate and rival. 'She was good tactically, but even better in terms of her determination. She didn't ride away from people because she was stronger than them, she was just more determined to. She could push herself right to the absolute limit and her limit was way more than most people's. I think that was why she was so successful.'

The dominance of a relatively small cabal of riders, which also included German trio Judith Arndt, Ina-Yoko

Teutenberg and Petra Rossner, could produce what were effectively two-tier events. 'If a break went in with good riders in it and they opened up a gap of a minute then it would often be the end of the race,' recalls Jean-Paul van Poppel, who managed a women's team for eight seasons after the end of his pro career. 'In men's racing, a break can get a minute, five minutes, even ten, and anything could still happen, the break could still be brought back. But in women's racing that wouldn't happen if good riders went away and got a couple of minutes. More often than not, that would be it, done.'

The former sprinter adds that when races did conclude in a bunch finish, these often had a very distinctive aspect. 'Teams weren't that organised when it came to sprinting back then. There were some very fast German sprinters, but they didn't really depend on a lead-out. They were so much quicker that they could win without one. Petra Rossner, for instance, was so fast that there would be twenty metres between her and the second-placed rider at the finish. She was like Marcel Kittel is now. She didn't need any help to win.'

The consensus is, though, that the pool of talent has been getting deeper in recent seasons. Heal believes that there is a growing number of teams that are right up to the standard of the powerful Saturn and Highroad outfits that used to bag dozens of victories each season a decade or more ago. 'There are more teams that are able to race at that kind of level, more teams that work really well as a team when they need to,' says Heal. 'Before it was more a case of the strongest riders that would win and you might have one or two of them on each team. Now there are plenty of teams that are winning races through tactics rather than just strength.

'You can see that evening out at an individual level as well. There have been riders in recent years who've had incredibly good seasons or parts of seasons, but there isn't anybody now who stands out as unbeatable. There are more riders at the top level who can be competitive and can win races. It is more about who is on form than having one rider who is going to dominate for a season or years at a time.'

While teams have got stronger, the ongoing lack of investment in the women's side of racing means that they haven't got any bigger. Yet, from a tactical perspective this appears to benefit both teams and their riders. Unlike in men's racing where the rosters include up to thirty riders, making cohesiveness in relationships and tactics quite difficult to obtain, the bond and level of understanding is stronger. 'I think women's teams are more solid from that point of view,' says Tiffany Cromwell. 'On a men's team you might see a teammate at a training camp at the start of the season and not see them again until a camp at the other end of the season. Because we're racing together more often, we do know more precisely what everyone's capable of.'

Smaller teams also mean that riders have to be adaptable. Nairo Quintana or Dan Martin, for example, would never consider riding the northern Classics, whereas every big-hitter in the women's peloton would make them a priority, alongside the season's major stage races. 'We have to have a skillset that means we can adapt to any kind of race, because we don't have the luxury due to numbers of being able to focus on a certain kind of event like the men do,' Cromwell explains. 'Men's teams have riders who are aimed at more specific targets, the Classics, the Grand Tours. A rider with a small build like me who's basically a climber would rarely ride the

Classics, for instance, but I've had to adapt, to get stronger, so that I can not only ride races like that but also contribute to my team's effort.'

With this comes another benefit, and one that the organisers of most men's races wish they could replicate – the best racers face each other many times during the season and not just at one or two of the very biggest races. 'You see them challenging each other right through the year. They're racing on the flat and in the crosswinds in Qatar at the start of the year, on the cobbles and in the hills in the spring, and on the hills over the rest of the season beyond that. We don't need to specialise in the same way that many men do in order to be successful,' says Ellen van Dijk. 'But the flip side of that you do need to be in good shape for the whole season. It's harder to periodise your year in that way. You can't say I'm just going to focus on the Giro Rosa, a bit like Chris Froome peaking for the Tour de France. You've got to commit yourself throughout the year. Everyone in women's cycling has to commit in that way and no doubt that also helps to keep things equal.'

The 2017 edition of the Tour of Flanders highlighted many of the qualities that make women's racing so captivating as a spectacle, but also underlined why it continues to struggle to gain an audience. Run on the same day as the men's event and covering much of the same course with the finish also in Oudenaarde, it is regarded as the biggest race of the season alongside the World Championships, attracts the best start list all year and huge roadside crowds. Yet few fans who weren't in Flanders would have been aware of that as live coverage was only available over the internet.

The Sunweb team's six-rider line-up featured both 2014 Flanders winner Ellen van Dijk and American sprinter Coryn Rivera. Having done a full recon as a team the week before the race, sporting director Hans Timmermann drew up a strategy in which Lucinda Brand and van Dijk would try to get in the move that was likely to come towards the end of the race and feature the strongest performers on the day, with Rivera as the fall-back option if a large group came to the finish together.

With just half a dozen riders per team, marking and controlling rivals is of fundamental importance. As a result, for the first ninety-odd kilometres, until the peloton reached the Muur at Geraardsbergen, every one of the many breakaway attempts was rapidly closed down. On the Muur, around fifty riders split away off the front, and soon after Sunweb's Rozanne Slik clipped away on her own, enabling her teammates to sit in for the next twenty kilometres until the climb of the Kanarieberg.

'Unfortunately, Rozanne got caught on the climb, so we couldn't use her for the rest of the race,' Rivera says, highlighting Heal's point about the ever-present difficulty of knowing when and where to commit racing resources. 'After that, the race really unfolded. Ellen was in some moves but they came back, and Lucinda tried a couple of times to get in a move, but couldn't quite get away. The moves that we didn't manage to get into we tried to pull back.'

Van Dijk's victorious solo break in 2014 began on the Kruisberg, with thirty kilometres remaining, and she knew that this was likely to be a critical point once again. 'My form was really good, but perhaps just a little bit short of what it needed to be and I missed the key move,' she says. 'Four girls went, Anna van der Breggen, Kasia Niewiadoma, Elisa Longo

Borghini and Annemiek van Vleuten, and I was the fifth and just couldn't bridge up to those four. I end up isolated between them and the group and realised that the best thing to do was sit up and wait for the group to come back up to me so that we could switch our tactics. Our only chance then was with Coryn in the sprint and for that to work out we'd have to race full gas to get those four girls back.'

Realising her chance had also gone, Brand committed to what Rivera describes as 'a suicide pull' to get the chasing group as close as possible to the four leaders at the bottom of the Oude Kwaremont, before dropping away from the main action. 'My role was much more important now and that put more responsibility on me for actually staying up near the front,' Rivera explains. 'I got dropped on the Kwaremont, but I looked ahead and saw that Ellen still hadn't got across to the break, so I fought hard and made a big effort to get back into the group. Once we got over the Paterberg, where I got tailed off again, I managed to get back into the group and join Ellen. Then we made the decision to chase the lead group down and go for the sprint.'

Van Dijk, one of the world's best time triallists, confesses that she's not good at hiding her strength, that bluffing is an art she still has to master. 'People tell me that I should do it but I'm not a very good actor when it comes to hiding how strong or weak I am. I'm not really someone who's very good at playing games like that,' she says. 'I think sometimes my rivals do tend to take advantage of my strength, they let me ride full gas. At that point, though, all that mattered was giving absolutely everything that I had to try to bring the break back.'

Rivera tried to lend a hand, but van Dijk yelled at her to return to a place hidden in the pack behind the Dutchwoman.

'She told me to save energy for the sprint. I had to sit back in the wheels,' Rivera recounts. 'When there was about 5k to go and the gap was coming down, I was sitting there thinking, "It would be really cool to podium." I felt that would have been a good day. But there was some disruption in the breakaway and we caught them going under the one-kilometre banner.' The breakaway's collaborative rhythm ended when van der Breggen was ordered to stop working as her Boels-Dolmans team opted to implement its plan B and put its faith in its sprinter.

'When it came to it, I knew I couldn't count on Ellen for a lead-out after all the work she'd done, so I just had to go with my instincts in the sprint,' says Rivera. 'Once someone opened up the sprint, I just kept pushing and going for the line. The line was actually a bit further away than I hoped and perhaps I was a bit lucky that no one passed me. I couldn't quite believe it. When I woke up that morning I didn't think I'd be the one who would win it for the team.'

Rivera, a Californian who spent three seasons racing under Rachel Heal's direction at the UnitedHealthcare team prior to joining Sunweb in 2017, admits that she has had to make plenty of adjustments when racing almost full-time in Europe. 'It has taken time to get used to some aspects of it, particularly dealing with the wind on tight, narrow roads. I've improved a lot in that area this year thanks to the work that I've done with some of the Dutch girls. I've found myself being in the front echelon group much more often, although the Dutch girls are also savvy enough to be able to let you back into the echelon when you do miss it.'

Heal points out this kind of adjustment is common among American men as well. 'I feel that at times you're dealing with two different beasts when you're looking at racing in the US and Europe. The fields in the US tend to be a little bit smaller and the roads are wider, so the focus on good bike-handling and positioning skills isn't as immediately important as it is in Europe,' says Heal, who adds that the problem is often most acute among stronger riders.

'In the US you can move from the back to the field to the front quite quickly just by riding around the outside of everybody. But when you're on a Belgian goat track that's not possible. It's seven hundred metres from the back of the field to the front and there's no room to get past anybody. If you're on a super windy little road and you can get to the front and then get off the front, then there's only a limited number of people who can actually chase you, those in the front five or ten places because everyone behind is stuck. But if you're on a highway seventeen lanes wide, anyone in the field can chase. Adapting to that can take time.'

With UCI president David Lappartient promising a greater focus on women's racing, suggesting that he's prepared to invest the ruling body's own money by funding the organisation of races that would be televised with the objective of boosting sponsorship opportunities and, as a result, investment in teams, there is reason to believe that its profile will rise. The establishment in December 2017 of the Cyclists' Alliance is another reason for optimism. The brainchild of former pro Iris Slappendel, who became the women's representative at the UCI, this riders' union aims to tackle key issues such as the need for a minimum wage within the peloton, working conditions and team ethics. The long-term aim for both organisations is for a fully professional women's peloton. This will inevitably raise the depth of competition even more.

There are calls too for the Tour de France Féminin, last run in one of its several variations in 2009, to be reinstated and run in conjunction with the men's race, as is the case with Flanders, Flèche Wallonne, Amstel Gold, and a number of other one-day races. Tour organisers ASO have been tinkering with a format that might, eventually, lead to this, but hitherto their La Course by Le Tour has done little more than highlight their reluctance to move towards a twin-Tour solution.

Many believe, however, that broadening the competitive level by making the career of a pro racer more financially viable is more vital to the development of women's racing, Britain's 2015 world champion Lizzie Deignan among them. Sweden's two-time Olympic road race silver medallist Emma Johansson is another who insists the focus should be on building strong teams that will make bigger races more competitive and exciting to watch, rather than on bringing the Tour back to life, even as a ten- rather than a twenty-one-day race.

'You need a lot of contenders for the GC and the stages [for a race like that], but at the moment you don't have professionalism spread that wide in women's cycling. Instead of having twenty top riders in the women's peloton you need at least forty, and instead of having maybe four big teams you need at least eight,' says Johansson. 'There have been some steps taken in the last few years, but asking for another big tour adds pressure and there are very few teams that can handle that,' she adds.

Propitiously, new teams have been appearing while existing ones are attracting more financial backing, so Johansson's target of eight big teams is well within reach. There is already, though, good reason for those who relish racing packed with attacks and tactical ploys to devote more of their viewing time to women's races. While its financial aspect may resemble the men's side of the sport up to the mid-1980s, with many riders often turning out for no more than a bike and a jersey, the competitive side also compares with men's events in that period as the peloton is not completely controlled. As a consequence, the racing has a more anarchic aspect and, as Rachel Heal suggests, it is harder for riders and sporting directors to assess who is going to be doing what and when.

'There's not that same templated feel to the racing that you often get on the men's side,' says Tiffany Cromwell. 'It can be really boring watching men's races where teams are riding according to what their meters are telling them and preventing rivals from attacking, or at the very least knowing that they'll be able to close down an attack very quickly. You don't see that in women's racing and I think that's one reason why it's often more interesting to watch and, from our perspective, more interesting in terms of competition.'

It is racing without manacles, where smart thinking is not only as important as good legs, but also very apparent. It is, as Mark Cavendish sugggests, the perfect showcase for the tactical aspects of bike racing, which is one more very good reason why every cycling fan and stakeholder should cherish and support it.

CHAPTER 19

SIMPLE, BUT EXTREMELY COMPLEX

Let's just dare to get back to racing and nothing else.
— *Laurent Fignon*, We Were Young and Carefree

Just as Henri Desgrange indicated back in 1894, it all comes down to the head and the legs, to having the right combination of both. What has changed in the century and more since he wrote his seminal training manual is the way in which those qualities need to be applied. When Desgrange went on to establish the Tour de France in 1903, he watched a race in which tactics were essentially back to front, with a bunch sprint away from the start line and the racers gradually slowing all the way into the finish, where the gaps between them could be measured in hours. The riders are now so evenly matched that a 3,500-kilometre Grand Tour won by a margin of a handful of minutes is a crushing victory.

Over that period, tactics have changed beyond recognition too. Pacing, teams, sprints, mountains, descents, technology and many other factors have all necessitated a new approach, and as a result tactical change has been continual. The one constant is that tactics remains largely a question of strength. 'You can be really smart but if you haven't got the legs to take advantage then it doesn't make the slightest bit of difference,' as Ellen van Dijk puts it.

Inevitably, given this amount of change, it is difficult to compare riders' tactical prowess and crown the greatest tactician. A case can be made for many of the legendary names in the sport, including Fausto Coppi, who almost always finished alone, Eddy Merckx, who established *la course en tête* as the benchmark against which all great champions are judged, and Bernard Hinault and Marianne Vos, who dominated when and where they wanted thanks to tactical insight, strength and unfailing belief. All rode and won with panache, a quality that is now regularly said to be absent among the star names.

More interesting, though, than an assessment of the best tacticians is what tactics and the approach to strategy say about bike racing in a particular era. Looking back to 1903, for instance, what may seem to modern eyes like a madcap approach can be largely explained by what French journalist Victor Breyer described as 'the hideous Fairy Dust that caused conjunctivitis, without talking about serious cases of hampering vision'. In contemporary times, tactics are mostly about defending until the possibility arrives when an attacking move has the greatest chance of success.

Merckx isn't impressed, declaring dismissively, 'These days the tactics are different. They're afraid – they're afraid of each other.' But his frustration says more about the way the Belgian super champion used to race than how the peloton does now. With everyone training at altitude, doing similar intervals, racing a more focused programme, it's harder to find the 2 or 3 per cent required to beat a rival. This is where tactics come in and why they are still vitally important. By working on positioning, descending and analysing where best to take advantage of these skills, riders can still find ways to improve and gain a little more of an edge on their rivals.

'Tactics are something I've thought a lot about and especially after realising that, great as it is sometimes to be the strongest guy and just use the simple tactic of waiting until the hardest moment and then pushing on, there are moments when you maybe don't feel like the strongest guy and those are the times when you really have to rely on tactics over pure brute force to win you the race,' says Chris Froome, who admits that during his first years in the sport, 'I was just following wheels and didn't really know what was going on.'

His sporting director at Sky, Nicolas Portal, is adamant that any assessment of a rider's ability with regard to tactics has to be viewed through the prism of road racing as it is in the second decade of the twenty-first century. 'Cycling nowadays is completely different to what it was in 1970, it's not at all the same as it was when Eddy Merckx was racing. When people say that Chris is looking at his power meter or whatever, you've got to remember that we're in 2017 and cycling has changed. The margins between the guys at the very top are so small,' says Portal.

To my mind, the rider who has consistently shown in recent years that he is capable of finding and exploiting any slight advantage is Vincenzo Nibali, whose qualities have been heightened more than any other in my eyes during the research for this book. Max Sciandri describes his Italian compatriot as representing the old style of racing, of not being 'afraid to go for it from a long way out if the opportunity's right'.

Often pigeon-holed as the ultimate daredevil descender, Nibali is much else besides, as he emphasised in taking the 2014 Tour title when he outperformed his rivals on the cobbles, on the climbs, in the time trials as well as on the descents. 'If an opportunity to attack comes up along the way – and Alberto Contador is probably like this, too – I'll take it. I don't even know how to explain it. They're such small moments, you sort of have to feel them. It's not a question of tactics; it's a question of invention,' he says of an approach that makes him so watchable because it always has that 'what's going to happen next?' aspect.

On the women's side, Ina-Yoko Teutenberg, who won 200 races before a serious injury forced her out of the sport in 2013, had that same quality. 'She was always very sharp tactically,' says Rachel Heal, who raced against the German and directed teams trying to get the measure of her. 'She'd be one of those riders you'd always worry about, regardless of whether the terrain or the course suited her. There are some riders you race with and against and you know that the only way they are going to win is if they are absolutely the strongest, but someone like Ina would find a way to win regardless of who she was up against.' More recently, Poland's Kasia Niewiadoma and Dutch duo Anna van der Breggen and Anna van Vleuten have proved that they race in a similar style.

Like the riders, race organisers, who provide them with the platform on which to perform, are also adapting to the changing face of racing, and particularly in multi-day events. Concern that the narrowing of the competitive level and increasing strength in depth is choking the possibility of spontaneity from races, and none more so than the Tour de France, where the leading teams field their best riders, has led to many of the events receiving a dramatic makeover. Stages have been shortened, finishing climbs steepened, descents made more critical, all with the aim of encouraging greater variation in tactics, reducing the control any one team or kind of team can have in order to raise the thrill potential.

As a consequence, several of cycling's biggest events have been revitalised. The week-long Paris–Nice and the Critérium du Dauphiné stage races stand out in this respect, thanks to both the variety and quality of action they deliver. The Vuelta a España has also been given a new lease of life. The 2018 Tour is set for another injection of vitality with a longer than usual stage over some of Paris–Roubaix's cobbles and an unprecedentedly short mountain stage extending to a mere sixty-five kilometres. Other races require similar treatment, none more so than the Ardennes Classics of Flèche Wallonne and Liège–Bastogne–Liège. Among the toughest one-day races on the calendar, both have become stale, reduced to the most predictable of sprints despite taking place on terrain that should encourage the audacious.

Yet, as these makeovers take place and become ever more dramatic in their remodelling of races, there is a counter-concern that organisers might be pushing these revamps too far in the search for action and, fundamentally, higher TV ratings. Vuelta organisers Unipublic, for instance, have been widely criticised for searching out so many summit finishes that the season's third Grand Tour is effectively shunning certain types of rider, primarily sprinters, but also time-trial specialists. Tour director Christian Prudhomme is also doing all he can to flush the overall favourites out of the sanctuary of the peloton on as many days as possible, setting traps such as cobbled stages, dirt roads, and short, steep finishing ramps in an attempt to catch them out and to draw them away from set-piece contests in the mountains. The danger is that by upping the stakes in the battle for the yellow jersey, they are changing the strategic aspect of races, perhaps in a detrimental manner.

GC contender Tejay van Garderen suggests that they could also be making the exciting mundane and threatening the pacing that makes the Grand Tours in particular so special. 'I think you should savour that kind of day and be excited when they happen. I don't think you should seek them out and try to manipulate the course to encourage more days like that,' the American says of stages like the Tour's sixty-five-kilometre sprint through the Pyrenees. He draws an interesting comparison with boxing. 'Everyone's into MMA these days and boxing is becoming less popular, even though it's by far and away the better sport. People just want to see quick knockout punches now, and that's not really what boxing is. It's more strategic, it takes ten to twelve rounds during which you land strategic punches, and that's what cycling's like too,' he says.

'Sometimes you have days when the race is more under control and there's a summit finish, which is where the fight's decided. You have time trials. Sometimes you might have a medium mountain day when it completely explodes and people lose control of the race. But it seems to me that organisers are trying to manipulate the *parcours* because they only want to see climbing, only explosions, they want something unforeseen to happen every day. Sprinters' stages are almost non-existent. At the 2017 Vuelta, they didn't exist at all. They're trying to make every race exactly the same with exactly the same guys winning, with lots of attacking. It's definitely changing cycling.'

Van Garderen fears that these innovations might end up damaging the chess-like aspect of races, that by adding more stages intended to produce GC thrills organisers will inevitably end up undermining the impact of those hard-to-control days too. 'It's sad to think that aspect is being eroded. Cycling should have that long-term strategic characteristic that boxing has. Sometimes boxers have more endurance, so they can save themselves for a couple of rounds and let the other guy punch himself out, and then they pick a round and they really go at them,' he explains.

Cycling's legendary stage races thrive on that too, and especially the Grand tours, twenty-one-day marathons that are sport's ultimate strategic tests. A lot of the enjoyment comes from appreciating the mindset, strategy and tactics. If it's a flat day, the overall favourites will sit in and try to save some energy in order to do battle another day while the sprinters get the chance to throw their punches. The GC riders have to pick when they're going to make their moves, when they're going to attack, and it's often on those crazy days when everything explodes.

'If it's a flat day, you often hear people say, "Well, that's boring. No one's attacking, everyone's just sitting in the bunch." But it would be stupid if you saw a GC rider trying to ride everyone off their wheel on the flat. It wouldn't make sense,' van Garderen affirms. 'You have to see a day like that as part of the overall strategy. They're sitting in and saving energy because they're going to attack tomorrow. I think people need to learn to value that.'

Tinkering of this nature, which is widely hailed as a means of revitalising racing, could well end up doing quite the opposite by diluting the tactical aspect. Climbs, after all, are the one area where the legs almost always trump the head, where strength alone counts. It is also undertaken on the assumption that the GC battle needs to be forced front and centre as much as possible, that other types of racing and rider aren't as exciting or important. Yet, better understanding of what's going on in the mad melee of a bunch sprint or when a breakaway and the peloton are each vying for control of the other can make them as gripping as the action on any summit finish.

The skills and tactics employed by those involved are harder to decipher and even cryptically complex at times, but are actually more fundamental to the racing repertoire of the professional cyclist. Highlighting these via the use of on-board cameras, individual rider tracking and data, and other technology will help those watching make sense and appreciate the beauty of tactics and the astonishing bike-handling ability and courage of racers. Let's see and appreciate how a rider works their way from the back of the bunch to the front, towing a sprinter in their wake, or how a bunch finish unfolds, or watch the *gruppetto* railing it down a Swiss mountain pass.

Simple but extremely complex at the same time, bike racing requires explanation more than gimmicks to expand its audience. I say this as a life-long fan who has spent a quarter of a century reporting and writing about the sport and its protagonists, and who is, I confess, often clueless as to precisely how a rider has won a race. That fog of unknowing has lifted as I've begun to watch bike racing in a quite different way, with less focus on what racers do and say off the bike and far more on how they're performing on it, and I've relished every moment of it.

Road cycling is a beautifully chaotic sport of infinite variations, where strength is much but not everything, where forethought generally wins. Rather like chess – at four hundred watts.

BIBLIOGRAPHY

Chany, Pierre, *La Fabuleuse Histoire du Cyclisme* (Éditions ODIL, Paris, 1975)

Chany, Pierre, *La Fabuleuse Histoire du Tour de France* (Éditions de la Martinière, Paris, 1995)

Desgrange, Henri, *La Tete et Les Jambes* (Imprimerie La Pochy, Paris, 1894)

Fignon, Laurent, *We Were Young and Carefree* (Yellow Jersey Press, London, 2010)

Fotheringham, William, *Merckx: Half Man, Half Bike* (Yellow Jersey Press, London, 2012)

Fotheringham, William, *Put Me Back on My Bike* (Yellow Jersey Press, London, 2014)

Fotheringham, William, *Fallen Angel* (Yellow Jersey Press, London, 2010)

Fotheringham, William, *The Badger* (Yellow Jersey Press, London, 2015)

Goddet, Jacques, *L'Équipée Belle* (Robert Lafont / Stock, Paris, 1991)

Guimard, Cyrille, *Dans Les Secrets du Tour de France* (Éditions J'ai Lu, Paris, 2012)

Leonard, Max, *Lanterne Rouge* (Yellow Jersey Press, London, 2014)

Leonard, Max, *Higher Calling* (Yellow Jersey Press, London, 2017)

Millar, David, *The Racer* (Yellow Jersey Press, London, 2015)

Moore, Richard, *Slaying the Badger* (Yellow Jersey Press, London, 2011)

Nicholson, Geoffrey, *The Great Bike Race* (Hodder and Stoughton, London, 1977)

Simpson, Tommy, *Cycling is My Life* (Yellow Jersey Press, London, 2009)

Wegelius, Charly, *Domestique* (Ebury Press, 2014)

Whittle, Jeremy, *Ventoux* (Simon and Schuster, London, 2017)

Wiggins, Bradley, *My Time* (Yellow Jersey Press, London, 2013)

ACKNOWLEDGEMENTS

I would like to thank all those riders, team staff and expert observers for the time and insight they granted me while researching this book, particularly Dave Brailsford, Tiffany Cromwell, José De Cauwer, Thomas De Gendt, Koen de Kort, Dirk Demol, Rod Ellingworth, Chris Froome, Rachel Heal, Greg Henderson, Patrick Lefevere, Marco Pinotti, Richard Plugge, Nicolas Portal, Coryn Rivera, Max Sciandri, Marc Sergeant, Ellen van Dijck, Tejay van Garderen, Jean-Paul van Poppel, Thomas Voeckler, Matt White, and Simon and Adam Yates.

As always, in order to reach many of those just mentioned, I am indebted to the press officers who managed to accommodate my interview requests, with particular thanks to Ben Wright and George Solomon (Team Sky), Matt Rendell (Trek-Segafredo), Phoebe Haymes (BMC), Emily Brammeier (Team Sunweb), Arne Houtekier (Lotto Soudal), and Taryn Kirby (Orica-GreenEdge). Fellow journalists José Been, Pierre Carrey, Leon De Kort, Laura Meseguer, Vern Pitt, Owen Rogers also provided invaluable insight and contacts for which I'm extremely grateful.

Once again, it has been a real pleasure to be able to collaborate with Fran Jessop, my editor at Yellow Jersey. Fran has been my *capitaine de route* throughout the production process, providing encouragement, tactical expertise and a much-required cutting edge to deal with the almost inevitable hurdles that unexpectedly appear when writing about professional cycling. My thanks also to the rest of the Yellow Jersey team – Anna Redman for directing the publicity side, production editor Phil Brown, Rowena Skelton-Wallace, Graeme Hall, copyeditor Justine Taylor, proofreader Josh Ireland, and to Rosie Palmer for the wonderful jacket design.

I would also like to express my gratitude to my *directeurs sportifs* at David Luxton Associates – David himself and Rebecca Winfield. That this book has seen the light of day is largely down to their support in the idea and their faith in me.

Finally, my love and gratitude goes to my wife, Elaine, and my children, Lewis and Eleanor, who have spent far too much time hearing about the finer points of tactical niceties and have provided unwavering support throughout.

EST.1998

Yellow Jersey Press celebrates 20 years of quality sports writing

Yellow Jersey Press launched in 1998, with *Rough Ride*, Paul Kimmage's William Hill Sports Book of the Year. In those early days, the Yellow Jersey list sought to give a platform to brilliant stories, which happened to be framed within a sporting environment. Over the past two decades, its name has become synonymous with quality sports writing, covering all sports from the perspective of player, professional observer and passionate fan.

Sport is about more than simple entertainment. It represents a determination to challenge and compete. It binds individuals with a common goal, and often reflects our experiences in the wider world. Yellow Jersey understands this as much as its readers.

This edition was first published in the Yellow Jersey Press 20th Anniversary Year.

YELLOW JERSEY PRESS
LONDON